which?
essential guides

FINANCE YOUR
RETIREMENT

❝ People living longer is often presented as a problem for society and the economy. But let's get this in perspective: a longer, healthier life is good news. To make the most of this good fortune, we need a sound financial plan. ❞

Jonquil Lowe

About the author

Jonquil Lowe is an economist who worked for several years in the City as an investment analyst, and is a former head of the Money Group at Which?. She now works as a freelance financial researcher and journalist, holds the Diploma in Financial Planning and works with the Open University on developing and tutoring personal finance courses. Jonquil writes extensively on all areas of personal finance and is the author of over 20 books, including the *Which? Essential Guide* to *Giving and Inheriting*, the *Which? Essential Guide: Pension Handbook*, the *Which? Essential Guide: Save and Invest*, *Be Your Own Financial Advisor*, *Money in Retirement* and, as co-author, *The FT Guide to Personal Tax*.

FINANCE YOUR
RETIREMENT

JONQUIL LOWE

Which? Books are commissioned and published by Which? Ltd,
2 Marylebone Road, London NW1 4DF
Email: books@which.co.uk

Distributed by Littlehampton Book Services Ltd, Faraday Close, Durrington, Worthing,
West Sussex BN13 3RB

British Library Cataloguing in Publication Data
A catalogue record for this book is available from the British Library

Copyright ©Which? Ltd 2009

ISBN 978 1 84490 057 2

1 3 5 7 9 10 8 6 4 2

Birmingham City Council

MG

C2 000 004 372594	
Askews	Feb-2009
332.024014	£10.99
MERE GREEN	

Although th   n this book
is accurate   financial,
legal, or me   who can
consider yo   rdingly
accept liabili   in the
information

The *Which?*   and
includes me   nformation
on budget   get-
changes/inc

Acknowledg   ng Asset
Management, Laing & Buisson and Consumer Focus for permission to use their
copyright material on pages 110, 114, 187 and 194, and Ian Robinson at Which? for
his helpful comments on the draft.

Project manager: Claudia Dyer
Edited by: Emma Callery
Designed by: Bob Vickers
Index by: Lynda Swindells
Cover photographs by: Alamy
Printed and bound by Stanley L Hunt (Printers) Ltd., Northamptonshire

G-Print Matt is an elemental chlorine-free paper produced at Grycksbo Valun Mill in
Dalecarlia, Sweden, using timber from sustainably managed forests. The mill is
ISO14001 and EMAS certified, and has PEFC and FSC certified Chain of Custody.

For a full list of Which? Books, please call 01903 828557, access our website at
www.which.co.uk, or write to Littlehampton Book Services.
For other enquiries call 0800 252 100.

Contents

Introduction   6

1 Building up pensions   11
The power of pensions • Your State Pension • Occupational pensions • Personal pensions •
Divorce and pensions • Consolidating pensions • Retiring abroad

2 Pension choices at retirement   41
Key decisions • Consolidating your pensions • Protecting your survivors •
Taking a tax free lump sum • Annuities • Deferring and phasing •
Income withdrawal • 'Third-way' products

3 Continuing to work   69
Your right to stay on • Your rights at work • Running your own business •
National Insurance • Top up for low earnings

4 Boosting your budget   89
Keeping track • Extras because of age • If you have a disability • If your income is low •
Money-saving ideas

5 Income from your home   113
Downsize or stay put? • Equity release schemes • Is equity release for you? •
Lodgers and B&B • Cash from your garden

6 Investments   131
Investments and risk • Investment goals • Income from property •
Complaints and compensation • Getting help

7 Tax   161
How your income is taxed • How capital gains are taxed • Tax and investments •
Tax-saving tips

8 Decisions about care   181
Care options • Moving to a care home • Planning ahead for care

9 The next generation   193
Family matters • Inheritance Tax on your estate • Lifetime gifts

Glossary   204
Useful addresses   211
Index   216

Introduction

If you look up 'retire' in a dictionary, the definitions focus on withdrawing from society, from work, from active life. Maybe 30 or 40 years ago that was a reasonable description, but these days retirement is no longer a period of withdrawal, just a different and potentially exciting phase of life.

The retirement phase of life is typically characterised by less stress and greater freedom to pursue your own agenda. You are likely to be more involved in society than ever before; you may still be working, perhaps in a new area you've always wanted to experience; and you'll probably be more rather than less active. In fact, a common remark from anyone who has retired is: how did I ever find time for the day job?

CHANGING ATTITUDES

A key factor in making the most of retirement is to plan and manage your finances appropriately. The financial needs and goals of retirement are different from those of the earlier years of life. Try the quiz overleaf and then ask yourself: how many of these questions

and answers would have been important to you before you were fifty years old? How many are important to you now? As our priorities change with age, so good financial planning adapts to each new phase of life. This *Which? Essential Guide: Finance Your Retirement* provides a handbook of good financial planning if you are looking at retiring within the next ten years or so or have already retired. It focuses on the needs and goals that are typical in this phase of life and shows how you can achieve them.

In these worrying times of international financial turmoil and worldwide recession, financial understanding and planning are all the more important. Your experiences and the risks you face will vary depending, for example, on whether you have access to a good pension scheme through work or have to take your own pension decisions, how secure you feel in your job if you are still working, the scope you have for deferring retirement, and the decisions you have taken so far if you have already retired. Whatever your circumstances, this *Essential Guide* is designed to help you consider your best course of action.

“ In these worrying times of international financial turmoil and worldwide recession, financial understanding and planning are all the more important. ”

6

Greater wealth

Your experience of retirement is likely to be very different from that of your parents' or grandparents' generation. The Government's Office for National Statistics (ONS) has published a study comparing the different life experiences of people who are retired now and people born in the 1940s and 1960s and how this is likely to affect retirement. It suggests that the younger generations are likely to be wealthier than people who are retired now, because of greater membership of occupational pension schemes and higher levels of home ownership (with the potential to release the wealth they have tied up in these properties, for example, by trading down at retirement).

Longer retirement

Government data show that you are likely to live longer than your parents or grandparents. The table below shows how life expectancy for people reaching age 65 has been rising steadily. For example, women who reached age 65 in 1991 can expect on average to live to 84 years and 4 months – though, of course, individuals may survive to younger or older ages. By contrast, women who will reach age 65 in 2031 can expect on average to survive to age 90 years and 6 months. But the ONS study notes that the general level of health is not increasing in a comparable way, although age related disabilities may be less severe than for previous generations.

> **❝** Younger generations are likely to be wealthier than people who are retired now, because of pension schemes and home ownership. **❞**

How long an average person aged 65 can expect to live

If you reach age 65 in	Men	Women
1991	16 years	19 years 4 months
2001	19 years 5 months	22 years 1 month
2011	21 years 2 months	23 years 7 months
2021	22 years 4 months	24 years 7 months
2031	23 years 2 months	25 years 6 months

Source: Government Actuary's Department (online).
www.gad.gov.uk/Demography_Data/Life_Tables/docs/2006/wUKcohort06.xls.

The retirement phase of life is an exciting time when you have more freedom to focus on the things you want to do. Putting your finances in good shape is key to making the most of these opportunities. Try this quiz to test how much you know already. Don't worry if you are not sure of the answers right now. Once you have read the *Which? Essential Guide: Finance Your Retirement*, you will have all the answers and be fully equipped to create the retirement you want.

		Where to find the answer
1	If you have ten years to go until you retire, how much might you need to save each month starting now to provide yourself with an extra £20 a week pension? **a)** £50 a month **b)** £100 a month **c)** £150 a month **d)** £300 a month	Chapter 1 page 12
2	Roughly how much would you need to have saved up as a lump sum to provide yourself with as much pension as you get from the full basic State Pension (£95.25 a week in 2009–10)? **a)** £20,000 **b)** £50,000 **c)** £150,000 **d)** £300,000	Chapter 1 page 15
3	If at age 65 you have a pension fund of £100,000, even if you pay no more into the fund, how much extra pension could you get if you put off retiring until age 70? **a)** £10 a month **b)** £50 a month **c)** £100 a month **d)** £150 a month	Chapter 2 page 62
4	At what age can you be forced to retire?	Chapter 3 page 70

5	Which of the following state benefits are means tested (ie only available if you are on a low income)? **a)** Pension Credit **b)** Winter Fuel Payment **c)** Council Tax Benefit **d)** Attendance Allowance	**Chapter 4** page 101
6	How could you turn a house you own into extra income without moving home?	**Chapter 5** page 114
7	If you have a fixed income and inflation averages 4 per cent a year, how much buying power would your income have lost after 20 years? **a)** One-quarter **b)** One-third **c)** Half **d)** Three-quarters	**Chapter 6** page 137
8	For someone aged 70, what proportion of their wealth should they sensibly invest in share-based investments?	**Chapter 6** page 137
9	How much income can a 65-year old have before he or she starts paying Income Tax?	**Chapter 7** page 163
10	What proportion of people aged 65 and over are providing informal care to family, friends or neighbours? **a)** One in fifty **b)** One in nine **c)** One in six **d)** One in three	**Chapter 8** page 182
11	How much can you leave your family free of Inheritance Tax?	**Chapter 9** page 194

Living alone

Finally, the ONS study suggests that people born in the 1940s and 1960s are more likely to be single in retirement because more people in these younger generations have either chosen to live alone or get divorced. This has implications for social care. Currently, the vast majority of carers are husbands, wives or children. The ONS report finds that, apart from more people living without a partner, one in five of the 1960s' generation are likely to remain childless (compared with one in eight of people born in the 1930s). Moreover, children whose parents have split up may be less willing to provide care.

STAY FOCUSED

When the economy or your investments go through a bad patch, it can be hard to feel optimistic. Even though your retirement planning may take some knocks from time to time, stay calm and focused on your goals. Try to carry on saving for retirement through good times and bad, take advantage of opportunities – say, to invest extra when investments look cheap – and, if you can, be flexible, about when to start your pensions.

LOOKING FORWARDS

Financially, therefore, your concerns are likely to centre around the key areas described below:

- **Building up as much wealth as possible** while you still work (see Chapter 1).
- **Making the most of your wealth,** investing it well with the main focus being on providing income once you retire (see Chapters 2, 5 and 6).
- **Maximising your income** in other ways if you have less than you need (see Chapters 3 and 4).
- **Funding care needs** – either your own or those of an elderly parent or other close relative (see Chapter 8).
- **Ensuring that your wealth, including your home,** is passed on as you would wish (see Chapter 9).
- **Doing all of this as tax efficiently as possible** (see Chapter 7).

The *Which? Essential Guide: Finance Your Retirement* takes you through each of these issues, highlighting the important aspects and pitfalls to watch out for. It shows you how to build a robust financial plan so you can enjoy this phase of life to the full.

 To see how deferring retirement could increase your eventual pension, see pages 28, 42 and 61 and for up-to-date information on budget changes, go to: www.which.co.uk/advice/tax-basics-explained/budget-changes/index.jsp.

Building up pensions

The most important influences on your finances in retirement are the pensions you build up while you are working. Even if retirement is already on the horizon, decisions you make now can affect how much your pensions will pay out and there is still a lot you can do to boost the amount you will get.

The power of pensions

Private pensions account for much of the difference between 'poor' and 'rich' pensioners. Even if you are within striking distance of retirement, you still have time to boost your pension.

Ensuring you have your own pension is the key to being comfortable in retirement. In 2005–6 (the latest data available), the poorest fifth of pensioners were getting by on just £109 a week, most of which came from State Pensions and other state benefits. The richest fifth had incomes of £461 a week with their private pensions providing £160 of this. Their investments and some continuing earnings also make a substantial contribution. The message is clear: although your State Pension is a valuable start, if you want to be comfortable in retirement, you need to save up through your own private pensions as well. This chapter looks at the different types of pension that are available and how to maximise your income from them.

IT'S NEVER TOO LATE

You're probably thinking: that's all very well, but I don't have enough time left to save before I retire. The answer to Quiz question 1 (right) shows you can still make a difference, although it may not be cheap.

- Even if you are fairly close to retiring, you can still enhance your retirement income. For example, if you are a man with ten years to go, starting to save £100 a month could provide an extra £14 a week (around £750 a year) from age 65, assuming it is **index-linked** throughout retirement.
- If you can put off your retirement for a while, your extra pension multiplies.

Pit your wits   Answers

Question 1
If you have ten years to go until you retire, how much might you need to save each month starting now to provide yourself with an extra £20 a week pension?
A: (c) £150 a month. If you plan to retire at age 65, you would need to save around £140 a month if you are a man and around £160 a month as a woman (because women tend to live longer, which makes their pensions more expensive).

 For guidance on boosting your retirement income through work or by clever investments, see Chapters 3 and 6. For more detail about building up pensions, see the *Which? Essential Guide: Pension Handbook*.

For example, saving £100 a month could provide the same man with an extra £33 a week instead of £14 if he retired at 70 instead of 65 years.

- **Pensions are expensive.** If you can afford only modest savings, check on pages 101–8 to see if it is worth saving at all or whether you would just be doing yourself out of means-tested state benefits.

> **“** Ensuring you have your own pension is the key to being comfortable in retirement. **”**

How saving can boost your retirement income

The table shows the extra weekly pension you might get for every £100 a month you start to save now. It is based on assumptions about how well your invested savings grow: 4% a year after charges if you are within ten years of retiring (the dark blue boxes) and 6% a year after charges if you have longer to go (the white boxes). All values are in today's prices and assume the amount you save increases each year with earnings inflation and the pension you get rises each year with price inflation.

Your age now	Weekly pension you might get for each £100 a month you save, if you retire at age:					
	50	55	60	65	70	75
MEN						
45	£4	£10	£22	£38	£66	£108
50		£5	£12	£26	£48	£82
55			£6	£14	£33	£59
60				£7	£18	£41
65					£9	£22
70						£11
WOMEN						
45	£4	£9	£19	£34	£57	£90
50		£4	£10	£23	£41	£68
55			£5	£13	£28	£50
60				£6	£15	£34
65					£8	£19
70						£9

To explore further the effect of extra savings on your retirement income, see www.pensioncalculator.org.uk or the CD-based tool, MoneyTrail, from www.ageconcern.org.uk/moneytrail.

Your State Pension

Although the State Pension is not enough on its own to fund a comfortable retirement, it does provide a valuable foundation for your finances.

There are two main parts to the **State Pension: basic and additional**. Nearly everyone builds up at least some basic pension. Employees and some people who cannot work may get additional pension too.

> **❝ The full basic State Pension is £95.25 a week (£4,953 a year) for a single person. ❞**

HOW MUCH STATE PENSION WILL YOU GET?

In 2009–10, the full basic State Pension is £95.25 a week (£4,953 a year) for a single person. Due to recent changes in the law (see page 17), from 2010 onwards, most people will retire on this full rate. The maximum additional pension could add another £140 a week or so, but very few people qualify for anything like that amount. In autumn 2007, the average additional pension was £15.37 a week (£800 a year).

State Pensions are increased each year in line with price inflation (or 2.5 per cent if more), so they retain their buying power throughout retirement. From a future date yet to be set, but possibly 2012, the basic pension is due to be increased in line with earnings inflation, which is typically around 2 per cent a year higher than price inflation. This is part of a package of government measures to improve the State Pension in order to reduce the reliance of future pensioners on **means-tested benefits** (see Chapter 4) and so encourage greater private saving for retirement.

Pages 17–21 explain how you build up the basic and additional State Pension and the amount you personally might get. Although the State Pension on its own is unlikely to be enough to support a comfortable retirement, it is a valuable foundation on which to build the rest of your retirement savings. Therefore, it is important to find out how much State Pension you are on track for to help you decide how much extra you might need to save. You can keep track by getting a State Pension forecast from the Pension Service (the government department that deals with pensions). There are several ways to do this (see the box below for website and phone details):

- An instant online forecast. If you have not used the online service before, first you need to register and wait to be posted an activation code (allow seven days).
- Print off form BR19, or complete the interactive form BR19 online and then print it off. Post the form to the address shown on the website. To request the form in writing, write to the Future Pension Centre (see Useful addresses, page 211).
- Request a forecast by phone. The call centre will fill in the form for you while you are on the line.

Except for the instant online service, it usually takes about 12 working days from the receipt of your request to send out your forecast.

““ Find out how much State Pension you are on track for by getting a State Pension forecast. ””

WHEN CAN YOU START YOUR PENSION?

You can get your State Pension once you reach State Pension age, which, if you are retiring today, is 65 for a man or 60 for a woman. For women retiring on or after 6 April 2010, State Pension age is gradually increasing until it matches that for men. In the longer term, State

You can find out how much State Pension you might get when you reach State Pension age by requesting a State Pension forecast - see www.thepensionservice. gov.uk/state-pension/forecast/home.asp. To request a forecast by phone, telephone 0845 300 0168.

Pension age is rising in stages to 66, 67 and then 68 for both men and women, but this will affect you only if you were born on or after 6 April 1959. The table below summarises the changes.

You can start your pension later than State Pension age – called deferring your State Pension. In that case, you earn either extra pension or a cash lump sum (see page 42 for details). You cannot, however, start your State Pension earlier than State Pension age.

 Under no circumstances can you start your State Pension before State Pension age. So, if you plan to retire earlier, you will need to think how you are going to finance the gap until it is time for your State Pension to kick in.

State Pension age

To check your State Pension age and the date from which you can claim your pension, use the State Pension age calculator at www.thepensionservice.gov.uk/state-pension/age-calculator.asp.

If your date of birth is:	Your State Pension age will be:	
	Women	Men
Before 6 April 1950	60	65
6 April 1950–5 April 1955	Between 60 and 65. Add one month[a] to age 60 for each complete month by which your birth date falls after 6 April 1950.	65
	Men and women	
6 April 1955–5 April 1959	65	
6 April 1959–5 April 1960	Between 65 and 66. Add one month[a] to age 65 for each complete month by which your birth date falls after 6 April 1959.	
6 April 1960–5 April 1968	66	
6 April 1968–5 April 1969	Between 66 and 67. Add one month[a] to age 66 for each complete month by which your birth date falls after 6 April 1968.	
6 April 1969–5 April 1977	67	
6 April 1977–5 April 1978	Between 67 and 68. Add one month[a] to age 67 for each complete month by which your birth date falls after 6 April 1977.	
6 April 1978 onwards	68	

a A month runs from the 6th of one month to the 5th of the next.

THE BASIC STATE PENSION

Generally, you build up an entitlement to basic State Pension by paying **National Insurance contributions** while you are working, either as an employee or a self-employed person (see pages 84–5). But in some situations you can be awarded credits that count as if they were contributions you had paid (see table, overleaf). Also, there are special rules that help women in particular to build up a basic pension (see below right). HM Revenue & Customs (HMRC) keep a computer record of all your contributions and credits and this is used to calculate your pension entitlement when you reach State Pension age. In most cases, credits and protection through the special rules should be given and recorded automatically.

The amount of basic pension you get depends on how many **qualifying years** of contributions and/or credits you build up over your **working life**. If you will reach State Pension age on or after 6 April 2010, you need 30 qualifying years in order to get the full basic pension. If you have fewer years, the pension is reduced pro rata – for example, 15 years would qualify you for half the full rate. Even a single qualifying year earns you some pension.

If you reach State Pension age before 6 April 2010, 90 per cent of your working life must be qualifying years if you are to get the full basic pension. Moreover, at least 10 per cent of your working life must be qualifying for you to get any basic pension at all. For example in 2009–10, a woman with a State

Pension age of 60 years and a working life of 44 years would need to have 39 qualifying years for her to get the full basic pension of £95.25 a week. She would need at least ten qualifying years to get any basic pension and, in that case, would get £24.77.

Carers and women

The State Pension system started in 1948 and in some ways still reflects a society where women were expected to marry and rely on their husbands for financial support:

- A wife can claim a pension (maximum £57.05 a week in 2009–10) using her spouse's National Insurance record if this would be more than she can get on her own record. From 6 April 2010, this right is being extended to husbands and civil partners.

Jargon buster

National Insurance contributions A tax paid by most people who work. Some types of contribution – Classes 1 (full-rate), 2 and 3 (see pages 84-5) – entitle you to build up State Pension

Qualifying year A tax year in which you have paid or been credited with enough National Insurance contributions for it to count towards your State Pension

Working life The tax years from the year in which you reached age 16 up to the last complete tax year before you reach State Pension age. For example, if your State Pension age is 65, your working life is the 49 tax years from age 16 up to 64 inclusive

---

- Some wives and widows still pay National Insurance at the married women's reduced rate (see page 84), which does not count towards the State Pension. These women are expected to rely on their husband.

Whether you are a man or a woman, currently, if you are unable to work or earn less than the lower earnings limit (£95 in 2009–10) because you are caring for a child under age 16 or an adult with a disability, you can get Home Responsibilites Protection (HRP). This is a scheme to help you protect your entitlement to State Pension if you are not paying National Insurance contributions. Years for which you get HRP are deducted from the number of qualifying years you need to get a given level of basic pension, though you still need at least 20 qualifying

years under the current rules in order to get the full-rate pension.

From 6 April 2010 onwards, past years of HRP will be converted into credits and you will then be awarded a National Insurance credit for each week that you are caring for a child under the age of 12 years or a person with a disability. HRP and the new carer credits can cover a maximum of 22 years in your National Insurance record (because the Government is keen that you should have participated in the labour market for at least some of your working life), so to get the full basic pension you would need at least another eight years of actual contributions or credits awarded for other reasons.

Filling in employment gaps to get extra pension

If you are not paying National Insurance and do not qualify for credits, you will have a gap in your record that could reduce your pension. This might be the case if, say, you have taken early retirement (unless you are a man aged 60 or over in which case you will be getting credits) or took a break from work (say, to study or travel). You can voluntarily pay Class 3 National Insurance contributions (see page 84) to fill such gaps. In effect your voluntary contributions buy extra qualifying years.

If you will reach State Pension age before 6 April 2010, check whether you

> **!** Bear in mind that, if you will reach State Pension age from 6 April 2010 onwards, you need only 30 qualifying years to get the full basic State Pension. You can have 19 years of gaps in your record without losing any pension, in which case it would not be worth paying voluntary contributions.

 If you believe credits you were entitled to have not been correctly recorded on your National Insurance record, contact NICO Contributor Group, Benton Park View, Newcastle upon Tyne NE98 1ZZ.

National Insurance credits

Periods when you are not paying National Insurance (because you are not working or earn too little) normally appear as gaps in your record and reduce your basic pension. This table shows the main situations when you get credits to fill the gap.

Situation	Credits for:	How you get them[a]
At school	Years you reached ages 16-18, provided you were born on or after 6 April 1957.	Awarded automatically.
Training	Years you took part in approved training, provided you were born on or after 6 April 1957. University does not count.	Awarded automatically if the course was government sponsored. Otherwise, you may hve needed to claim.
Low earnings	Periods you earn less than the lower earnings limit (£95 a week in 2009-10) and are claiming or claimed Working Tax Credit, Working Families Tax Credit or Disabled Person's Tax Credit.	Automatic. In case of a couple, only credited to one of the couple (usually the claimant).
Working abroad	These periods count if the UK has a reciprocal agreement with the country where you work and you pay contributions there.	By paying the equivalent contributions abroad.
Unemployed	Periods when you are unemployed and getting state benefits	Automatic, providing you claimed the relevant benefit. If eligible for benefit but not claiming it, you had to notify the relevant social security office/Jobcentre Plus in writing within a year of the end of the tax year of your claim.
Ill or pregnant	Periods when you were off work for these reasons and getting state benefits.	You had to give notice in writing to the relevant social security office/Jobcentre Plus in writing within a year of the end of the tax year of your claim. If you got sick pay or maternity pay from your employer that came to at least the lower earnings limit (£95 a week in 2009-10), you would have paid contributions as normal.
Caring	Periods when you are getting Carer's Allowance (see page 97) or its predecessor, Invalid Care Allowance. Periods before 6 April 2010 for which you got HRP (see opposite). Periods from 6 April 2010 when you are caring for a child under age 12 or a person who is disabled.	Automatic credits if you claim Carer's Allowance (or claimed Invalid Care Allowance). HRP and credits should be awarded automatically if you are getting Child Benefit, but in other circumstances you may need to claim the protection, usually within three years.
Older man and not working	Being over 60 but under State Pension age, but these credits are being phased out over the period 2010-2020 as women's State Pension age is aligned with men's.	Automatic.

a The rules about credits are extremely complicated and have changed several times over the years - the notes here are just a rough guide. Married women paying National Insurance contributions at the reduced rate (see page 84) are not eligible for credits.

would benefit from voluntary contributions by first ordering a State Pension forecast (see page 15). Here are some points to consider:

- If, even after paying the voluntary contributions, fewer than 25 per cent of the years in your working life are qualifying, you will not qualify for any basic pension. It will not be worth paying the extra contributions.
- If you already have enough qualifying years for a full basic pension, paying extra contributions cannot increase your pension. It will not be worth paying the extra contributions.
- In other cases, each extra qualifying year you buy could increase your basic pension by between around £1.90 to £4.60 a week (in 2009–10).
- It may not be worth getting extra basic pension if it would simply prevent you from getting means-tested Pension Credit (see page 101) or you can claim just as much on your husband's record (see page 17).

- If you would benefit and you have already started your State Pension, you may get a back payment as well as an increased pension from now on.

If you will reach State Pension age on or after 6 April 2010, it will not be worth making voluntary contributions if you already have the 30 qualifying years needed for the full pension. In addition, it may not be worth paying the extra contributions if your income in retirement will still be low and extra pension would simply be offset by lower means-tested benefits or you can get just as much on your spouse's record (see page 17). In other cases, each extra qualifying year you buy will increase your basic pension by around £3.20 a week in 2009–10.

Normally, HMRC sends you a letter (called a deficiency letter) after the end of the tax year if you have paid or been credited with too few contributions for that year to be a qualifying year. Under the rules as they stood at the time of writing (October 2008), you normally

Exception to the six-year rule

For the years 1996-7 to 2001-2, by mistake the Government sent out the deficiency letters very late. So that you are not disadvantaged by this, it has extended the normal six-year time limit described above. Under the extension, if you have a gap during that period, you can still apply to pay voluntary contributions (at a special rate set at the rate that applied when the gap arose) subject to the following time limits:

- If you reached State Pension age before 24 October 2004, you must pay the contributions by 6 April 2010. In fact, the amount you are owed in back pension could exceed the contributions, in which case you will get a lump sum for the balance.
- If you reached State Pension age on or after 24 October 2004, you need to pay the contributions by 6 April 2009.

have six years in which to plug the gap by paying voluntary contributions.

On 24 October 2008, the Government announced that it is changing the law so that, if you reach State Pension age between 6 April 2008 and 5 April 2015, you can buy a further six years of voluntary contributions in addition to those described in the rules above. You must already have at least 20 qualifying years in your National Insurance record. The Government also announced a 50 per cent increase in voluntary Class 3 contributions to £12.05 a week from 2009–10.

THE ADDITIONAL STATE PENSION

Employees build up additional State Pension if they earn more than the lower earnings limit (£95 a week in 2009–10) and are not contracted out of the additional scheme. Self-employed people cannot belong to this part of the State scheme.

The additional State Pension used to be called the State Earnings Related Pension Scheme (SERPS) and changed in 2002 to the State Second Pension (S2P). The additional pension you get depends on the rights you have built up under both SERPS and S2P.

SERPS and, so far, S2P are both earnings-related, which means the more you earn, the larger the pension you can

build up. However, if you earn less than a given amount – called the low earnings threshold (LET) (expected to be £13,900 in 2009–10) – you build up S2P as if you had earnings equal to that amount.

Similarly, the following people who are unable to work are credited with S2P as if they had earnings equal to the LET:

- People caring for children, currently under age 16, reducing to under age 12 from 6 April 2010 onwards.
- People caring for someone with a disability who qualify for Carer's Allowance or the disabled person is getting certain state benefits.
- People who are off work because of long-term sickness and meet certain conditions.

S2P is due to become a flat-rate scheme. This change will be phased in from 2010 onwards.

Jargon buster

Contracted out While you are contracted out, instead of building up additional State Pension rights, you build up pension through a private scheme (an employer's occupational scheme or a personal pension). You either pay less in National Insurance or part of your contributions are rebated and paid direct to the private scheme

For details of the special arrangements for paying voluntary contributions to fill gaps in the years 1996-7 to 2001-2, see www.thepensionservice.gov.uk/resourcecentre/factsheets/home.asp.

Occupational pensions

While working, you may be able to join an occupational pension scheme run by your employer and this is likely to provide the backbone of your retirement finances. Although leaving the employer means you stop paying into that scheme, you keep the pension rights already built up.

The advantage of saving for retirement through any pension scheme is the tax treatment. You get tax relief on what you pay in (within limits – see table, opposite), pension funds grow largely tax-free and you can take part of the proceeds at retirement as a tax-free lump sum (see page 52). The big advantage of an occupational pension scheme over other pension arrangements is that your employer pays a substantial part of the cost of building up your pension. Therefore, even if retirement is only a few years away, it is usually worth joining an occupational scheme if you can – not joining is like turning down a pay rise.

Most occupational schemes require you to contribute, too, and let you pay in extra if you want. Pages 29–32 consider the pros and cons of making extra contributions and boosting your pension through **salary sacrifice** schemes.

The pension you will get from an occupational scheme depends in part on how the scheme works. There are two main types:

- **Salary-related schemes** (see opposite to page 25).
- **Money purchase schemes** (see page 26).

Not all pension arrangements offered through the workplace are occupational schemes. You might instead be able to join a group personal pension scheme (see page 34) or a stakeholder scheme (see also page 34).

 If you have changed jobs in the past, you may have pensions from several different employers' schemes. Page 39 considers whether it might be worth consolidating these before you reach retirement.

Jargon buster

Relevant earnings UK earnings on which you have paid tax, including salary, taxable fringe benefits, profits, and rental income from commercial furnished holiday lettings but not other property income

Salary sacrifice Scheme where you give up some basic pay in return for fringe benefits from your job, such as extra pension rights. The tax treatment of pay and perks means that both you and your employer may be better off as a result (see pages 31-2)

Limits on your pension savings

These limits apply collectively to all the private pensions (occupational schemes and personal pensions) you may have.

Type of limit	Description	Amount		
Annual contribution limit	The maximum contributions on which you can get tax relief. You can continue contributing until your 75th birthday.	£3,600 or 100% of your UK relevant earnings for the year, whichever is greater.		
Annual allowance	The maximum addition to your pension savings in any one year (including, for example, employers' contributions). Anything above the limit normally triggers a tax charge, but this does not apply in the year you start to draw the pension.	Tax year	Amount	
		2008-9	£235,000	
		2009-10	£245,000	
		2010-11 to 2015-16	£255,000	
Lifetime allowance	The cumulative value of benefits that can be drawn from your pension savings. Any amount drawn that exceeds the limit triggers a tax charge.	Tax year	Amount	
		2008-9	£1.65 million	
		2009-10	£1.75 million	
		2010-11 to 2015-16	£1.8 million	

SALARY-RELATED OCCUPATIONAL SCHEMES

In a salary-related scheme (also called a defined benefit scheme), the pension you get is worked out using a formula based on your pay and how long you have been in the scheme (see the case study, overleaf, for a typical example). Two common types are the final salary scheme and career average scheme.

- Final salary scheme. Your pension is a proportion of your pay at or near retirement multiplied by your time in the scheme. This has been the dominant salary-related scheme in the past and is common throughout the public sector.
- Career average scheme. Your pension is a proportion of your pay each year you have been in the scheme. Usually,

To check what sort of pension scheme(s) you belong to through your current or former employer(s), see the scheme booklet(s) or talk with the human resources department.

each year's amount is increased in line with inflation up to the time you retire or leave the scheme. Some employers are switching to this type of scheme because it is often cheaper to provide than a final salary scheme.

While you are building up an occupational pension, the scheme should send you a benefit statement each year, which is a forecast of the amount of pension you could get at retirement expressed in **today's money**.

The law requires that most pensions from salary-related schemes, once they start to be paid, must be increased each year in line with inflation but only up to a limit. Different limits apply depending on when the pension was built up and whether it is a contracted out pension (see page 21). But the statutory increases could be as low as 2.5 per cent a year, which means the pension will lose buying power if inflation is higher. Schemes can choose to pay bigger increases.

The credit crunch that started in 2007, resultant stock-market crash and economic recession increased the

pressure on employers already struggling with the rising cost of salary-related pension schemes. If you work in the public sector, your pension scheme is ultimately backed by the Government and should continue to be a secure way to save for retirement. In the private sector, poor economic conditions may hasten the rate at which remaining final-salary schemes are closed in favour of cheaper, money purchase arrangements. If you are concerned your employer might fail, be aware that there are safeguards to ensure that pensions built up so far are protected, but only up to a maximum limit – see page 50.

Case Study Aleah

Aleah is coming up to age 65 and earns £34,000 a year. She has been in her company's final salary scheme for 14 years. She will get a pension of 1/60th of her final pay for each year she has been in the scheme. Based on her current pay, she would get a pension of 1/60 x £34,000 x 14 = £7,933 a year.

Because salary-related pensions are worked out according to a formula, the amount you will get if you are about to retire is not directly affected by current economic conditions.

" An occupational pension scheme should send you a benefit statement each year. "

Benefit statement

This is an example of a combined benefit statement for a final salary scheme.

The percentage is multiplied by the current salary. Salary for pension purposes may be defined in a special way, eg it might exclude overtime and bonuses.

This is the accrual rate for the scheme (in this case, 1/60th) multiplied by the number of years the person has been in the scheme.

On retirement
Assuming you remain in the scheme until normal pensionable age of 65, you will receive a pension equal to this percentage of your final pensionable salary: **23.33%**

Because your pension automatically rises with your pay, this is the pension you might get in today's money.

Based on your current final pensionable salary of £34,000, your pension would be: **£7,933 pa**

Which would be paid as   **£661.11 monthly**

Based on the amount you have earned so far if you pay, or are credited with, enough full-rate National Insurance contributions, the State Pension payable from State Pension age would be:

Some statements, like this one, are 'combined benefit statements'. They include a forecast of your State Pension, which has been supplied from the Government's computer.

Total State Pension   **£433.33 monthly**

Assuming that both your pensions were payable on the same day you would receive a Combined Pension (before tax) of: **£1,094.44 monthly**

To find out how much pension you might get from an occupational pension scheme, check your most recent benefit statement.

MONEY PURCHASE OCCUPATIONAL SCHEMES

In a money purchase scheme (also called a defined contribution scheme), you build up your own pension fund that is used at retirement to buy a pension. The size of your pension fund depends on:

- **The amount paid in** by you and your employer.
- **How the invested contributions** grow.
- **How much is deducted** in charges.

The other key factor is how much pension you can buy with your fund – this and the different types of pension available are considered in detail in Chapter 2 (pages 55–68). Your scheme might offer to provide the pension, but whether or not it does, you have the right to take your fund and shop around elsewhere for a better pension. It is up to you what type of pension you buy, so you choose whether or not your pension will increase each year to maintain its buying power.

Unlike a salary-related scheme, it is hard to predict how much pension you might get at retirement. You get a benefit statement each year with a forecast of your possible pension in today's money and based on assumptions about how your invested fund might grow in future and what the rate of inflation might be. But, as is painfully evident in the current economic climate, changes such as a slump in the stock market can have a big impact on the forecast – see the case study. Therefore, it is important to:

- **Check your benefit statements each year** and, based on what they say, consider whether you might need to save extra.
- **Stay calm if the stock market falls** and you are more than ten years from retirement. As a long-term investor, you do not need to worry about short-term fluctuations in the value of your investments. You can sit tight and wait for recovery.
- **Shift out of stock-market investments into more stable bonds and cash** once you are within ten years of your chosen retirement date. This strategy protects you from the effects of a stock market fall just before you need to use your fund to buy a pension. Some money purchase occupational schemes make the investment choices for you, but these days many let you choose from a menu of different investment funds. If you are approaching the ten-years-to-go point but the stock market is still very low, you might want to wait for some degree of recovery before you start shifting your existing fund into more stable investments. However, you can make a start by investing new contributions in bonds and cash rather than shares.

 For information on how much pension your fund might be able to buy, see pages 55-68 and the *Which? Essential Guide: Pension Handbook.*

How charges can affect your pension

	Value of each £1,000 of your pension fund in today's money[a] by age 65 if you had been saving regularly since age:			
	20	30	40	50
Before deducting charges	£1,000	£1,000	£1,000	£1,000
After charges of 0.5% a year	£875	£905	£933	£961
After charges of 1% a year	£770	£821	£873	£924
After charges of 1.5% a year	£680	£747	£817	£889
After charges of 2% a year	£603	£682	£766	£856

[a] Assuming the pension fund grows by 7% a year before charges, inflation averages 2.5% a year and you increase your contributions each year in line with average earnings (assumed to average 4% a year).

Source: author's own calculations.

WHEN YOU CAN START YOUR OCCUPATIONAL PENSION

By law, you must normally start your pension between the ages of 50 (increasing to 55 from 6 April 2010) and 75 years. Between those limits, schemes set their own normal pension age from which your full pension is payable. Age 65 is common.

You have the right to ask to carry on working beyond age 65, though your employer can turn you down and does not have to give a reason. Provided your employer agrees and the pension scheme rules allow it, you do not have to retire in

Case Study Pete

Pete, who is coming up to the age of 65, has been in a money purchase occupational scheme for the last 14 years. He pays contributions equal to 5 per cent of his salary and his employer adds another 6 per cent. (At his current salary of £34,000, this means around £312 a month is being invested in the scheme.) His last benefit statement showed a pension fund worth £61,000, which could buy him a level pension of £4,470 a year. But since the date on the statement, the stock market has lost 15 per cent of its value and his fund, which was completely invested in shares, is now worth only £51,900, which would reduce his pension to £3,800 a year.

 For guidance on investments and strategies to manage the level of risk, see Chapter 6. For a more detailed look at investments, see the *Which? Essential Guide: Save and Invest*.

> Do not confuse pension age and retirement age. Since 1 October 2006, under anti-age-discrimination laws, it has become illegal for employers to set a normal retirement age below 65 unless there is an objective reason for doing so – for example, on health and safety grounds. The legislation specifically excludes occupational pension schemes from most of the anti-age-discrimination requirements, so schemes can still set a normal pension age.

pension age for your scheme. This may entitle you to a larger pension once it does start, but you need to check the rules for your scheme and whether you are already on the maximum permitted amount. In a salary-related scheme, there might be an overall cap of, say 45/60ths of your final pay. In a money purchase scheme, your fund will normally simply be left invested and so has the potential to grow further, but you need to check whether your employer will continue to contribute and at what rate. Retiring later might be a useful option to consider if you have a money purchase scheme and your expected pension is currently very low because of the stock-market crash.

order to start drawing a pension from that employer's scheme. And you are completely free to start your pension but take on work elsewhere.

Retiring later

Many schemes let you put off starting your pension beyond the normal

Retiring early

The law lets you retire before the age of 50 (55 from 2010) if you have to because of ill health. Salary-related schemes usually pay fairly generous ill-health pensions based, for example, on the number of years' membership you would have had if you had stayed until normal pension age rather than your actual years of membership. Some employers have **group income protection insurance** to provide a replacement income for employees who have to stop work because of ill health.

In other cases, retiring before the normal pension age for your scheme will usually mean taking a much lower pension. For example, in a salary-related scheme, your pension will be based on fewer years of membership and the

Jargon buster

Actuarial reduction A cut in your pension if you retire early to reflect the extra cost of paying your pension for longer. Often 6 per cent for each year of early retirement

Group income protection insurance Income protection insurance pays out a replacement income if you are unable to work because of a long-term illness or disability. Usually, the income is paid out until you recover or reach retirement age, whichever comes first. A group scheme is a perk of the job, organised by your employer to cover all, or a section, of the workforce

Case Study Paul

Paul has belonged to a salary-related scheme, paying 1/80th of his final pay for each year of membership, for 20 years. Based on his current salary of £40,000, Paul (now aged 60) can expect a pension at the normal pension age of 65 equal to 25 x 1/80 x £40,000 = £12,500 a year. But he would like to retire now. This means his pension would be based on 20 years' membership and the scheme would also make an actuarial reduction of 6 per cent for each year of early retirement (in this case 30 per cent). Paul's pension from age 60 would be 70% x (20 x 1/80 x £40,000) = £7,000 a year. Retiring five years early causes his pension to fall by 44 per cent.

TOPPING UP YOUR PENSION

You may want to top up your retirement savings if your expected pension looks too low or you want to take early retirement. You have several options:

- Some salary-related schemes, particularly in the public sector (covering for example, NHS and local government workers) let you buy **additional pension** (see overleaf). These schemes have typically replaced added-years schemes.
- Most occupational schemes let you pay in Additional Voluntary Contributions (AVCs) on a money purchase basis (see page 33).
- You could save extra through your own personal pension (see page 33).
- Some employers offer salary sacrifice arrangements (see page 31).

scheme will probably make an **actuarial reduction** to reflect the extra cost of paying your pension over a longer period (see the case study, above).

If you retire earlier than the normal pension age from a money purchase scheme, your pension will be lower because fewer contributions will have been paid, the fund will have been invested for a shorter time and also the fund will buy less pension, reflecting the fact that the pension has to be paid out for longer. If your employer is asking for voluntary redundancies, however, you might be offered an enhanced early retirement package.

Jargon buster

Added-years schemes Scheme formerly available with final salary schemes in the public sector, which allowed members to buy extra years that, via the pension formula, increased the value of the pension and other benefits. As final salary schemes have become increasingly expensive, most of these schemes have been withdrawn and replaced by additional pension schemes

Additional pension scheme Scheme where you buy a sum of future pension, paying either by lump sum or regular contributions

Added years schemes

These are schemes that used to be available with final salary schemes in the public sector. They allowed members to buy extra years in exchange for extra monthly contributions or a lump sum. Via the pension formula, the extra years increased the value of the pension and other benefits. For example, if you earned £20,000, expected to have been a member of the scheme for 20 years by the time you reached retirement and the scheme offered a pension of 1/80th of your final salary for each year of membership, you would have been on track to get 20 x 1/80 x £20,000 = £5,000 a year pension. Buying two added years would increase your expected pension to 22 x 1/80 x £20,000 = £5,500 a year. As final salary schemes have become increasingly expensive, most of these schemes have been withdrawn and replaced by additional pension schemes.

❝With additional pension schemes, you can typically choose to buy any amount from £250 a year up to £5,000.❞

Additional pension scheme

Many final salary schemes in the public sector used to offer added years schemes (see box above). If you have already bought extra years in this way, the arrangement continues. But if you are newly looking to boost your pension, most added years schemes are now closed and instead you are likely to be offered an additional pension scheme.

Additional pension schemes work in a similar way, but instead of buying years that boost your pension only indirectly via the pension formula, you buy the pension direct. In the public sector, you can typically choose to buy any amount from £250 a year up to £5,000, in multiples of £250. Additional pension schemes typically have the following features:

- **The pension is increased in line with inflation** from the time it is bought and throughout retirement.
- **The cost is set by the scheme** (and varies from scheme to scheme). It **depends on** your age now, chosen pension age, gender and whether you want your survivors to carry on getting part of the pension if you die – see the case study, opposite. (See page 51 for information about survivors' pensions.)
- **You choose whether to pay** through an increase in your regular contributions to the scheme or in a single lump sum.
- **Your payment should qualify for tax relief** provided that your total contributions are within the limits described on page 23.

Case Study — Claire

Claire, aged 55, spent over ten years away from paid work while her children were young and then returned to full-time nursing. Currently she is on track to complete 27 years membership of the NHS pension scheme by the age of 65 years. Based on her current salary of £25,000 a year, she would get a pension of 27 x 1/80 x £25,000 = £8,438 a year. Claire is looking at buying £2,000 extra pension, which (according to the current NHS pension scheme) will cost her either:

- A single lump sum of just under £27,680, or
- An increase in her regular monthly contributions of £342 a month if she opts to pay over nine years. In that case, the total payments will be £36,893.

Additional Voluntary Contributions (AVCs)

AVC schemes are offered by most occupational schemes. All AVC schemes work on a money purchase basis, so your extra contributions are invested and build up a fund. This can be used to buy extra pension, other benefits or an increased tax-free lump sum (see page 52). Typically AVC schemes are run for your employer by an insurance company or other financial provider and work in much the same way as personal pensions (see page 33) except for:

- **Matched contributions.** Some employers pay extra towards your pension if you do, agreeing to match your contributions up to a maximum level – for example, 3 per cent of your pay.
- **Charges.** Your employer may have negotiated a good deal on charges, so they are lower than for a personal pension.
- **Investment choice.** The AVC scheme might offer a smaller choice of investment funds than you would like.

Salary sacrifice

A salary sacrifice scheme lets you give up some pay in return for fringe benefits from your job, such as extra pension rights. If you are under State Pension age, there can be advantages for both you and your employer when you receive part of your pay in the form of employer's pension contributions instead of normal pay, because you can both save on National Insurance contributions.

You get Income Tax relief on your own contributions to an occupational pension scheme, but you do not get any relief from National Insurance. But whatever

 If you are in a public sector pension scheme, check the scheme website for details of buying additional pension (or added years if still available). Some have online calculators that let you work out the cost.

Over State Pension age, you do not pay National Insurance anyway (see page 85) and in that case salary sacrifice would not be worthwhile.

your employer pays into the scheme for you counts as a tax-free fringe benefit on which you pay neither Income Tax nor National Insurance. Furthermore, your employer also saves National Insurance on money they pay into a pension scheme for you. (The savings also work just as well if your employer pays into a personal pension for you.)

As a result, some employers offer salary sacrifice schemes that let you choose to have varying amounts of your pay package in the form of employer's pension contributions instead of normal pay. Even if your employer does not operate such a scheme, they might be willing to set up such an arrangement if you ask. But think carefully before opting for salary sacrifice. It may affect, for example, the additional State Pension you are building up (see page 21) and your entitlement to other benefits, such as Working Tax Credit or sick pay.

Case Study Arif

Arif, aged 58, earns £36,000 a year. He and his employer both pay 5% of his pay into the pension scheme, making a total of 10% x £36,000 = £3,600. His employer offers a salary sacrifice scheme under which the employer will pay an extra £1,500 into the pension scheme if Arif accepts a pay cut of £1,400 a year. The table below shows how Arif's take-home pay falls by £910 in 2009-10, but the contributions to his pension scheme increase by £1,360 a year, so Arif gains £450 a year from the salary sacrifice.

	Before the salary sacrifice	After the salary sacrifice	Change
Arif's gross salary	£36,000	£34,600	-£1,400
Arif's take-home pay (after pension deductions, tax and National Insurance)	£25,324	£24,414	-£910
Arif's pension contribution	5% x £36,000 = £1,800	5% x £34,600 = £1,730	
Employer's pension contribution for Arif	5% x £36,000 = £1,800	(5% x £34,600) + £1,500 = £3,230	
Total pension contributions	£3,600	£4,960	+£1,360
Arif's net pay plus pension contributions	£28,924	£29,374	+£450

Personal pensions

Personal pensions provide a tax-efficient way to save – or save extra – for retirement. If you cannot save through an occupational scheme (for example, there is no scheme at work, you are self-employed or you are already retired), a personal pension is often the next best option.

Like occupational pension schemes, personal pensions have tax advantages: tax relief on your contributions (up to the limits shown on page 23), the pension fund builds up largely tax-free and you can take part of the proceeds as a tax free lump sum (see page 52).

All personal pensions work on a money purchase basis, so your savings build up your own pension fund, which is used at retirement to buy a pension (see pages 55–68). The size of your fund depends on the amount paid in, how well the invested contributions grow and charges. Bearing this in mind, you might want to consider the special types of personal pension summarised in the table, overleaf.

As with all money purchase pensions, if you invest your fund in the stock market, you should consider moving to less volatile investments, such as bonds and cash, if you are within ten years of the date on which you want to start your pension. The recent stock-market crash has provided a vivid example of the risks of staying invested in shares right up to the point of retirement.

Tax relief on your contributions

When you pay into a personal pension, the amount you pay is treated as if it has been paid net of tax relief at the basic rate (20 per cent in 2009-10). The pension provider claims basic rate relief from HM Revenue & Customs (HMRC) and adds it to your scheme. You get this basic-rate relief even if you are a non-taxpayer. If you are a higher-rate taxpayer, you can claim an extra relief (a further 20 per cent in 2009-10) through your tax return.

 For guidance on choosing an appropriate investment strategy for your pension fund, see Chapter 6. To compare the personal pensions offered by different providers, use the Financial Services Authority's Compare products service at www.fsa.gov.uk/tables.

Special types of personal pension

The table shows how some special types of personal pension differ from a standard scheme. For definitions of the different schemes, see the Glossary on pages 204–10.

	Personal pension (no special type)	Group personal pension scheme	Stakeholder scheme offered through your workplace	Stakeholder scheme you arrange for yourself	Self-Invested Personal Pension (SIPP)
Available through your workplace	✗	✓	✓	✗	✗
Your employer is likely to contribute	✗	✓ at least 3% of pay	✗	✗	✗
Contributions may be deducted direct from your pay	✗	✓	✓	✗	✗
Charges may be lower than average	✗	✓	✓ maximum 1.5% pa in first ten years and 1% pa thereafter	✓ maximum 1.5% pa in first ten years and 1% pa thereafter	✗
May be a very wide choice of investments	✗	✗	✗	✗	✓

WHEN YOU CAN START YOUR PERSONAL PENSION

You must start to draw your personal pension by the age of 75 years. The soonest you can start is normally at the age of 50 (increasing to 55 from 6 April 2010 onwards), though an earlier pension is possible if you cannot work because of illness. The earlier you start the pension, the lower it will be because your contributions will stop early, the fund has less time to grow and the pension has to be paid out for longer. Conversely, the later you start your pension, the larger the pension is likely to be (see page 61).

Case Study Dan

Dan is 63 years old, self-employed and pays Income Tax at a top rate of 40 per cent. He's hoping to retire in a few years' time and is putting as much as he can afford into his personal pension. In 2009–10, he paid in £30,000. The provider claimed basic-rate relief of £7,500 from HMRC to add to the scheme. Dan was able to claim back a further £7,500 relief through his tax return. In this way, Dan has paid a net amount of £22,500 but £37,500 has gone into his pension scheme.

Divorce and pensions

The law takes pensions into account when married couples and civil partners split up, but unmarried partners have no legal rights to each other's pensions.

Couples, particularly if they raise a family together, often organise their finances – including pension savings – at the household level. Typically, the main breadwinner saves on behalf of the couple and the main carer relies on his or her partner for future security in retirement. Splitting up can leave your retirement planning in tatters. The law does offer protection for wives, husbands and civil partners, but unmarried couples have no rights to an ex-partner's pension savings.

❝ Couples often organise their finances at the household level, so splitting up can leave your retirement planning in tatters. ❞

THE STATE PENSION AND DIVORCE

The State scheme has special rules to help people who get divorced. You can substitute your ex-spouse's or ex-civil partner's National Insurance record for part or all of your own if this would result in a higher basic pension than you can get based on your own record. You lose this right if you subsequently remarry or enter a new civil partnership.

Bear in mind that, if you will reach State Pension age on or after 6 April 2010, you need only 30 qualifying years to get the full basic pension (see page 17), which means you are much more likely than in the past to qualify for a full pension on your own record without using your ex's contributions.

To check your position, get a State Pension forecast (see page 15). When you apply for the forecast, you will be asked for details about your ex, so that his or her National Insurance record can be taken into account if relevant. Ideally

 To get a State Pension forecast, see www.thepensionservice.gov.uk. There are several ways to apply for a forecast, including an instant online service (see page 15).

you need to supply your ex's name, date of birth, National Insurance number and last known address. The Pension Forecasting Service does not contact your ex-partner.

On top of your basic pension, you get any additional pension that you have built up in your own right. The State Pension rules do not allocate you any of your ex-partner's additional pension, but a court will take this into account in arriving at a divorce settlement (see below).

> ❝The court can order that part of one spouse's pension rights must be transferred to the other. ❞

PRIVATE PENSIONS AND DIVORCE

Courts must take each person's occupational and personal pension rights and any additional State Pension into account when deciding how to share the family's assets. There are three ways they can be done.

- **Offsetting.** The person with less in pensions may be granted a bigger share of other assets to compensate for the lost pension rights. For example, the wife might be given a large lump sum or the family home and the husband retains his pension rights in full.
- **Earmarking** (more formally called 'attachment orders'). The court can order that part of one spouse's pension once it starts and/or any tax-free lump sum must be paid to the other. This can also be applied to a pension that has already started. In Scotland, only lump sums not pensions can be earmarked in this way.
- **Pension sharing.** The court can order that part of one spouse's pension rights be transferred to the other. The other person then becomes a member of the pension scheme in his or her own right and, except in the case of most public sector schemes, can transfer the rights to another scheme if desired. Pension sharing orders first became possible for divorces started on or after 1 December 2000.

If you arrange your divorce without going to court, you should still make sure that whatever settlement you agree takes pensions into account. However, if you

For more information about dividing your assets when a relationship breaks down, see the *Which? Essential Guide* to *Divorce and Splitting Up.*

want to use pension sharing, you will have to go to court because only a court can order a pension scheme to transfer pension rights from one spouse to the other.

“ Make sure that whatever settlement you agree takes pensions into account. ”

Comparing options for pensions on divorce

	Offsetting	Earmarking	Pension sharing
Creates a clean break between you and your spouse	✓	✗	✓
You will be unaffected by your ex's future pension decisions (eg when starting the pension or his or her death before retirement)	✓	✗	✓
Can be used even if the family has few other non-pension assets	✗	✓	✓
Ensures you get a retirement pension even though your ex made most of the family's retirement savings	✗	Maybe[a]	✓
Ensures you keep your retirement pension if you made most of the family's retirement savings	✓ Full pension retained	✓ Part pension retained	✓ Part pension retained

a If your ex dies before retirement, there will be no pension. Furthermore, if your ex decides to make future contributions to a new pension scheme to which you will have no right, the pension that has been earmarked could be small.

 Sorting out pensions on divorce is complicated – use a solicitor, who will be able to draft in pension experts as necessary. To find a solicitor who is an expert in divorce, contact Resolution at www.resolution.org.uk.

Consolidating pensions

If you have accumulated several different pension schemes over the years, deciding whether or not to consolidate them before retiring is no easy matter. You are likely to need expert advice.

Few people these days stay in the same job all their lives. As you have moved around, you may well have accumulated pension **rights** with several employers and perhaps have more than one personal pension as well. When you get to retirement, you might want to consolidate some or all of these pensions into a single pot (see Chapter 2), but should you tidy up your pension collection now while you are still working?

There is no simple answer to this, but there are a number of important factors you should check out before making any changes – see the box opposite.

Jargon buster

Rights In the context of pensions, 'rights' means an entitlement to receive a pension at some future date. Usually you build up rights year-by-year while you are a member of a scheme. If you stop being a member, you stop building up new rights but generally do not lose rights that you have built up during previous years

In general, you should be very wary of transferring from a salary-related pension scheme to any type of money purchase scheme (occupational scheme or personal pension). A salary-related scheme promises you a given level of pension worked out according to a formula. You are insulated from the ups and downs of the stock market and the rising cost of pensions due to people living longer. If you switch to a money purchase scheme, you will be giving that up and for a pension whose value cannot be predicted in advance – in other words, you will be taking on extra risks.

Comparing different pension schemes to see what you might get from each is complex and always involves making assumptions because no one can be sure of the future. For expert help making your decision, go to an independent financial adviser IFA) who is authorised to give pension transfer advice – you can check whether this is the case by looking at the IFA's entry on the Financial Services Authority's register (see below).

 To find an IFA, see www.unbiased.co.uk. To check what type of advice an IFA is allowed to give, check the advisers' entry on the Financial Services Authority register at www.fsa.gov.uk/register/home.do.

The pros and cons of consolidating your pensions before retirement

Pros

- Convenience. It is easier to keep track of just one scheme rather than several.
- Fears about a former employer's solvency. If your former employer's business fails, there is some risk that any salary-related pension scheme might be unable to pay the promised pensions (but see page 50). Moving your pension now avoids that risk.
- Better deal. You might reckon your current scheme is likely to produce a higher pension than your old scheme(s). Your current scheme might offer a wider range of investments than your old scheme(s).
- Future benefit improvements. An old occupational pension scheme might not be interested in improving the benefits of former employees. But your current employer's scheme, when making improvements, might take into account both the rights that you have built up while working for the new employer and rights you transferred from a previous scheme.
- Economies of scale. With personal pensions, charges are often lower for bigger funds.

Cons

- Blocked by the rules. Not all employers' schemes accept transfers from other pension schemes.
- Extra risk. Consolidating your pensions in one scheme means putting all your eggs in one basket. Transferring from a salary-related to a money purchase scheme, means you take over the risk of a lower pension because of stock-market volatility or poor terms when you come to convert your fund into pension (see Chapter 2).
- Loss of guaranteed benefits. Some money purchase schemes (for example, some older types of personal pensions) offer guarantees about the amount of pension your fund will buy. These guarantees will be lost if you transfer and may be impossible to beat.
- Reduced pension from salary-related schemes. Because each scheme uses different assumptions, the benefits you are promised in your current scheme might be lower than the benefits you give up in the old scheme(s).
- Extra charges. The scheme(s) you leave may deduct a surrender charge. If you switch from an occupational scheme to a personal pension, the charges will almost certainly increase.

If you have lost track of pensions you built up in a previous employer's scheme or an old personal plan, get help from the Pension Tracing Service at www.thepensionservice.gov.uk/atoz/atozdetailed/pensiontracing.asp.

Retiring abroad

A warm climate, a gentler pace of life or joining family are attractive reasons for retiring abroad but, before you pack your trunk, check the impact on your pension.

YOUR STATE PENSION

Wherever you live in the world, you can still claim any UK State Pension that you have built up. However, you will get the yearly State Pension increases only if you live in another European Economic Area country, the Isle of Man, Sark or other countries with which the UK has a social security agreement. Note in particular that you will not qualify for increases if you retire to these popular destinations: Canada, New Zealand, Australia and South Africa. Without the increases, the buying power of your pension with fall each year.

PRIVATE PENSIONS

Occupational and personal pensions can be paid to you anywhere in the world and you should receive the same increases and benefits as UK-based pensioners. Make sure that the scheme has your current address and bank account details.

RESIDENCY AND TAX

If you are a UK resident, you are liable for UK tax on your worldwide income. To escape UK tax on your pensions, you need to count as non-resident. This is a complex area, but essentially you will need to:

- Satisfy HM Revenue & Customs (HMRC) that you intend to live abroad indefinitely.
- Be abroad for at least a whole tax year.
- Spend fewer than 183 days of the tax year in the UK.
- Over the most recent four years, spend on average less than 91 days per tax year in the UK.

You need to check the residency and tax rules of the country abroad to find out what taxes you may be liable for there.

! Bear in mind that a UK pension will be paid in sterling so you will need to exchange it into local currency and may gain or lose as the exchange rate fluctuates.

 For more on State Pensions paid abroad, contact the International Pension Centre at www.thepensionservice.gov.uk/ipc/home.asp. For guidance on tax, contact the Centre for Non-Residency section of HMRC at www.hmrc.gov.uk/cnr/index.htm. See also the *Which? Essential Guide* to *Moving Abroad*.

Pension choices at retirement

The choices you make at the start of retirement set the financial tone for all your retirement years. They determine the income you will get, the financial risks you face and the financial protection for any survivors. These are among the most important decisions you will ever make and it pays both to shop around and to get good advice.

Key decisions

You have important decisions to make when you reach State Pension age and when you decide to start drawing a pension from your occupational and/or personal pension scheme(s).

Reaching State Pension age and starting a private pension may happen at the same time or different times. They may or may not coincide with giving up work. Whether or not you consider yourself to be 'retiring', this chapter looks at how the decisions you make when these events occur will shape all of your retirement.

DECISIONS AT STATE PENSION AGE

The main decision when you reach State Pension age is whether or not to start drawing your State Pension (see pages 14–21 for how much you might get). This section describes the deferment deal the State offers. On the whole, the terms seem generous but will be worth considering only if you can budget without the pension for now. This is most likely to be the case if at present you are carrying on doing some work.

The Pension Service should contact you four months before you reach State Pension age to find out whether you want to claim or defer your pension. If this has not happened by the time you have three months to go, initiate contact yourself. The pension is normally paid straight to your bank or building society account and you can choose whether it is paid every four or 13 weeks.

Deferring your State Pension

If you reach State Pension age but do not immediately need the pension, you could opt to defer it. In return, either your pension will be higher when it does start or you can receive a cash lump sum.

You have to defer for at least five weeks in order to earn extra pension

The value of index linking

A valuable feature of the State Pension is that it is index-linked. This means generally it automatically maintains its buying power throughout retirement (see page 46). The rules are due to change so that the basic State Pension (but not the additional pension) for both new and existing pensioners will be increased in line with earnings inflation rather than price inflation. As earnings tend to increase at a slightly faster rate than prices, this should be good news for pensioners. The Government must announce by 1 April 2011 when the rule change will come into effect. It has already suggested the start date might be 6 April 2012, but this is by no means guaranteed.

How to defer your State Pension

As you approach State Pension age, the Pension Service will normally contact you to find out whether you want to start claiming your State Pension (see opposite). It will send you a claim form and booklet, BR33, which gives you general information about State Pensions and how to claim. There is space on the claim form to say that you would instead like to defer your pension start to a future date. For detailed information, get the Pension Service's free booklet SPD1 'State Pension deferral – your guide' from www.thepensionservice.gov.uk/pdf/spd/spd1may08.pdf.

or at least a year to get a lump sum. You can defer for as long as you like, but you can take deferral only once, either from State Pension age or, if you have already started your pension, by cancelling your pension (and so restarting it later on).

You have to put off your whole State Pension, not just part of it, and if you are a married man and your wife is getting a State Pension based on your National Insurance record (see page 17), her pension must be deferred as well and it also earns the increase or lump sum.

- If you opt for extra pension, you get 10.4 per cent extra for each year you defer (and pro rata for a part year). This increases the total State Pension you get and, as with all State Pensions, the higher total will be increased each year in line with inflation.

- If you opt for the lump sum, you are treated as if your deferred pension had been invested and earned interest at the Bank of England base rate plus 2 per cent. The base rate varies, so you cannot know in advance precisely how much you will get. The table below gives some examples.

Extra pension or lump sum?

The table gives an example of how much extra pension you could get if you defer your State Pension. Alternatively, you could opt to receive a lump sum and the table gives examples of the amount you could get assuming the Bank of England base rate was 3% throughout the deferral period.

If you defer your pension for:	Your weekly pension would rise to:	OR you could have a lump sum of, say:
No deferral	£95.25	£0
1 year	£105.16	£5,078
2 years	£115.06	£10,410
5 years	£144.78	£28,060

Deferral and tax

State Pensions count as taxable income, so any increase you earn will also be taxed if you have enough income to be a taxpayer – see Chapter 7 for information about tax.

Case Study Andy

Andy is a retired engineer but has carried on doing some consultancy work. He's just had his 65th birthday and could have started a State Pension of £103.50 a week. But he does not need this income yet and has decided to defer the pension for five years. Using today's rates, this means giving up £26,910 of pension over the five years. In return he could have a pension of £157.32 a week once it starts. He would need to survive nine years and seven months to break even on the deal and the average life expectancy for a man reaching 70 in 2013 is over 18 years.

Alternatively, Andy could take a lump sum. If the Bank of England base rate was 3 per cent throughout, he would get a return of 5 per cent a year, which is higher than he could get from many banks or building societies. By the end of five years, the lump sum would have grown in value to just over £30,491. But, if inflation averaged 2.5 per cent a year over the five years, the real value of the lump sum would be about £26,949. Andy decides to opt for the increased pension.

If you opt for the lump sum, this is also taxable, but only at the top rate of tax you were paying before getting the lump sum. So the lump sum cannot push you into a higher tax bracket. You also have the option to delay receiving the lump sum until the next tax year. This can be useful if, say, you are stopping work and your income and top tax rate will be lower next year.

DECISIONS ON STARTING A PRIVATE PENSION

You may have built up occupational and/or private pensions from one or more sources over your working life. The decisions you now face depend in part on the type of pension scheme(s) involved as summarised in the boxes opposite and then elaborated upon throughout this chapter.

Each scheme should contact you about three months before the normal pension date for the scheme to tell you that your pension is due and explain your options. If you don't hear from a scheme, make contact yourself.

> **"** The decisions you now face depend in part on the type of pension scheme(s) involved. **"**

If The Pension Service has not contacted you to claim or defer your State Pension, call the Retirement Pension Teleclaim Service on 0845 300 1084. To find out more about claiming your State Pension, see booklet BR33 from www.thepensionservice.gov.uk.

Your key private pension choices

If you have a salary-related pension

- Taking the pension offered is likely to be better than switching to another scheme at this stage (page 48).
- Your main choice is whether to take a lump sum (page 52).
- The other key decision is whether you need to protect any survivors (page 51).

If you have money purchase pensions

- If you have more than one, you may want to consolidate your schemes (page 48).
- Generally, it's worth taking a lump sum even if you need to maximise your income (page 51).
- Consider whether you need to protect any survivors (pages 51 and 60).

How will you cope with inflation?

- Put aside some savings during the early years (see Chapter 6).
- Put off drawing part of your pension, for example, deferring your State Pension (page 42) or phasing your retirement (page 61).
- Increasing annuity (page 57).
- Income withdrawal (page 63).
- Some third-way products (page 66).

Want a flexible income?

- Put off drawing part of your pension, for example, deferring your State Pension (page 42) or phasing your retirement (page 61).
- Income withdrawal (page 63).
- Third-way products (page 66).

Looking for a higher income than an annuity?

- Income withdrawal (page 63).
- Third-way products (page 66).

Want to pass on at least some of your pension savings if you die young?

- Annuity with guarantee (page 59).
- Capital-protected annuity (page 59).
- Income withdrawal (page 63).
- Some third-way products (page 66).

INFLATION AND RETIREMENT INCOME

Some of your retirement income automatically increases each year to keep pace with inflation. This includes your State Pension (see page 14), any state benefits (Chapter 4) and many salary-related occupational pensions (see page 24).

With some other types of income – such as money purchase pensions (see pages 26 and 33) and investments (Chapter 6) – you may have a choice about building in protection against inflation; for example, by opting for an index-linked annuity as described on page 57. Before making such choices, make sure you really think about what

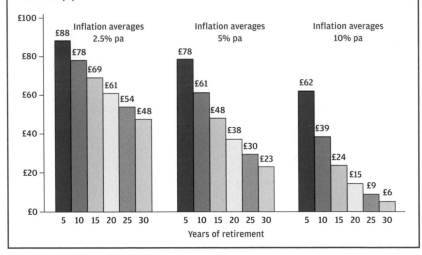

The impact of inflation

The chart shows how inflation eats into the buying power of £100 over the years in three different scenarios with inflation averaging 2.5%, 5% or 10% a year. For example, if you have a level income of £100, after 25 years of inflation at 2.5%, that income will buy only the same as £54 today. If that were your only income, your standard of living would halve. Higher rates of inflation cut into your income even more sharply.

Inflation averages 2.5% pa: £88, £78, £69, £61, £54, £48
Inflation averages 5% pa: £78, £61, £48, £38, £30, £23
Inflation averages 10% pa: £62, £39, £24, £15, £9, £6

Years of retirement

To claim a pension from a private scheme, check your last benefit statement or other scheme documents for the address to contact.

inflation can do to your standard of living over the years. Rising prices reduce the amount you can buy if part or all of your income is fixed. That may seem like stating the obvious, but it is easy to underestimate the impact of even a low rate of inflation when it is eating into your money year after year – see the chart, opposite.

>> **Make sure you really think about what inflation can do to your standard of living over the years. "**

Case Study **Emily**

In 2009-10, Emily receives £6,000 a year in State Pension and a fixed pension of £5,000 a year from a personal pension. She finds the total of £11,000 a year is just about enough to live on. Ten years later, her State Pension still has the same buying power but, if inflation has averaged 2.5 per cent a year, her level pension buys only the same as £3,900 today. She effectively has to live on £9,900 a year, implying a 10 per cent cut in her living standards.

The Pension Tracing Service, www.thepensionservice.gov.uk/atoz/atozdetailed/pensiontracing.asp, can help you contact a scheme with which you have lost touch and you think owes you some pension.

Consolidating your pensions

Consolidating money purchase pensions at retirement may be a good idea, but be very wary of giving up any salary-related pensions. This is a complex decision so, as explained on page 38, get professional advice.

These days it is common to reach retirement with several pensions due to you from, say, your current employer, one or more past employers and also personal pensions that you arranged for yourself. Chapter 1 (page 38) considered the pros and cons of consolidating these pensions into one while you were still working.

If you have kept a variety of separate schemes, the question now is: should you draw a pension from each one or pool them all into a single pension pot? Certainly it would be simpler to deal with just one pension provider. But you also need to look at what pensions you would give up and what you might gain, and the answer depends largely on the types of scheme that you have.

SALARY-RELATED PENSION SCHEMES

Because salary-related schemes tend to offer more generous pensions than money purchase schemes, in general, you will be better off drawing the pension offered by any salary-related scheme rather than transferring your pension rights at this stage to another scheme. So you should be very wary of transferring to a personal pension or occupational money purchase scheme. There are exceptions.

- **Your current employer's scheme is also salary-related,** will accept a transfer from another scheme and would give you a better pension than the one you are giving up. To compare what each will offer, you need a benefit statement from the old scheme, a statement showing the **transfer value** it will pay to the replacement scheme and a statement from the new scheme showing how much pension it will give you for the transfer value.
- **You are worried that the scheme is in financial difficulties** and might not be able to keep up the promised pension payments throughout retirement – see overleaf on how your pension is protected.

The above situations are complex so consider getting advice from an independent financial adviser authorised to give pension transfer advice (see the adviser's entry in the Financial Services Authority's register at www.fsa.gov.uk/register/home.do).

MONEY PURCHASE SCHEMES

You convert money purchase pension funds into pension by buying an **annuity** (see page 55) or using **income withdrawal** (page 63). In general, consolidation of money purchase schemes is likely to be a good idea because:

- Pooling your pension funds from two or more money purchase schemes may mean you can get a better annuity rate.
- Your existing money purchase schemes might not offer income withdrawal, so if that option attracts you, you will have to transfer and consolidating is likely to make **drawdown** more manageable and possibly cheaper (see page 63 for details).

But, if you belong to any money purchase scheme that offers you a guaranteed annuity rate, be wary of giving this up unless you are sure the new scheme offers a better deal.

The Association of British Insurers (the trade body that covers most personal pension providers) recommends that transferring your pension fund from one provider to another at retirement should be completed within ten working days, though research by the Financial Services Authority (FSA) suggests that delays are common. If you lose the best pension rates because of unacceptable transfer delays, complain and ask for redress (see page 158).

Jargon buster

Annuity An investment where you exchange a lump sum (your pension fund) for income that is usually payable for life, but can be for a set period. You cannot get your original investment back as a lump sum

Annuity rate Usually expressed as the amount of income (pension) you get each year for each £10,000 of lump sum

Drawdown Another name for income withdrawal

Income withdrawal Arrangement where you leave your pension fund invested and draw an income direct from the fund. The income will tend to vary with the value of your investments

Transfer value The cash sum that is passed from an old scheme to a new one when you transfer your pension rights. If the old scheme is a money purchase scheme, the transfer value is simply the amount that you have built up in your pension fund. If the old scheme is a salary-related scheme, the transfer value is the lump sum that would need to be invested today in order to provide the promised pension given assumptions about, for example, investment growth

PENSION PROTECTION

If a salary-related scheme does not have enough money to pay all the promised pensions, the employer concerned must pay in extra. If the employer has gone bust, the Pension Protection Fund (PPF) steps in to ensure that the promised pensions are paid up to certain limits. For pensions that are already in payment (rather than still building up) the PPF ensures you get:

- **Your full pension up to a maximum limit,** if you retired at the normal pension age for your scheme or retired early because of ill health.
- **Ninety per cent of your pension** up to a maximum limit if you retired early for other reasons.

The maximum limit varies with age. In 2008–9, at age 65, the 100 per cent limit is £30,856.35 and the 90 per cent limit is £27,770.72. The PPF is funded by a levy on pension schemes. Claims for compensation from the PPF are dealt with by the trustees of the scheme concerned, not you.

❝ If the employer has gone bust, the PPF steps in to ensure the promised pensions are paid up to certain limits. ❞

 Comparing the pension you give up and the pension you might get if you transfer is complicated. Get advice from an independent financial adviser (IFA) authorised to give transfer advice. To find an adviser, see www.unbiased.co.uk. To check what advice an adviser can give, see www.fsa.gov.uk/register/home.do.

Protecting your survivors

The decisions you make now may have big implications for your partner's financial wellbeing as well as your own. Be wary of making choices that could leave your partner in financial distress.

Occupational pension schemes typically offer a package of benefits including a pension for your widow, widower, civil partner or unmarried partner (see box, right) if you die first. At the point of retirement, some schemes let you give up the survivor pension in exchange for a higher pension for yourself. Similarly, if you are buying an annuity (see page 60), you can choose whether to have a higher income for just your lifetime or a lower amount that continues (usually at a reduced rate) for your partner if you die first. In general, you should opt out of the survivor pension only if:

- You are single.
- Your partner has his or her own adequate sources of retirement income.
- Your partner would not be eligible for the survivor pension because, for example, your occupational scheme does not pay pensions to unmarried partners or because your partner is much younger than you and excluded under the scheme's or annuity provider's rules.

To check your scheme's rules for survivors' pensions, see the members' handbook or scheme website, or talk to the pension scheme administrator at work.

Unmarried partners

Most schemes, including public sector schemes (for example, those covering teachers, NHS workers and local government employees), now pay survivors' pensions to unmarried partners. There may be conditions, for example, you had been cohabiting for at least two years up to the time of death and were financially interdependent.

Case Study Ted and Siobhan

Ted and Siobhan enjoyed a comfortable retirement on a joint income of £18,460 a year from their State Pensions and Ted's occupational pension. In 2008-9, Ted suddenly died and his pensions died with him. Siobhan's State Pension increased (because the State Pension scheme includes rules that let a wife or husband effectively inherit part of their deceased spouse's pension) and she qualified for Pension Credit (see page 101), but her total income became just £6,450 a year. When he retired, Ted gave up the option of a widow's pension to boost his own pension from £7,680 to £9,120 a year. If he had kept the widow's pension, he and Siobhan would have had a joint income of £17,040 and, after his death, Siobhan would have had £8,740 a year, including the widow's pension.

Taking a tax-free lump sum

Being able to draw a tax-free lump sum is an attractive perk of pension schemes. Even if you need to maximise your income, it is often – but not always – still worth taking the tax-free cash.

Pension savings are sometimes referred to as 'tax-free', but this is not true. In the main, pension schemes offer 'tax-deferred' savings: you get tax relief on what you pay in and the contributions grow largely tax-free, but generally the proceeds must be taken out as taxable pension. The exception is the tax-free lump sum. Some schemes automatically provide a combination of pension and tax-free cash. But usually you can choose and taking cash reduces the pension you get. Broadly speaking, you can draw a quarter of your pension savings from any type of scheme as a tax-free lump sum.

In most cases, taking the tax-free cash will be a good choice. The exception is where you belong to a salary-related pension scheme – whether or not the choice is a good one depends on how much lump sum you are offered for each £1 of pension you give up (called the **commutation factor**) (see opposite and overleaf for details).

NON-TAXPAYERS

For most people, there's a big jump in their Income Tax personal allowance from age 65 (see page 163). If your taxable income will be no more than the allowance, your pension will be tax-free anyway. But taking the tax-free cash

upfront now is a lower risk strategy than receiving an equivalent sum bit by bit as tax-free pension – after all, you might die young or your tax position might change so that you end up paying tax after all.

TRIVIAL PENSION

If the total of your pension savings come to no more than 1 per cent of the lifetime allowance (see page 23) – in other words, £17,500 in 2009–10 – you don't have to turn any of it into pension. You can take the full amount as a lump sum. One quarter will be tax-free in the normal way, but the rest is taxable.

MAXIMISING INCOME

Where you have saved through money purchase schemes, you reach retirement with a pension fund. If you take a quarter of the fund as tax-free cash that leaves only three-quarters with which to buy your pension. So taking a tax-free lump sum reduces your pension, but you can invest the lump sum to provide a replacement income and, because only the return from your investment is taxed (not the capital itself), your after-tax income can be higher than if you had taken your whole fund as pension. See the case study, opposite, for how this can work.

SALARY-RELATED SCHEMES

Some salary-related schemes – particularly public sector schemes – automatically pay you a pension and a tax-free lump sum at retirement. Other salary-related schemes offer you a choice of a higher pension or a lower pension plus tax-free cash. The rate at which you swap pension for cash – called the **commutation factor** – determines whether or not taking the cash is a good deal. The tax-free lump sum calculator, overleaf, aims to help you decide whether the deal that your scheme offers is worth accepting by comparing the scheme's deal with the rate at which you could turn the lump sum back into pension if you use it to buy an **annuity**. It will give you a basis for starting any discussion with your pension scheme.

Case Study Rasheed

Rasheed, 65 is a basic-rate taxpayer (20 per cent in 2009-10). He has a pension fund of £40,000 and could use a quarter of this to provide a before-tax, index-linked pension of £456 a year (£365 after tax). Instead he takes £10,000 as a tax-free lump sum. He invests the lump sum in a purchased life annuity, which will give him an index-linked before-tax income of £440 a year. Around two-thirds of each payment he gets from this annuity counts as return of his original £10,000 investment and is tax-free. Because only the remainder is taxed, his net income from the purchased life annuity is £407 a year – in other words more than the net pension he gave up.

Jargon buster

Commutation factor In salary-related pension schemes, the amount of tax-free lump sum you get for each £1 of pension you give up

Pension annuity The type of annuity you buy with a pension fund. All the income you get is taxable

Purchased life annuity Type of annuity you buy with your own lump sum. Part of each payment counts as return of your original investment and only the excess is taxed as income. Say you invest £10,000 and are expected to live ten years, £1,000 a year would be tax free

 See pages 55–60 for a guide to the different types of annuity that are available and how to choose between them. See Chapter 6 for guidance on making investments and Chapter 7 for more about tax.

Tax-free lump sum calculator

Use this calculator for a rough idea of whether you are being offered a high enough lump sum for the pension you are giving up. It can give only an indication and you should discuss the details of the deal with your pension scheme administrator or adviser before making any decision.

		Example	Your figures
How much lump sum are you being offered?	A	£38,000	
What is the reduction in your yearly pension?	B	£3,167	
Commutation factor you are being offered C = A / B	C	12	
Is the pension you are giving up: 1 A level pension (ie likely to stay the same amount year after year) without any survivor's pension? 2 A level pension with a survivor's pension? 3 An increasing pension (ie likely to increase each year – say, in line with inflation) without any survivor's pension? 4 An increasing pension with a survivor's pension? D = the number of your answer above.	D	4	
Select the commutation factor from the table below using the column that corresponds to the number you have entered at D, your age and your sex.	E	26	
Is the answer at C higher or lower than the figure at E?	F	Lower	

If F is 'Lower', swapping pension for a tax-free lump sum might be a poor deal.
If F is 'Higher', swapping pension for a tax-free lump sum might be a good deal.

Commutation factors based on annuity rates available August 2008

Age at which you are making the swap	1		2[a]		3		4[a]	
	Man	Woman	Man	Woman	Man	Woman	Man	Woman
50	17	18	18	18	36	38	40	40
55	16	17	17	17	31	33	35	36
60	15	16	16	16	26	29	30	31
65	14	14	15	15	22	24	25	26
70	12	13	13	14	18	20	21	22
75	10	11	12	12	15	16	17	18

a Assumes you and your partner are the same age and that the survivor's pension is half your pension.

Source: Annuity rates used to calculate these factors are from Financial Services Authority (online). www.fsa.gov.uk/tables. Accessed 5 August 2008.

Annuities

An annuity is an investment where you swap a lump sum – such as your pension scheme – for an income, usually payable for life. You cannot get your original investment back as a lump sum. A lifetime annuity combines investment with insurance so you can be confident of a stable income however long you live.

With occupational money purchase schemes, personal pensions and all other money purchase arrangements, at retirement you need to turn your accumulated pension fund into a pension. If you had perfect foresight, you could invest your fund somewhere safe and draw off just the right amount of pension each month so that your fund was run down to zero exactly on the day you died. In practice, there are two problems with this strategy:

- **The return on your investments** will either be at a guaranteed but low rate or a higher but unpredictable rate, and
- **You do not know when you will die,** so you have no set term over which to run down your fund.

These two problems are at the heart of the dilemma over whether to go for safe but unexciting traditional annuities or whether to opt for newer variations that aim to deliver a higher income, but inevitably involve risks. This section looks at annuities, the next section considers income withdrawal (see pages 63–5), and finally we look at new 'third-way'

products that aim to give you some of the security of annuities combined with some of the flexibility and potential extra return from drawdown (see pages 66–8).

❝ You have the right to shop around for the best pension deal you can find. ❞

 You do not have to accept the pension offered by your current occupational money purchase scheme or personal pension provider. You have the right (called your open market option (OMO)) to shop around for a better deal elsewhere. The difference between the highest and lowest annuity rates can be as much as 40 per cent. This can make a substantial difference to your income throughout retirement. Use your OMO!

LIFETIME ANNUITIES

The traditional – and still most popular – way to turn your pension fund into pension is to buy a **lifetime annuity**. You hand the whole fund over to an insurance company and in return get an income for the rest of your life. This is a one-off decision – once you have bought the annuity, you cannot change your mind or get your lump sum back.

The insurance company invests your fund in relatively safe, long-term investments (mainly **gilts**, but sometimes corporate bonds) so that it can be sure of being able to provide the promised income year in, year out. It also promises to pay you the income however long you live. To do this, it pools you with lots of other pensioners. The pensioners who die young subsidise the cost of paying continuing pensions to those who live well beyond average. In other words, an annuity has built-in insurance against living longer than your savings would otherwise have lasted. Like all insurance, not everyone claims (in this case, not everyone lives longer than average), but you are buying peace of mind in case you do need to claim.

Jargon buster

Corporate bond A loan to a company that can be bought and sold on the stock market

Enhanced annuity A lifetime annuity paying a higher than normal income because you are likely to have a shorter than average life due to your lifestyle or a health condition (for example, smoking, diabetes)

Escalating annuity Annuity where the income paid out increases by a set percentage each year (for example, 3 per cent or 5 per cent a year)

Gilt A loan to the British Government that can be bought and sold on the stock market. If the loan is held for its full term, the investment produces a fixed return and, because the Government is unlikely to default, these are considered to be very safe investments

Impaired life annuity A lifetime annuity paying a significantly higher than normal income because your poor health means you are likely to have a much shorter life than average

Lifetime annuity Investment where you swap a lump sum for an income that continues for the rest of your life, however long you live

Level annuity An annuity where the amount of income paid out stays the same year after year

Retail Prices Index (RPI) A common measure of price inflation. RPI measures changes in a basket of goods and services chosen to reflect the way the average household spends its money

RPI-linked annuity Annuity where the income paid out increases each year in line with price inflation as measured by the Retail Prices Index (RPI). If prices fell (deflation), the income would fall

LEVEL, ESCALATING AND RPI-LINKED ANNUITIES

The most basic type of annuity provides a level income throughout retirement. Despite the certainty that inflation will reduce the future buying power of a level income (see page 46), a **level annuity** is still the type most commonly bought.

An alternative is an annuity where the income increases each year, either by a set amount (often called an **escalating annuity**) or in line with price inflation – usually measured by changes in the **Retail Prices Index (RPI)**. This provides partial or full protection from inflation, but the starting income is much lower and it may take many years before you catch up with the total that a level annuity would have paid out – see the table, overleaf. Because there are relatively few buyers and sellers of **RPI-linked annuities** and escalating annuities, these rates are not always particularly competitive. Therefore, a level annuity may be the sensible choice, provided you plan how you will cope with rising prices over the years – for example, by saving during the early years of retirement to boost your spending later.

❝ Inflation will reduce the buying power of a level income. ❞

Annuity rates

Annuity rates are set by market conditions and so are varying all the time. Their general level tends to reflect the return on long-term gilts and projections about how long people on average will live. (As people generally are living longer, annuity rates have been falling. This does not necessarily mean that annuities now offer a poor deal – the lower rate reflects the expectation that on average the promised income will have to be paid out for longer.)

The rate you individually are offered will be based mainly on your age (the older you are, the higher the annuity rate) and your sex (women get a lower rate than men because they tend to live longer).

However, if your lifestyle or health is poor, so that you are expected to live for a shorter length of time than the average person, you can often get a higher rate by shopping around for an enhanced or impaired life annuity.

 To check out current annuity rates and compare what different providers are offering, see the Financial Services Authority's Compare products service at www.fsa.gov.uk/tables. For details of specialist IFAs who can help you shop around for the best annuity, see Useful addresses (page 213).

Level, escalating and RPI-linked annuities compared

The table shows, for a man aged 65, how the income and buying power of different types of annuity change over the first five years and selected years thereafter. It also shows the total paid out in today's money. If inflation is low (2.5% a year), it takes 44 years before the RPI-linked annuity has paid out as much in today's money as the level annuity – as shown by a dark blue box. If inflation is higher (5% a year), the breakeven point comes after 23 years (again indicated by a dark blue box). Average life expectancy for a man aged 65 is 20 years and 10 months.

Year	Level annuity			Escalating annuity: increasing at 3% a year			RPI-linked annuity		
	Yearly income in £s	Yearly income in today's money	Total paid to date in today's money	Yearly income in £s	Yearly income in today's money	Total paid to date in today's money	Yearly income in £s	Yearly income in today's money	Total paid to date in today's money
IF INFLATION AVERAGES 2.5% A YEAR									
1	£732	£732	£732	£552	£552	£552	£456	£456	£456
2	£732	£714	£1,446	£569	£555	£1,107	£467	£456	£912
3	£732	£697	£2,143	£586	£557	£1,664	£479	£456	£1,368
4	£732	£680	£2,823	£603	£560	£2,224	£491	£456	£1,824
5	£732	£663	£3,486	£621	£563	£2,787	£503	£456	£2,280
21	£732	£447	£12,143	£997	£608	£12,175	£747	£456	£9,576
44	£732	£253	£19,886	£1,968	£680	£27,018	£1,319	£456	£20,064
IF INFLATION AVERAGES 5% A YEAR									
1	£732	£732	£732	£552	£552	£552	£456	£456	£456
2	£732	£697	£1,429	£569	£541	£1,093	£479	£456	£912
3	£732	£664	£2,093	£586	£531	£1,625	£503	£456	£1,368
4	£732	£632	£2,725	£603	£521	£2,146	£528	£456	£1,824
5	£732	£602	£3,328	£621	£511	£2,657	£554	£456	£2,280
23	£732	£250	£10,367	£1,058	£362	£10,359	£1,334	£456	£10,488
24	£732	£238	£10,606	£1,089	£355	£10,714	£1,401	£456	£10,944

Source: Annuity rates used to calculate these projections are from Financial Services Authority (online). www.fsa.gov.uk/tables. Accessed 7 August 2008.

INVESTMENT-LINKED ANNUITIES

With traditional annuities, the provider invests your fund mainly in gilts to produce a safe, dependable return. But the return from safe investments tends to be much lower than you can get from riskier investments, such as shares (see page 137). By investing your fund in shares, over the long-term, a higher income should be possible. The snag is that shares are volatile. As the stock market rises and falls, so does your income.

Investment-linked annuities typically let you choose what combination of income and risk you want. They work like this:

- You use your pension fund to buy an annuity where the income will be linked to the performance of an underlying fund of investments. Usually you can choose from a range of different funds.
- You assume what level of investment growth you expect in future. If you choose a high assumed growth rate, your starting income is high. If you choose a low assumed growth rate, your starting income is low.
- Each year your income is reviewed. If the growth rate over the past year has been higher than your assumed rate, your income for the coming year increases. If the growth rate has been lower than your assumed rate, your income is cut.

Investment-linked annuities are suitable only if you can cope with an income that may fall. You may need an adequate, stable income from other sources.

GUARANTEES AND CAPITAL PROTECTION

Like any insurance, lifetime annuities are great if you 'claim' (that is, live longer than average), but can seem like a poor deal if you don't – in annuity terms, if you die younger than average. In response to such concerns, the following variations have developed:

- **Annuity with guarantee.** This is a lifetime annuity where the provider guarantees to pay out the income for at least a chosen term (usually five years, but can be as long as ten), even if you die before the term is up. You can nominate who should get the income if you do die within the guarantee period.
- **Capital-protected annuity.** This lifetime annuity is guaranteed to pay out at least as much as you invested. For example, if you paid £10,000, but the annuity had paid out only £8,500 by the time you died, your survivors would get the balance of £1,500.

With both these options, the level of income you get is lower than from an annuity without the feature, but the

 If you are attracted to investment-linked annuities, you might also want to consider income withdrawal (see page 63) or the new 'third-way' solutions (see page 66).

reduction may be small. For example, in August 2008, a ten-year guarantee for a 65-year-old man reduced the pay-out from a level annuity by around £12 a year for each £10,000 invested.

SHORT-TERM ANNUITIES

Once you buy an annuity, you are normally locked in for the rest of your life. That's bad luck if, with hindsight, you bought when annuity rates were particularly low. Short-term annuities let you keep your options open. You can invest just part of your pension fund in an annuity that pays out for up to five years. At the end of that time, you can use another part of your fund to buy a further annuity, and so on. But this can continue only to age 75 by which time the balance of your fund must normally be used to buy a lifetime annuity (but see page 63).

Protecting your partner

So far this section has assumed you are buying an annuity that will pay out just for your own lifetime – called a 'single life annuity'. But, if your partner depends on you financially or you share expenses, you may need an annuity that will carry on paying out until the second of you dies – a 'joint-life-last-survivor annuity'. You can choose annuities that pay out the same income or a reduced amount to your survivor if you die first. The amount of income you select and the age of your partner will affect the annuity rate you can get. The table shows examples for a man aged 65 buying a level annuity (see page 57). The first row shows the income the man could get if he bought a single life annuity just for himself. In the subsequent rows, you can see that the income is lower if he buys an annuity to pay out an income until both he and his partner have died, especially if his partner is a lot younger (and so might survive him for many years) and if there is no reduction in the income for his survivor if he dies first.

Annuities taken out by a man aged 65	Starting income £ a year for each £10,000 invested	
Type of annuity	Female partner same age	Female partner 10 years younger
Single level annuity	£732	£732
Joint-life level annuity – no reduction in income on death	£636	£576
Joint-life level annuity – one-third reduction in income on death	£660	£624
Joint-life level annuity – half reduction in income on death	£684	£648

Source: Annuity rates are from Financial Services Authority (online). www.fsa.gov.uk/tables. Accessed 7 August 2008.

Deferring and phasing

Putting off the start of retirement is a simple way to increase your pension. Staggering the start is another option and can also be a way to protect your income against inflation.

If your pension savings are not enough to support the lifestyle you want in retirement, one way to improve the position could be to retire later – see the table, below. Your fund will have extra time to grow, you may be able to carry on paying in contributions and, since your pension will not have to be paid out for so long, you will get a better annuity rate when you do finally start your pension.

Another option might be to phase your retirement, by converting your pension savings into pension in stages, in other words using part of your pension fund to

Retiring later to boost your pension

The table shows, for a person who has a pension fund of £100,000 in August 2008, how much extra pension they might get each month from putting off their retirement for five years even if they did not pay any further contributions during those five years. If they carried on paying in to their pension scheme, the extra pension at the end of five years would be even greater.

	If they put off retiring from age:			
	55-60	60-65	65-70	70-75
MEN				
Total pension given up over 5 years	£16,200	£19,200	£22,800	£27,600
Extra pension once it starts £/month	£108	£128	£163	£212
Number of years they need to survive to break even	12 years 6 months	12 years 6 months	11 years 8 months	10 years 10 months
WOMEN				
Total pension given up over 5 years	£15,000	£17,400	£21,000	£25,200
Extra pension once it starts £/month	£92	£123	£146	£182
Number of years they need to survive to break even	13 years 7 months	11 years 10 months	12 years	11 years 6 months

buy a lifetime annuity on one date, using a further part to buy a second lifetime annuity on another date, and so on. This could help you, for example, to:

- **Reduce your working hours,** while drawing some of your pension to make up the shortfall in your income. You can draw further tranches of pension as you cut back further on work.
- **Leave some of your pension fund invested for now** so that you can gradually draw more pension later to offset the effects of inflation.

Most modern personal pensions let you phase your retirement. Income withdrawal (see opposite) could be another way to achieve the same effect. If your current money purchase arrangements do not allow phasing or income withdrawal, consider switching to another that does (see Consolidating your pensions on pages 48–50).

‟ Another option might be to phase your retirement. This could help you reduce your working hours. **”**

Income withdrawal

This route offers flexibility and the chance of a higher pension than you could get from an annuity, but only by taking on substantial extra risks and charges.

Rather than buying an annuity at retirement, you could instead leave your pension fund invested and draw a pension direct from the fund – called income withdrawal or income drawdown. This can be attractive if you want to vary your income as retirement progresses and/or have the chance of a higher income than an annuity can provide. But this route is suitable only if you will be comfortable with a pension that may fluctuate quite violently, so, in general, you need a large (say, six-figure) pension fund or other sources of income to fall back on.

Unlike an annuity, with income withdrawal, there is no insurance element to ensure that your pension will carry on however long you live. You will be relying purely on your own pension fund for a continuing income. To guard against running down the fund too fast, there are rules about how much pension you can draw off:

- Under the age of 75 years. Your pension must be in the range nil–120 per cent of the single-life level annuity without guarantee that could be bought with your fund for someone of your age and sex (see the case study, right). The pension is reviewed every five years or earlier if you request it.

(Opting initially for a nil pension lets you take your tax-free lump sum – see page 52 – while deferring the start of your pension). Under the age of 75, an income withdrawal pension is known as an unsecured pension.

- Aged 75 and over. Your pension must be in the range 55–90 per cent of the single-life level annuity without guarantee that could be bought with your fund for someone of your sex but aged 75. The pension is reviewed each year. From the age of 75, an income withdrawal pension is known as an alternatively secured pension.

Case Study Joanna

Joanna, 65, has a £400,000 pension fund. She draws a quarter of this as a tax-free lump sum. The remaining £300,000 could buy a level annuity without guarantee for a 65-year-old woman of £20,880. Joanna is allowed to draw a pension between £0 and 120% x £20,880 = £25,056 a year for the first five years. She draws the maximum amount. Five years later, despite modest investment growth, her remaining fund is worth £219,400. Being five years' older, Joanna qualifies for a higher annuity rate but rates generally have fallen by 10%. The maximum pension she can draw over the next five years is only £20,537.

Important differences between lifetime annuities and income withdrawal

	Lifetime annuity[a]	Income withdrawal
Investment risk	The promise to pay you a set income is backed by the annuity provider investing in gilts, which produce a fixed, low-risk return or sometimes good quality corporate bonds.	To beat the income from an annuity, you need to invest your fund in investments that offer the chance of a higher return than gilts, but these investments will also be more risky (see Chapter 6).
Longevity risk	An annuity is partly insurance and promises to pay out however long you live.	To guard against your fund running out, rules limit the yearly income you can have.
Income	Set from the time you retire. Depending on the type of annuity you choose, the income may be fixed, escalating or inflation-linked.	Your income is reviewed every five years up to age 75 and yearly thereafter. If your investments and/or annuity rates have fallen, your income will be cut. If your investments have performed well or annuity rates have risen, your income can rise.
Charges	Charges are built into the annuity rate you are offered. You may have to pay a fee for advice when you first buy. Otherwise, no explicit charges.	Ongoing charges for managing your investments and carrying out the reviews. You may also pay fees for investment advice.
Inheritance	You can arrange a modest sum for your heirs if you die soon after buying the annuity and/or a pension for a surviving partner.	Before age 75, your surviving partner can draw a pension or your heirs can inherit your remaining fund subject to a tax charge of 35% in 2008–9. From age 75 onwards, your partner can draw a pension or you can leave the fund to charity. Other options are usually subject to a tax charge of over 80%.

a Other than investment-linked annuities.

In the past, income withdrawal was frequently viewed as a good way of passing on tax-efficient pension savings to your heirs. But the Government has changed the tax rules to make this use of withdrawal no longer worthwhile beyond age 75 (see the table, opposite) and to encourage most people to buy an annuity by that age. However, you can continue with income withdrawal if you want and this may be attractive if, say, you have religious objections to annuities (as a form of gambling on life).

REINVESTING YOUR TAX-FREE LUMP SUM

Income withdrawal opens up a novel way to boost your pension savings. If you are under 75, you can draw a quarter of your pension fund as a tax-free lump sum but opt for nil pension. You can then reinvest the lump sum as a contribution, picking up tax relief on the way – the case study, right, shows how this works.

Although tax anti-avoidance rules generally ban recycling the tax-free lump sum in this way, there is an exception where the lump sum involved is no more than 1 per cent of the lifetime allowance: £17,500 in 2009–10 (see page 23). Bear in mind that the gross value of the contribution must also be within the limits set out on page 23 if it is to qualify for tax relief.

Case Study — Phil

Phil, 58, is a self-employed plumber making around £40,000 a year who intends to carry on working for a while yet. He has £70,000 in a personal pension. If he starts income withdrawal now, he can take 25% x £70,000 = £17,500 as a tax-free lump sum, but put off drawing any pension. He can invest the £17,500 in a new personal pension. The plan provider adds basic-rate tax relief of £4,375, so Phil now has total pension savings of £74,375. However, Phil needs to factor in any extra charges for the income withdrawal arrangement.

> **❝ Income withdrawal opens up a novel way to boost your pension savings, recycling the tax-free lump sum. ❞**

 Income withdrawal is complex and risky, so always get independent financial advice. To find an adviser, see www.unbiased.co.uk.

'Third-way' products

Income withdrawal is too risky for most people, but lifetime annuities offer a seemingly poor deal. This has spurred a market in new products that aim to tread a middle course, offering some of the advantages of each while damping down the disadvantages.

A third-way product combines some of the features of annuities with a few of the features of income withdrawal to provide a pension that may be flexible and may be higher than that offered by an annuity but with lower risk than income withdrawal. Like income withdrawal, third-way products aim to cater for people seeking to turn a pension fund into income and who want one or more of the following features:

- **Opportunity to vary your income** as your circumstances change. For example, you gradually wind down work, take more holidays in the early years, or cope with care costs in the later years.
- **Opportunity to take advantage of changing external circumstances.** For example, if annuity rates improve later on or the Government relaxes pension scheme rules.
- **Chance of a higher income** than traditional annuities offer.

- **Ability to pass on at least some of the pension fund to survivors** in the case of early death.

However, in all cases, the aim is to offer more security than income withdrawal. At the time of writing, there are just half a dozen or so third-way products available in the UK. They all work in different ways and can be thought of as lying on a spectrum from annuities with flexible features to income withdrawal with guarantees – see the chart, opposite.

HOW THIRD-WAY PRODUCTS WORK

You pay for the extra flexibility or guarantees of these third-way products either through the charges for the product or lower annuity rates. In addition, as with income withdrawal, you may be paying ongoing charges for leaving your pension fund invested or linking your pension to some underlying

 Get advice from an independent financial adviser (IFA) with knowledge and experience of these products. To find an IFA, fo to www.unbiased.co.uk. See also the *Which? Essential Guide: Pension Handbook*.

A spectrum of third-way products

EXAMPLES OF THE THIRD WAY

Income withdrawal (see page 63)

UNCERTAIN INCOME

HIGH FLEXIBILITY

Flexible income. Guaranteed minimum fund at age 75 but reviewed, say every 3 years to lock-in any gains which would increase this maturity value.

Guaranteed minimum income with potential to increase. Guaranteed sum at age 75, less amount withdrawn as income, that can be used to buy a lifetime annuity.

Short-term annuity that pays a fixed income for, say, 3 or 5 years. You get a guaranteed minimum sum at age 75 (or earlier) that can be used to a buy a lifetime annuity.

Investment-linked lifetime annuity. Income fixed for, say, 5 years at a time. Change in income at review depends on investment performance and annuity rates.

Traditional annuity
(see pages 55–60)

INCOME CERTAINTY

NO FLEXIBILITY

investment funds. You need to weigh up the impact of all these charges on your pension fund or the income offered. There is a risk that any advantage in the form of investment performance, rather than flowing to you, may be creamed off by the providers of the product and the underlying investment funds. However, if the market for third-way products grows, charges might become more competitive. As with all complex investments, where these products offer guarantees, check how they are to be met and whether there are circumstances when the guarantees could break down.

❝Think carefully about the features you personally want.❞

CHOOSING BETWEEN THE PRODUCTS

With so much variation in the products, there is no simple way to choose between them. You will need to think carefully about the features you personally want (such as fixed or variable income, how much variation in income you would be comfortable with, whether you want a guaranteed minimum income, and length of time between review periods) and then sift through the products for the most suitable match. It is best to do this with the help of an IFA (see page 160). So far, however, many advisers have a low awareness of these third-way products, so check that the advisers you approach have both an interest and expertise in these options. For example, try asking: what proportion of your customers over the last year have taken out a third-way product? Although take-up is currently very low (less than 3 per cent), you will be looking for an adviser who has sold at least some of these products or whose reply shows a good knowledge of them.

Continuing to work

Deferring retirement or continuing to work after you have started to draw a pension might be a financial necessity, especially if you are nursing a pension fund damaged by falling share prices. But equally it could be a lifestyle choice, with work providing, for example, stimulation, companionship and a sense of self-worth. This chapter explains the opportunities, rights and rules that apply to working in your later years.

Your right to stay on

In general, it is illegal for employers to discriminate against workers on the grounds of age. But the legal protection is weak once you reach the age of 65 years.

AGE DISCRIMINATION LEGISLATION

On 1 October 2006, new legislation came into effect in the UK to ban age discrimination in the workplace. As a result, normally you cannot be forced to retire before the age of 65 years. In theory, your employer could legally set a lower normal retirement age or require you personally to retire earlier if he or she can show some objective justification for this policy or action – for example, genuine health and safety grounds. In practice, it is very unlikely that an employer could make an objective case for doing this, since inability to carry out a job is seldom if ever due directly to age. It will be for the courts to decide each case on its merits. If your employer tries to retire you before age 65 and you don't

 Your employer must give you at least six months' notice that you are coming up to your expected retirement date so you can plan ahead and have plenty of time to put in a request to stay on if you want to.

agree with the reason given, you can appeal (see page 75).

Beyond the age of 65, you have the right to ask to stay on and your employer must consider your request. However, he or she can turn you down and does not have to say why. The Government has said it will review the default age of 65 in 2011, so there is a chance it could be raised in future. But, for now, you have no legal right to stay beyond the age of 65 years.

CHANGING JOB

There is nothing to stop you drawing a pension from one employer's scheme and taking a job elsewhere. The age discrimination rules apply to recruitment and so place a general ban on turning down an applicant on the grounds of age. However, there are various exceptions. You can legally be turned down because of age if:

- **You are older than age 65** (or the employer's normal retirement age if younger) or you are within six months of reaching that age.
- **There are objective grounds for turning you down.** For example, it is unlikely you could work for a reasonably long enough period following training.
- **There is a genuine occupational reason,** such as, needing a younger person to act in a particular role in a play.

On top of that, it can be very hard to pin down why you have been rejected. Although application forms frequently no longer ask for your date of birth or age (and there's no reason to include these details on your CV), it is easy for an employer to estimate your age from your qualifications and employment history. If you believe you have been discriminated against, you have the right to take your complaint to an **employment tribunal**, which can award compensation. As part of the process of gathering the evidence you need, you have the right to send the employer a questionnaire seeking information about the interview and selection criteria – see page 75 for more information.

Jargon buster

Employment tribunal A body like a court, but less formal, that resolves disputes between employees and employers about, for example, unfair dismissal and discriminatory treatment

Pension age

Do not confuse retirement age with pension age. In the main, pension schemes are exempt from the age discrimination rules and can set any normal pension age they like – this applies to any current employer's scheme and also any occupational pensions you are due to receive from previous employers' schemes. In April 2006, there was a change in the Government's rules so that it is now possible to stay on in your current job and simultaneously start drawing a pension from your current employer's occupational scheme, provided the scheme rules allow this. Continuing to work does not affect your right to draw your State Pension or any personal pensions you may have.

 For a list of recruitment agencies that specialise in helping older people to find work, see www.agepositive.gov.uk/resource/links.asp.

Your rights at work

Since the age discrimination rules came into effect, if you are over State Pension age, you now have mainly the same rights as younger workers. Exemptions from the rules often work in your favour.

PAY AND BENEFITS

Any employee aged 22 or over, with no upper age limit, must be paid at least the national minimum wage. In the year from 1 October 2008, this is £5.73 an hour. In general, employers should not base pay scales on age or length of service, but a few exceptions are allowed. In particular, people whose service record is longer than other workers by up to five years can be given extra pay and/or benefits. For example, it is legal for an employer to give extra paid holiday to employees who have completed, say, two years with the firm. Longer service can also be rewarded, if the employer can objectively justify it – for example, by showing that more experienced staff are more efficient, and you can be paid extra to reflect higher qualifications and skills.

Sick pay

There is now no upper age limit for statutory sick pay. In 2009–10, if you are off work sick for more than three days and you earn at least £95 a week, you are entitled to sick pay at a standard rate of £79.15 a week for a maximum of 28 weeks. (The daily rate is normally £79.15 divided by the number of days you work each week.) Employers often run their own more generous schemes, so you may get more than this.

Company pension scheme

An important benefit while you are working and still building up a pension is that your employer may be paying contributions to the company pension scheme on your behalf (see page 22). If this applies, the age discrimination rules say the employer contributions must not stop simply because you have reached a particular age. However, the scheme rules are allowed to set a maximum pension entitlement – say two-thirds of your pay. If you have already reached that maximum, there is no point in either you or your employer paying in any extra, so the law says your employer's contributions (and your own) can stop.

 For help and advice enforcing your right to receive the national minimum wage, call the HM Revenue & Customs National Minimum Wage Helpline on 0845 600 0678.

Hours and holiday

The laws about hours and holiday entitlement do not have any upper age limit. Your main rights are:

- Each year: At least 4.8 weeks off. This applies pro rata, depending on the length of your working week. For example, if you work five days a week, you are entitled to 4.8 x 5 = 24 days off a year. From 1 April 2009, the entitlement increases to 5.6 weeks. Bank holidays count as part of the entitlement – they are not extra.
- The working week: A maximum 48 hours a week unless you have agreed in writing to longer hours. At least one day off per week or two days per fortnight.
- Every 24 hours: At least 11 continuous hours off.
- Your working day: A rest break of at least 20 minutes if the working day is longer than six hours.

FLEXIBLE WORKING

Some examples of flexible working that might help you strike a balance between work and retirement are working part-time, condensed hours (for example, working a full week but in four days), flexitime and working partly from home or in a job share.

If you have been with your current employer for at least six months and you are looking after a family member who needs care, you have a legal right to request flexible working. Your employer must consider your request, but can turn you down if he or she has good business reasons for doing so. But, even if you do not have a legal right to request flexible working, many employers are happy to consider flexible arrangements if you ask.

Either way, the onus is on you to decide what arrangement you want and to show how it could work. Any switch to flexible working will be a permanent change in your contract of employment and may, of course, affect your pay and other benefits.

Family emergencies

By law, you are entitled to time off to deal with a family emergency where someone who is dependent on you needs your help. 'Dependant' includes your husband, wife, partner, child, parent or someone else who lives with you as part of the family. This must be a genuine unforeseen emergency, for example, someone falling ill, having an accident or normal care arrangements unexpectedly breaking down. You must

The Department for Business Enterprise and Regulatory Reform has produced a form to help you set out your request for flexible working. You can download form FW(A) from www.berr.gov.uk/files/file37031.doc.

Making a request to work flexibly

Your request should be in writing and include the following points:

- If you are a carer, your relationship to the person you care for, the nature of the care you provide and that you are making the request under your statutory right.
- The type of flexible work pattern you want.
- The effect you think that pattern would have on your employer and how any problems could be overcome. (You might want informally to talk to colleagues and perhaps include their reactions and suggestions here.)
- The date on which you want to start working flexibly. Allow at least 14 weeks for your request to be considered and put into effect.
- Whether you have made any previous requests to work flexibly and, if so, when.
- Date of your request.

tell your employer as soon as possible why you haven't turned up for work and when you will be back. Your contract of employment will say whether or not you will be paid, but your employer is not required to give paid leave for this purpose.

TRAINING AND PROMOTION

Your employer may not withhold training or deny you promotion on the grounds of age, unless he or she can show an objective reason for doing so. For example, your employer might argue that it would not be cost effective to pay for your training given that you are likely to retire in a few years. But this would not necessarily be justifiable if younger workers are free to leave soon after receiving training.

Similarly, external providers of training – such as further education colleges and universities (but not schools) – must no longer set age limits for entry onto their courses, unless there is an objective reason. For example, it might be lawful for a community centre to organise computer courses for people over, say, age 60, provided it could show that discriminating in favour of older people was justified because in that geographical area older people lacked computer skills and this was putting them at a disadvantage finding work compared with younger workers.

REDUNDANCY

Since 1 October 2006, it is illegal for an employer to select workers for redundancy on the grounds of age unless

 To check your rights, contact the Association for Conciliation and Arbitration Services (ACAS) Helpline on 08457 47 47 47.

he or she can show objective justification for the policy. It is very unlikely that an employer could justify an age-related policy. In general, using age as a criterion amounts to unfair dismissal.

Whatever your age, if you are made redundant, you are entitled to receive statutory redundancy pay. This now applies even if you are over 65. The rate at which you build up redundancy pay is as follows:

- **Half a week's pay** for each full year of service you completed while aged less than 22 years.
- **One week's pay** for each full year of service completed while aged 22 or above, but less than 41 years.
- **One-and-a-half weeks' pay** for each full year of service completed while aged 41 or more.

This calculation is based on your pay at the time of your redundancy notice, but capped at a maximum of £330 a week. There is also a cap on the maximum number of years that can be taken into account – this is 20 years. Your employer might offer you a more generous pay-off.

You can see that the rates of redundancy pay described above are higher for older workers than for younger workers. This is, of course, an example of age discrimination. However, an exemption from the age discrimination laws means that older workers are allowed to build up redundancy-pay rights at these higher rates.

ENFORCING YOUR RIGHTS

If you feel you are being discriminated against because of your age (or have any other employment grievance, for example, you feel you have been discriminated against on sexual or racial grounds), first try to resolve the problem by talking to your employer.

The next step is to bring a complaint using your employer's formal grievance procedure – your human resources department, trade union or whoever in your firm deals with personnel matters will tell you how to do this. If that fails, you have the right to take your case to an employment tribunal.

In the case of age discrimination, to gather evidence that you need to present to a tribunal, you have the right to send your employer a questionnaire asking for relevant information. The questionnaire does not have to be in any specific format – you could just set out your queries in a letter – but the Government has produced a standard document that you can use (see below). The employer's answers, evasions or failure to respond can all be taken into account by the tribunal.

 For information about employment tribunals, go to www.employmenttribunals.gov.uk. You can download the Government age discrimination questionnaire at www.berr.gov.uk/files/file32724.pdf.

Running your own business

Being your own boss has the advantage of flexible hours and no fighting to stay on after the age of 65 years. But it can be hard work with uncertain rewards and difficult to wind down.

EASING OUT OF BUSINESS

If you are already self-employed, you may be thinking about winding down your business. A big advantage of being your own boss is no one saying that you must retire once you reach 65 years. On the other hand, cutting down your hours is often more difficult than it would be for an employee. With most businesses, you need to be readily available to your customers or clients and, depending on your type of work, may need to keep up a network of contacts. If you cut back your business too much, there is a risk of all the demand for your products or services drying up as customers go to new suppliers. Some possible solutions might be:

- Sharing the business with other family members, for example, grown-up children. They can gradually take over more and more of the day-to-day running as the years progress.

- Taking on an external partner or new director (if you are a company) who can perhaps progressively take over more of the work.
- Selling your business, but staying on as a consultant if the new owner agrees.
- Focusing your business on a smaller area. For example, if you have been selling worldwide, restricting your sales to the UK or your local region; if you have been providing different markets – say, selling knowledge to industry, charities and government – limit yourself to just one market.

❝ If you cut back your business too much, there is a risk of all the demand for your products or services drying up. ❞

 See Chapter 7, page 170, for guidance on Capital Gains Tax on any profit you make from selling a business.

STARTING A BUSINESS

Retirement can be the opportunity to strike out on your own, turning a hobby into a business or trying something completely new, pursuing a long-held dream to be your own boss or offering the chance of better pay than local jobs. There is no limit to the type of business you could choose, but here are a few ideas to consider:

- If you have green fingers and/or building skills, maybe landscape gardening or garden maintenance
- If you are good at making things, carpentry, potting, jewellery, silk printing, and so on. Many regions have local craft centres and fairs where you could sell your products.
- Catering for birthdays parties and other functions if you have a flair for cooking.
- Use your existing employment skills to work as a consultant for either a firm you are leaving or perhaps customers of that firm.
- Going freelance if, say, you work in a creative area, such as writing or publishing.

WORK-LIFE BALANCE

Choosing the right business is not just a matter of thinking about the skills you have. Think also about the work-life balance you want to achieve. Some

No soft option

Do not underestimate the challenges of running your own business:

- What is your unique selling point (USP)? Why will people buy your goods and services rather than those of someone else?
- Can you make a profit? Can you sell at a price that will cover your costs and give a reasonable return?
- Do you have sufficient time and resources? Starting up can be time consuming. You have to find suppliers, identify your market and promote your product, produce your goods or services and deal with the behind-the-scenes work of getting your business structure right and complying with relevant tax and other legislation. You can buy in help but this reduces your profits.

businesses take up a lot of time – for example, if you aspire to a high street shop, bear in mind that you will need to be open at the times when people want to shop. If your opening hours are erratic or limited, potential customers will quickly take their business elsewhere. Selling over the internet could give you more time to yourself, but you will need to check and respond to new orders in a timely manner, which may limit your scope, for example, to take extended holidays. Making and selling craft items at fairs could be a more flexible option.

 For information and advice on all aspects of starting a business, contact your local Business Link at www.businesslink.gov.uk (England); Flexible Support for Business at www.business-support-wales.gov.uk (Wales); Business Gateway at www.bgateway.com (Scotland); NI Business Info at www.nibusinessinfo.co.uk (Northern Ireland).

BUSINESS STRUCTURE AND TAX

One of your first decisions is whether to set up as a company, self-employed or in partnership. Key pros and cons of each are set out in the table, opposite.

Self-employment

By far and away the simplest structure is to become self-employed. There are no formalities. You simply start trading, but you must register your business with HM Revenue & Customs (HMRC) within three months of the end of the month in which you start trading. You will have to fill in a tax return after the end of each tax year. Any profit you make is added to your other income – such as your state and occupational pensions and any taxable investment income – to see if the total is high enough for you to have to pay tax.

Partnerships

From a tax point of view, partnerships are treated in the same way as being self-employed. So, as with becoming self-employed, you have three months to register that you have started up (see above) and must complete a tax return each year to ensure that you pay the correct amount of Income Tax on your share of the partnership profits.

You do not need to have any formal agreement between you and your partners, but you would be unwise to do business together without setting out your rights and responsibilities to each other – for example, in what proportion you will share the profits, what happens if one of you wants to leave the partnership, and so on. Get a solicitor to draw up a formal partnership agreement.

Trading as a company

If you opt to trade as a company, there are a number of formalities to go through. These include: drawing up the required legal paperwork; choosing a company name and ensuring that it is not a name already in use, offensive or prohibited; and registering the company with Companies House (or the Companies Registry in Northern Ireland). Although you could carry out these tasks yourself, it is better to use an accountant or company formation agent, who can give you advice and information and will already have standard legal documents

Jargon buster

Dividends Payments by a company to its shareholders. They represent a share of the company's profits
Limited liability Situation where the maximum you can lose is capped at the amount you have invested

---

 Chapter 7 looks in detail at the tax rules and how you pay your tax. See also the *Which? Essential Guide: Tax Handbook 2009/10,* published in Spring 2009. To find a company formation agent, use a business directory on an online search engine.

that you can use or adapt and even ready formed companies that you just need to register.

Companies House will inform HMRC that your company has been registered, but you should also contact your nearest tax office (get the address from *The Phone Book* or www.hmrc.gov.uk) to tell them that you have started trading. Companies must pay corporation tax and file annual reports with Companies House

as well as delivering an annual tax return to HMRC. There are strict time limits and fines if you miss the deadlines. You are strongly advised to use an accountant to help you meet these legal obligations.

❝ By far and away the simplest business structure is to become self-employed. ❞

Your business structure

The areas shaded dark blue highlight the most advantageous structure (or structures) in the context of the aspect being described.

Type of business	Self-employment	Partnership	Company
Start-up	Very simple. Just start trading.	Best to get a solicitor to draw up a formal agreement with your partners.	Form or buy a company. Get help from an accountant.
Limited liability	None. You personally are responsible for the debts of your business.	Usually none – you personally are responsible for the debts of the business, whether run up by you or your partners. See an accountant if you want to explore a limited liability partnership.	Company has a separate legal identity from you. Generally, the most you can lose is the money you have put into the company.
Paying yourself	Profits are automatically yours.	A share of the profits is automatically yours.	Profits belong to the company. You can receive salary as an employee or dividends as a shareholder. The company can lend you money.
Paperwork	Fairly simple. You might be able to manage your own tax returns and accounts.	Fairly simple. You might be able to manage your own tax returns and accounts.	Complex. You are almost certain to need help from an accountant.

COST OF STARTING UP

Whatever type of business you choose, an essential first step is to draw up a business plan. This sets out a statement of the goals of your business, the market you are targeting, the resources you have, the nature of your product or service, how you will operate and a financial analysis, including forecasts. The business plan will help you to clarify your ideas and the feasibility of your proposition. It is also essential if you will need to persuade others to put money into your business.

Having created your business plan, among other factors, you will have a clear understanding of your immediate financial needs for:

- **Start-up capital** for example, to pay for premises, computers, plant and machinery, vehicles, marketing, and so on. The details in your business plan of how you will operate will include a list of the items you need to buy and an estimate of their costs.
- **Working capital,** in other words the cash you need to cover the running costs, such as raw materials, stationery and printing, phone and internet connections, and so on, which you have to pay in order to bring your product or service to market. Even if you are able to sell your output immediately, with

many businesses there will be a delay before your customers pay you, so you need working capital to cover that gap. The cash flow statements in your business plan will help you work out how much working capital you need. Business Link suggest you allow enough to cover at least six months' running costs.

The sum of your start-up capital and working capital tells you how much initial funding you need to get your business off the ground. The next question is: where will the money come from?

SOURCES OF FUNDING

There are essentially five sources of funding for your business:

- Your own money.
- Family and friends.
- Banks.
- Outside investors.
- Grants and support.

Your own money

You will have no choice but to put in some of your own money. If you are going to persuade other people or organisations to lend or invest, they will want to see that you too are making a substantial commitment and have an interest in making your business a

To register as self-employed, see www.hmrc.gov.uk/selfemployed/register-selfemp.htm or call 0845 915 4515. For free guides on forming a company, see www.companieshouse.gov.uk. To find an accountant or solicitor, see Useful addresses on pages 211-15.

success. Being able to finance your business completely yourself is a good position to be in, because you have complete control and no risk of funds suddenly being withdrawn.

A big advantage of retirement is that you may already have a lump sum from your pension scheme or redundancy that you can use to get started. In either case, there are no restrictions on the way you use these payouts (but bear in mind that drawing a lump sum from your pension scheme will generally reduce the pension you get – see pages 52–4).

If you do not have a lump sum from these sources, you could consider some form of personal borrowing – for example, a mortgage or equity release (see page 117) on your home, a personal loan or even using personal credit cards. The latter is not recommended for anything more than very short-term borrowing, because credit cards are costly over the medium to long term.

Family and friends

Be wary of using this source. Family and friends may be your most loyal supporters, but you must make sure they understand the risks and you must consider how your relationship with these people will be affected if you lose their money. To avoid misunderstandings, set

down in writing exactly what they are committing to your business, when and how you will repay or reward them, and what happens if either you default or they urgently need their money back.

Banks

This is likely to be the first true test of your business plan. In general, banks are conservative organisations and will lend to your business only if you can convince the bank that you have a sound business proposition. There are two main ways to borrow from a bank: overdraft or business loan.

An overdraft: You can only arrange an overdraft with the bank where you have your business current account. An overdraft is flexible and economic because, having arranged an overdraft limit, you choose whether or not and when to use it and you only pay charges during periods when your account is actually overdrawn. An overdraft can be an ideal source of extra working capital, allowing you to respond easily to fluctuations in cash flow. The main drawbacks of an overdraft are that your bank can cancel the facility without notice (and is most likely to do this if it is worried about your business, in other words just at the time you probably most need the facility) and, if you go beyond

See the *Which? Essential Guide* to *Working for Yourself*. For courses and workshops that include drawing up a business plan, contact your local Business Link (www.businesslink.gov.uk) or equivalent regional organisation or LearnDirect (www.learndirect.co.uk).

The bank's security

A bank is likely to insist on some security for any money it lends you. Usually this will be a charge against your home. Think carefully before agreeing to this. If you fail to repay the loan, the bank can insist that your home is sold so the bank can get its money back. If you share your home with others, discuss the position with them before you go ahead. If you operate as a sole trader or in partnership, there is no legal separation between you and your business, so, if you default on your borrowing, the lender can, in any case, take you to court and claim against your personal as well as business assets.

If you are setting up as a company, it has a separate legal identity from you and, in theory, limited liability means that you personally should not be liable for the debts of your business. However, in the case of a small company, any bank lending to the company is likely to seek personal security (such as a charge on your home) from the directors for any loan to the business.

your overdraft limit, the charges are punitive. In addition, you need a certain amount of self-discipline to manage an overdraft – do not let it grow uncontrollably; always have a plan for getting back to black.

Business loan: You can take out a business loan with any lender. You do not need to stick to the bank with which you have your business or other accounts. Shop around for the best deal, for example, by using a web comparison site or a commercial broker. A loan can be a good option if you are buying large items and want to spread the cost over a number of years. The regular repayment structure provides extra discipline to help you stay on top of the debt.

When you are buying equipment or vehicles, an alternative to a loan could be a leasing arrangement. With this, the lender buys the item and then rents it to your business. You might have the option to purchase the item outright after a set number of years. A commercial broker is a good source of advice on the options available and help in shopping around.

Whichever form of borrowing you choose, the repayments and interest are costs to the business. (The interest qualifies for tax relief, which helps.) You have to pay those costs, regardless of whether you are currently making a profit or the size of that profit. This means debt can be a problem if your business is struggling but has less and less impact as your profits grow.

 To shop around for a business account or loan online see, for example, www.moneyfacts.co.uk. To find a commercial broker, contact the National Association of Commercial Finance Brokers (www.nacfb.org) for a list of its members who all abide by a code of conduct and have proper complaints procedures.

Outside investors

Outside investors share the risk of your business with you. They are useful when you are starting up because they are willing to put money in without seeing any immediate reward. But their reason for investing is to share in your profits once you become successful. It may be easy to part with, say, 40 per cent of your business when you are small and struggling, but you need to be comfortable with giving up 40 per cent of your profits when the money does start to roll in.

Outside investors can come in many shapes and sizes:

- **Through a partnership.** If you are sole trader, the main way in which you can bring in an outside investor is to create a partnership. The outsider will usually work with you in the business but could simply put in finance in return for a share of your profits.
- **By selling shares.** If you operate as a company, you can sell shares in your business to outsiders. The outsiders then share in your profits, through dividends, and are often looking eventually to sell the shares at a profit. You would have to become a very large business indeed to sell your shares on a stock exchange. Much more likely when you are small is that you will sell to friends or family (who might work in

the business with you or not), to another company operating a similar or complementary business (perhaps a supplier or customer), or to an investor (often called a **business angel**).

Grants and support

There is a vast array of grants and government support available for businesses. The easiest way to find out what is available in the area where you want to operate is to contact Business Link or your equivalent organisation – you can either talk to an adviser or use an online grant-finder.

If you are aged 50 or over, you are eligible for information, advice, networking events and other support from the Prince's Initiative for Mature Enterprise (PRIME) – a not-for-profit organisation linked to Age Concern designed to help mature people start in business. If you are unable to get a business loan from a bank, PRIME might even be able to help you raise the finance you need.

 To find a business angel, contact the British Business Angels Association at www.bbaa.org.uk. To contact PRIME, see www.primeinitiative.org.uk.

National Insurance

If you are an employee or self-employed, National Insurance payments stop when you reach State Pension age. But, if you run your own company, your business will still have to pay this tax.

National Insurance is a tax paid by employees, their employers and anyone who is self-employed (which includes being in partnership). There are different types of contributions (see table, below), some of which build up a right to receive the State Pension and other state benefits (payable, for example, if you are ill or unemployed). Mature workers don't pay contributions.

Main types of National Insurance [a]

Type	Who pays?	How much? (Main rates in 2009-10 tax year)	Entitles you to State Pension or benefits?
Class 1	Employees aged 16 to State Pension age	0% on the first £110 a week 11%[a] between £110 and £844 a week 1% on pay over £844 a week	Yes
	Employers (in respect of all employees aged 16 and over)	0% on the first £110 a week 12.8% above £110	Not applicable
Class 2	Self-employed aged 16 to State Pension age	£2.40 a week (you can apply to be exempted if your earnings are less than £5,075 for the year)	Yes
Class 3	Voluntary payments to fill gaps in record	£12.05 a week	Yes
Class 4	Self-employed aged 16 to year in which State Pension age reached	8% on profits between £5,715 and £43,875 for the year 1% on profits over £43,875	No

a Married women who have opted to pay at the reduced rate pay 4.85% on these earnings and do not build up any entitlement to State Pension or benefits.

EMPLOYEES

Any earnings payable after the birthday on which you reach State Pension age are exempt from Class 1 National Insurance. You must give your employer proof of your date of birth, which can be a birth certificate, passport or certificate of age exemption issued by HMRC. It is a good idea to sort this out a month or two in advance of reaching State Pension age, so that you get your pay with the correct deductions made, but you can claim back any National Insurance incorrectly deducted. If, when you claimed your State Pension (see page 43), you said you intended to carry on working, you should automatically have been sent a certificate, otherwise contact HMRC – see the box below. If you have more than one job, you may need more than one certificate.

SELF-EMPLOYED

Similarly, if you are self-employed, you are exempt from Class 2 National Insurance contributions from the date on which you reach State Pension age. Class 2 contributions are charged weekly and, if your birthday falls part way through a week, you are exempt for that particular week (and every subsequent week). HMRC may automatically stop collecting your payments but, to be on the safe side,

you could send your tax office a reminder shortly before your birthday.

Class 4 contributions (a tax on your profits if you are self-employed, which, unlike Class 2 contributions, do not build up any entitlement to state benefits) cease from the start of the tax year following the one in which you reach State Pension age. If your birthday falls on 6 April, you are treated as having reached State Pension age at midnight on 5 April. You can use your tax return (see page 168) to stop the payments.

RUNNING YOUR OWN COMPANY

If you are a director of your own company, technically you are an employee and your company is your employer. As an employee, your liability to pay National Insurance also stops from the birthday on which you reach State Pension age. However, age does not affect the employer's contributions, which carry on being due. So your company still has to pay employer's Class 1 National Insurance on any salary and other remuneration you get (but not any dividends you receive as a shareholder).

❝ Earnings payable after State Pension age are exempt from Class 1 National Insurance. ❞

To notify HM Revenue & Customs that you are approaching State Pension age and/or to request a certificate of age exemption, write to the National Insurance Contributions Office at HM Revenue & Customs (see page 214). See Chapter 7 for information about Income Tax on your earnings.

Top up for low earnings

If you work but your household income is low, you may be eligible for Working Tax Credit (WTC). There is no upper age limit for claiming this particular benefit.

WTC is a state benefit designed to top up low earnings and ensure that being in work pays. WTC has to be claimed (it is not paid automatically) and you make the claim for your whole household. A couple can choose which of them makes the claim. It is a means-tested benefit, so the amount you get depends on your household income and it reduces as your income rises.

WHO QUALIFIES?

There are several ways you can qualify for WTC, depending on your circumstances and how many hours you work, for example:

- You work at least 30 hours a week or, if you are a couple, either you or your partner works 30 hours or more.
- You (or your partner) have a disability that puts you at a disadvantage getting a job and you work at least 16 hours a week and you are getting state benefits because of your disability (see pages 96–100).
- You are aged 50 or over, you have been out of work for at least six months and claiming certain state benefits and you work at least 16 hours a week.

HOW MUCH?

WTC comprises a number of different elements that you qualify for depending on your circumstances – see the table, opposite. Everyone qualifies for the basic element. If, for example, you are a couple, you also get the couple element; if you work at least 30 hours a week, you get the 30-hour element.

Adding together all the relevant elements gives the maximum WTC you could potentially get. This maximum is reduced if your household income is more than a set threshold (£6,420 in 2009–10). In 2009–10, it is reduced by 39p for each £1 by which your income exceeds the threshold.

ASSESSING WTC

Your tax credit claim for a particular tax year depends on your household income for that tax year, which, broadly speaking, is the gross income that you declare for Income Tax (see pages 162–8). However, at the time you make a claim, you cannot be sure what your income for the whole year will be. So, in the first instance, it is usually assumed that your income this year will be the same as it was last year. For example, initially your claim for 2009–10 will be

Working Tax Credit elements

Element	Amount in 2009–10 £ per year	How do you qualify?
Basic	£1,890	Everyone who is eligible for WTC gets this.
Couple	£1,860	Two-person household unless you are claiming the 50+ working 16–29 hours element (see below).
30-hour	£775	You or your partner work at least 30 hours a week. (Unless you have a child under 16 or under 19 if still in full-time education; you cannot add together a couple's hours to make 30.)
Disabled	£2,530	You or your partner qualify for WTC because of disability. If you are a couple and both meet the conditions, you get two elements.
Severely disabled	£1,075	Paid in addition to the disabled element above, if you or your partner get the highest rates of state benefits payable due to disability. If you are a couple and both meet the conditions, you get two elements.
50+ working 16–29 hours	£1,300	You have been out of work for at least six months and claiming certain state benefits (the list is complex, so check with HMRC which benefits qualify). This element is paid for your first year back in work. If you are a couple and both meet the conditions, you get two elements.
50+ working 30 hours or more	£1,935	

based on your taxable income for 2008–9.

After the end of the tax year, your tax credit claim is reviewed:

- If it turns out that your actual income for the year was lower than last year, your tax credits are revised upwards and you get extra.
- If it turns out your income was higher, this could mean you have been overpaid and some of your tax credits have to be repaid. However, the first £25,000 of any increase in income is ignored. For example, you will have to repay some of your 2009–10 tax credits only if your income is more than £25,000 higher this year than it was in 2008–9.

You can ask for your tax credits to be based on your estimate of this year's income if you know it will be significantly different from last year. If you have been unemployed, your claim will be based on an estimate of this year's income.

Continuing to work

WTC calculator

If you qualify under the rules on pages 86-7, use this calculator to work out broadly how much WTC you might be able to claim in the 2009-10 tax year. The calculator indicates the total for the whole year assuming you make your claim within three months of the start of the tax year. Figures here have been rounded to the nearest pound but your actual tax credit award will be to the nearest pence.

To claim WTC or find out if you are eligible, see www.hmrc.gov.uk/taxcredits/index.htm or call the Tax Credits Helpline 0845 300 3900.

		Example	Example	Your figures
		Single, aged 55, returning to part-time work after two years unemployed and on benefits	Couple, husband works 35 hours a week	
STEP 1				
From the table on page 87, select all the elements that apply to you	A	£1,890 £1,300	£1,890 £1,860 £775	
Add together all the elements you have written down under A	B	£3,190	£4,525	
STEP 2				
What is your household income (usually insert here the figure for last year – see pages 86-7)?	C	£8,000	£15,000	
Income threshold	D	£6,420	£6,420	£6,420
C – D	E	£1,580	£8,580	
Rate of reduction (loss per £1)	F	0.39	0.39	0.39
E x F	G	£616	£3,346	
STEP 3				
Work out B – G	H	£2,574	£1,179	

If **H** is zero or less, you do not seem to qualify for any WTC. However, if your income this year turns out to be lower than amount **C**, you might qualify after all.

If **H** is greater than zero, this is the amount of WTC you qualify for based provisionally on last year's income. If your income this year turns out to be lower than amount **C**, you might qualify for more. If your income this year turns out to be more than £25,000 higher than amount **C**, you might qualify for less.

Keeping track

Knowing where your money comes from and where it goes can help you to carry on spending on the things you want and steer clear of debt problems.

If you have been in a reasonably well-paid job most of your life, the transition to living on a pension can be difficult. Although your outgoings might fall on retirement – no more commuting costs, expensive coffees and work clothes – your income is likely to drop too. If you have been used to a comfortable surplus once the bills were paid, maybe you haven't had to think about budgeting before. At least in the early months of retiring, it could be a good idea to track where your money goes to make sure you are keeping your spending within your new income limit.

If your spending exceeds your income, you have a budget shortfall. A shortfall means you are either dipping into your savings or running up debts. This might be sustainable for a short while but will soon lead to problems if you do nothing about it. Use this chapter to make sure you are getting all the State and other help you are entitled to and see pages 109–12 for tips on saving money. For ideas on boosting your income, see Chapters 3 (working), 5 (income from your home) and 6 (investments).

> **" If you have been used to a comfortable surplus, maybe you haven't had to think about budgeting before. "**

A spending diary

It's surprising how the little things add up. Keep a spending diary in a notebook for a week or two so you really know where your money goes. Each day start on a fresh page and list everything that you spend your money on, ranging from newspapers and groceries to coffees out and pocket money for the grandchildren.

 Don't ignore problem debts. Get free, independent help and advice from Citizens Advice (www.citizensadvice.org.uk for your local branch), National Debtline (www.nationaldebtline.co.uk) or the Consumer Credit Counselling Service (www.cccs.co.uk).

Boosting your budget

Once you approach or reach pension age, you qualify for a variety of extras, such as cheap rail travel, help with winter fuel and free prescriptions, just on the basis of your age and regardless of how well off you might be. Some other types of state help are available only if your income is low or if you have a disability – something that becomes more likely as we naturally age.

Financial help available

Here are the main types of help and perks if you are close to or have reached pension age.

Type of help	For details, see pages:	You may be eligible if you have: Reached a specified age	A disability (any age)	A low income (mostly any age)
Travel				
Free local bus travel	92, 96	✓	✓	
Cheap rail travel	92, 96	✓	✓	
Cheap coach travel	92, 96	✓		
Free passport	92	✓		
Free car tax and parking	96		✓	
Extra income				
Pension Credit	101	✓ [a]		✓ [a]
Attendance Allowance or Disability Living Allowance	97		✓	
Your health				
Free prescriptions	93, 97, 106	✓	✓ [b]	✓
Free or cheaper dental treatment	106			✓
Free sight test	93, 97, 106	✓	✓ [b]	✓
Voucher towards cost of glasses or contact lenses	106			✓
Free travel to receive some NHS treatment	106			✓
Some free equipment, such as raised toilet seats, lever taps and bed raisers	99		✓	
Help with bills				
Council Tax	100, 107		✓	✓
Rent	107			✓
Winter fuel bills	94	✓	✓	
Extra cash in cold weather	107			✓
Free TV licence	94	✓	✓ [c]	
Your home (owned or privately rented)				
Grant for insulation and heating system	108			✓
Small grant towards heating system	95	✓		
Free cavity wall and loft insulation	95, 108	✓		✓
Grant for major adaptations to help you live at home	100		✓ [a]	✓ [a]
Free minor adaptations to help you live at home	99		✓	
Advice and support to help you undertake repairs and adaptations	95, 100	✓	✓	✓

a Both conditions must apply. b But only you have specified health conditions. c A 50% reduction if you are registered blind.

Extras because of age

Some perks you get simply by reaching a specified age with no conditions about income or other hoops to jump through. These include travel concessions, some health benefits and help with fuel bills.

TRAVEL

- **Buses and trains.** If you are aged 60 or over and live in England, Wales or Scotland, you are entitled to travel free on local buses. In Northern Ireland, the scheme covers trains as well. The schemes vary – see table, below – and each local authority has discretion to set up its own additional concessions.
- **Coaches.** Some coach companies (National Express, Scottish Citylink, Berry's and Baker Dolphin) offer discounted fares on national routes to travellers aged 60 or over. People aged 60 and over can buy a Senior Railcard (costing £24 in 2008), which entitles them to one-third off most fares for rail travel throughout Britain.
- **Passport.** If you were born on or before 2 September 1929, you no longer have to pay for your passport (saving £72 in 2008). If you are

Free local travel schemes

Scheme	Age eligibility	Where you can travel	Travel time restrictions	More information
England: National Bus Pass	60 and over	Local buses throughout England	Not peak hours (before 9.30am weekdays)	Your local authority
Wales: Concessionary Bus Pass	60 and over	Local buses throughout Wales	None	Your local authority
Scotland: National Entitlement Card	60 and over	Local buses and scheduled coaches throughout Scotland	None	Your local authority, post office or Strathclyde Partnership for Transport travel centre
Northern Ireland: 60+ SmartPass	60–64	Buses and trains throughout Northern Ireland	None	Translink (Tel: 028 90 66 66 30) or bus and rail stations
Northern Ireland: Senior SmartPass	65 and over	Buses and trains throughout Northern Ireland and cross-border travel	None	Translink (Tel: 028 90 66 66 30) or bus and rail stations

Qualifying age

Many age-related concessions are available to both men and women from women's State Pension age, currently 60. From 2010, this age will gradually increase until it reaches age 65 by 2010 (see page 16).

eligible and have applied for a new or replacement passport since 19 May 2004, you can ask for a refund of the fee.

YOUR HEALTH

- **NHS prescriptions.** Once you reach age 60, you qualify for free NHS prescriptions (saving £7.10 per item in 2008). If you are eligible, simply sign the declaration on the back of your prescription. Scotland and Northern Ireland have announced that they will be phasing out charges for prescriptions, which will become free for everyone from April 2010 (Northern Ireland) and April 2011 (Scotland). Prescriptions are already free for all in Wales. There are no plans to phase out charges completely in England, though some health-related exemptions are already allowed or planned (see page 99).
- **NHS sight tests.** From age 60, you also qualify for free NHS sight tests

(instead of having to pay for private tests, which typically cost £20 or more), but you will still have to pay for your glasses or lenses (unless your income is low – see page 106). You can get free sight tests from age 40 if you are considered at risk of developing glaucoma because a close family member has this condition (or from any age if you already have sight problems – see page 99). Tell your optician you are entitled to a free test and fill in the form they supply.

Claims to free prescriptions and tests are checked and you can be fined if you were not eligible. Age does not entitle you to free dental care, however.

BILLS

- **Winter Fuel Payment.** This is a UK-wide scheme and provides a cash sum to every household with one or more people aged 60 or over in the 'qualifying week', which is the week beginning on the third Monday in September. You can use the cash in any way you like, but it is designed to help you cope with winter fuel bills. The standard payment is normally £200 per household or £300 for

For more information about free passports, call the Passport Adviceline on 0870 521 0410; to apply, get an application pack from larger post offices or go to https://www.ips.gov.uk/epa1r1a.

Proof of age

With most of the concessions described in this section, you need to provide proof of your age. This could be, say, a birth certificate, passport, driving licence or, in some cases, your National Insurance number (which is then used to check the details held on your National Insurance record).

households with someone aged 80 or over. But, for the winter of 2008, these are increased to £250 and £400, respectively. If you get a State Pension or have had Winter Fuel Payment in previous years, you should get your payment automatically without having to claim.

- **Television licence.** Anyone aged 75 or over can apply for a free television licence (saving £139.50 in 2008). It doesn't matter if there are younger people in the household as well, but the licence must be in the name of the person aged 75. If you are already the licence-holder, you can apply for a cheaper short-term licence for just part of the year in which you turn 75 and you will then automatically be issued a free licence for the period from your 75th birthday onwards. If you are not the current licence-holder, you need to apply. The free licence lasts for three years at a

time and should be automatically renewed on expiry. The licence covers just your main home – if you have a second home, you will have to pay the normal fee for a second licence.

- **Council Tax.** While not directly age-related, bear in mind that if you live alone (which is common particularly in later retirement), you can apply to have your Council Tax bill reduced by a quarter – contact your local authority for details.

YOUR HOME

There is help out there to make sure you can heat your home properly and use fuel efficiently. Some is available only if your income is low (see page 108) but, in addition to the Winter Fuel Payment (see page 93), you may be able to claim the following whatever your income:

- **Heating rebate of £300.** This is operated under the name Warm Front in England, but see Useful addresses (page 215) for the equivalent schemes in the rest of the UK. The eligibility conditions are: you are aged 60 or over, own your own home or rent privately and you have no central heating or the system you have does not work. You get a voucher/claim form to use when an approved supplier fits a new heating system.

 To claim Winter Fuel Payment for the first time, see www.thepensionservice.gov.uk/winterfuel or call 08459 15 15 15. For a free television licence, see www.tvlicensing.co.uk or phone 0844 800 6790.

- **Free insulation.** If you are aged 70 or over, you are entitled to free loft insulation and cavity wall insulation (saving around £500 each) under a central government scheme. Your local authority and local energy providers may offer other grant schemes and discounts.

estimates and oversee work, and may operate their own handyman and gardening schemes. 'Vulnerable' includes older people with no specific age limit. The initial visit is free and charges for managing a project will always be discussed first and can usually be included in any grant that is given.

Home improvement agencies (HIAs)

Home improvement agencies offer advice and support to vulnerable homeowners and private tenants regarding repairs, improvements and adaptations to your home. For example, they can advise on the condition of your home and what work needs doing; help you find out if you are eligible for any grants; get

❝ There is help out there to make sure you can heat your home properly and use fuel efficiently. ❞

 To find out about Warm Front grants (England), call 0800 316 2805. For equivalent schemes in the rest of the UK, see Useful addresses on page 215. For insulation and other grants, see www.energysavingtrust.org.uk or call 0800 512 012. To find your local home improvements agency, see www.foundations.uk.com/hiasearch.aspx.

If you have a disability

There are benefits and deals designed to help with the extra costs of disability. But, in some cases, eligibility depends on having a low income as well.

TRAVEL

- **Buses.** The free local bus schemes for England, Wales and Scotland (see page 92) are not just for older people. You are also eligible at any age if you have a disability. Contact the relevant scheme for details and conditions. In Northern Ireland, there are parallel schemes giving free travel if you are registered blind or war disabled, and normally you will automatically be sent an application form; if you have other disabilities, you may qualify for half-price travel on buses and trains – contacts in the table on page 92 for details.
- **Trains.** For discounted rail travel throughout Britain, you can apply for a Disabled Person's Railcard (for £18 in 2008). This entitles you to one-third off most fares for yourself and a companion.
- **Local transport schemes.** Check with your local authority to find out about any local transport schemes for people with disabilities, such as a community dial-a-ride scheme.
- **Car.** If you have mobility problems and qualify for state disability benefits (see below), you may be eligible for a free tax disc for your car (which may be driven by you or someone you have nominated as your driver). You might also qualify for a 'Blue Badge' permit that lets you park free in on-street restricted-parking zones and disabled public parking bays. As a Blue Badge holder, you could also qualify for exemption from the London congestion charge (see below).

EXTRA INCOME

There are two main state benefits for people with disabilities: Attendance Allowance if you are aged 65 or over at the time you claim, and Disability Living Allowance if you are younger. Both provide tax-free income with eligibility based on the effects of your disability, not your income, savings or record of

 For free car tax, get an exemption certificate from the Disability and Carers Service: 0845 712 3456. To apply for a Blue Badge, contact your local authority's social services department. Go to www.tfl.gov.uk for information about London congestion charge exemptions.

paying National Insurance. In either case, you get cash, which you can spend in any way that you like, though it is intended to help with the extra costs you incur because of your disability. Someone who looks after you may be eligible for Carer's Allowance.

Attendance Allowance (AA)

This is paid at one of two rates, depending on the extent of your disability (see table, overleaf). To qualify, you must need frequent help with personal care or continual supervision during the day, night or both.

Disability Living Allowance (DLA)

This allowance has two components and you can be eligible for either or both. The care component is payable at three rates and the mobility component is payable at two rates, depending on the severity of your disability. The table, overleaf, shows the amounts payable in 2009 10.

Carer's Allowance

If you are getting Attendance Allowance or the middle or higher rate of Disability Living Allowance, someone who looks after you may be able to claim the Carer's Allowance (£53.10 a week in 2009–10). This is a taxable benefit that depends on the caring situation and eligibility does not depend on the claimant's National Insurance record.

Your carer does not have to be related to you – for example, he or she could be a neighbour or friend – though most often carers are husbands, wives or grown-up children. Your carer must spend at least 35 hours a week caring for you, not be in full-time education (21 hours a week or more) and, if he or she works, earn less than £95 a week after tax and some other deductions.

Carer's Allowance interacts with other benefits. For example, if your carer gets State Pension as well, he or she will receive a total amount equal to the higher of the pension or Carer's Allowance. If the pension comes to more than the Carer's Allowance, your carer does not get the Carer's Allowance at all. Instead, he or she is said to have an 'underlying entitlement', which can increase the amount of other benefits that are available (such as Pension Credit – see page 101).

Fast-track Attendance Allowance or Disability Living Allowance

To claim Attendance Allowance, you must normally have needed help or supervision for at least six months. A similar rule applies to the care component of Disability Living Allowance, but the waiting period is three months. However, if you are terminally ill and not expected to survive longer than six or three months, you can get the benefit straight away without waiting.

Jargon buster

Underlying entitlement An entitlement to a state benefit that you do not actually receive because you are getting some other type of state benefit instead

YOUR HEALTH

● **NHS prescriptions.** Whatever the state of health, over-60s qualify for free prescriptions and NHS sight tests (see page 93). However, if you under 60 and have a medical exemption certificate, you can still get free NHS prescriptions. This is available only

The main disability benefits

Benefit	Main conditions[a]	Amount in 2009-10
Attendance Allowance		
Lower rate	You require help with bodily functions during the day; or continual supervision during the day or night to protect yourself or others from harm; or you require repeated or prolonged help with bodily function during the night.	£47.10
Higher rate	You need help as above during both the day and the night.	£70.35
Disability Living Allowance		
Care component		
Lowest rate	You require help with bodily functions during the day or cooking a main meal.	£18.65
Middle rate	You require substantial supervision to protect yourself or others from harm either during the day or the night. Alternatively, you require repeated or prolonged help with bodily function during the night.	£47.10
Highest rate	You need help as for the middle rate above during both the day and night.	£70.35
Mobility component		
Lower rate	You can walk but need guidance or supervision most of the time.	£18.65
Higher rate	You cannot walk or cannot walk far without sever discomfort or risk to your health.	£49.10

a Benefit rules are complex. This description gives only abroad outline.

To find out about or claim Attendance Allowance, Disability Living Allowance or Carer's Allowance see www.direct.gov.uk/en/DisabledPeople/index.htm. For more information about assessing your needs and benefits, see the *Which? Essential Guide* to *Care Options in Retirement*.

Case Study   Jack and Sylvia

Jack, 67, has had Parkinson's disease for nearly 12 years. Everyday tasks and walking have become progressively more difficult and now he relies on his wife Sylvia's help around the clock, though some days are better than others. They are surprised to learn that Jack's condition is now so severe that he qualifies for Attendance Allowance (and at the higher rate). Sylvia also meets the conditions for Carer's Allowance, but cannot claim it because she already receives a higher amount through her State Pension.

where you have a specified medical condition, including, for example, a permanent fistula (such as a colostomy) that needs continuous dressing, some forms of diabetes, epilepsy that requires continuous therapy, or any continuing physical disability that prevents you going out without another person's help. If you think you might be eligible, talk to your GP who can provide the necessary form. Prescriptions are free for all in Wales, regardless of age or type of health condition, and this will be the case in Northern Ireland from April 2010 and Scotland from 2011. For England, the Government has announced that prescription charges for cancer patients will be abolished from April 2009 and an intention to phase out charges for all people with long-term health conditions.

- NHS sight tests. If you are under 60, you may be eligible for free NHS sight tests if you have glaucoma or you are at risk of developing this condition, or you are registered as sight impaired, partially sighted or blind. If your income is low, you may be eligible for a voucher towards the cost of your spectacles or contact lenses worth between £13.40 and £196.10 in 2008-9, depending on the type you need. If the total cost comes to more, you have to pay the excess.

- Needs assessment (also called care assessment). You have a right to ask for a needs assessment, which will be carried out by your local authority's social services department. Contact them by phone or letter. There is no charge for the assessment. As well as potentially supplying a variety of services, the visiting social worker or care manager might suggest equipment that would be useful, such as aids for getting out of bed or raised toilet seats. Small items of equipment like these, and minor adaptations to your home costing no more than £1,000, are provided free, but it is up to your local authority to set its own general conditions on who is eligible.

❝ Prescription charges for cancer patients will be abolished from April 2009. ❞

BILLS

As well as the ways suggested on page 94 for lowering your bills, you may qualify for a reduction in Council Tax due to your disability.

Council Tax

Your household may qualify for a reduction in Council Tax if, due to your disability, you need to live in a larger home – for example, you need an extra bathroom or kitchen or extra space so you can get round your home in a wheelchair. In that case, the property band on which your tax is based is reduced by one band, for example, from Band D to C. If your home is in the lowest band, A, you get a cash reduction. For example, in 2008–9, assuming you would normally pay the average Band D charge of £1,373, a reduction to the average Band C charge of £1,220 would save you £153.

When your home was rated for Council Tax, any disability-related adaptations that reduce the value of your home – perhaps, concrete ramps – should have been taken into account, but any that would increase its value (say, a second bathroom) should have been ignored. If you think that changes have not been reflected in your rating, contact your nearest Valuation Office Agency.

A carer living with you who is not your husband or wife or a person in the household has a severe mental disability can be disregarded when counting up the number of adults in the household and so might mean that the 25 per cent single-occupancy discount (see page 94) applies.

YOUR HOME

- **Disabled Facilities Grant (DFG).** This is the main help available to help you live independently in your own home and it is administered by your local authority. The scheme provides grants up to £30,000 to adapt your home, but it is means tested, so you can qualify only if your income and savings are low. The grant could be used, for example, to install a bathroom, kitchen, ramps, stairlift, move electrical switches, and so on. This could be your own home or one you privately rent and a condition is that you will continue to live there for at least five years (unless, say, health problems make that impossible). Your local authority also has discretion to provide other help, for example, with moving to an alternative property if that is a better option.
- **Home improvement agencies.** Regardless of any disabilities, you can get advice and support from your local home improvement agency regarding any repairs, improvements and adaptations to your home – see page 95.

 To apply for a disability-related reduction in Council Tax, contact your local authority. To find your nearest Valuations Office Agency, go to www.voa.gov.uk. To find out about the Disabled Facilities Grant, contact the social services or housing department of your local authority.

If your income is low

Once you reach age 60, Pension Credit is the main financial help if your income is low. But there are a range of other benefits available whatever your age.

EXTRA INCOME

If you are retired or semi-retired but still working and your income is low, the state benefits most likely to be of interest to you are Pension Credit (see below) or Working Tax Credit (see pages 86-8). If you are working, you may be able to claim both.

66 Pension Credit provides regular tax-free cash to top up a low income if you are aged 60 or over. 99

Pension Credit – the basics

Pension Credit is a means-tested benefit that provides regular tax-free cash designed to top up a low income if currently you are aged 60 or over. For couples, whichever of you makes the claim must be aged 60 or over, but a partner can be younger. The minimum age of 60 from which Pension Credit can start is being gradually increased from 2010 onwards in line with the rise in women's State Pension age (see page 16).

Whether you qualify and for how much depends on the income and circumstances of you and your partner, if you have one – the circumstances are described overleaf. Not all of your income is taken into account – see the table on page 104.

Pit your wits Answers

Question 6

Which of the following state benefits are means tested (ie only available if you are on a low income)?

a) Pension Credit. YES, see this page.

b) Winter Fuel Payment. NO, see page 93.

c) Council Tax Benefit. YES, see page 107.

d) Attendance Allowance. NO, see page 97.

- If you are aged 65 or over and your financial circumstances seem unlikely to change much in the future, your Pension Credit award may be for a period of up to five years. If you expect to start getting a new source of income – an occupational pension, say – within the next 12 months, your award period is likely to be shorter. During your award period, you do not have to report changes to certain types of income or capital, such as annual increases to an occupational pension in line with the scheme's rules as you described them at the time you made your Pension Credit claim. However, if your income or capital fall so that you might be entitled to an increase in Pension Credit, you can ask for your award to be reassessed immediately.

- If you are under the age of 65 (or you are 65 or over but have not been given an award lasting several years), your Pension Credit is based on your actual income and capital and you must report any changes straight away so that the amount you get can be revised.

❝A Pension Credit award may be for up to five years, during which you do not have to report changes to certain types of income or capital.❞

There are two parts to Pension Credit:

- A guarantee credit payable from age 60.
- A savings credit, payable from age 65.

You might get just one part or both.

Applying for Pension Credit

To claim Pension Credit, contact the Pension Service by calling 0800 99 1234, where you will be talked through the claim process and, as part of that same process, you can also claim for Housing Benefit and/or Council Tax Benefit. When you call, make sure you have to hand your National Insurance number, information about the sources and amounts of your income and any savings and investments, together with details of the bank or building society account to which you would like your Pension Credit to be paid.

If you prefer, you can instead either download a paper claim form from the Pension Service website and post it or fill in an online claim form – in either case, go to www.thepensionservice.gov.uk/pensioncredit/form.asp.

Once you are getting Pension Credit, if you have any queries or think your award should be reviewed, contact the Pension Service using the contact details given on the letter you received telling you about your award.

Case Study Imran

In 2009-10, Imran gets £103 a week in State Pension and a further £10 each week from a personal pension, totalling £113 a week. He has no other income or savings. This means he qualifies for £130 - £113 = £17 in guarantee credit to bring his income up to the minimum guarantee of £130.

The guarantee credit

You may be able to claim this part of the Pension Credit either on its own or in addition to the savings credit (see right). Pension Credit guarantees that you will have at least a minimum amount to live on. In 2009-10, the standard minimum guarantee is £130 a week if you are single and £198.45 if you are a couple. You will be treated as needing more than the standard amount if you are severely disabled, care for someone who is severely disabled or have certain housing costs, such as mortgage interest or some types of service charge.

If the income you are assessed as having under the Pension Credit rules is less than the minimum guarantee, you get the amount of guarantee credit required to plug the gap.

❝ Pension Credit guarantees that you will have at least a minimum amount to live on. ❞

The savings credit

You may be able to claim this part of the Pension Credit either on its own or in addition to the guarantee credit (see left). If having an extra £1 of income meant losing £1 of Pension Credit, there would be no incentive for anyone on a low income to make their own savings for retirement. To address this problem, Pension Credit includes a savings credit to reward you for making your own (modest) retirement savings.

For savings credit purposes, your income is compared with a threshold called the savings credit starting point, which in 2009-10 is £96 for a single person and £153.40 for a couple. If your income is less than the starting point, you do not get any savings credit. If it is more, you can use the calculator, overleaf to work out how much you might get. The maximum savings credit is £20.40 for a single person and £27.03 for a couple in 2009-10. If your income is more than about £181 (single) or £266 (couple), you cannot get any savings credit.

The way the savings credit works means that once your income exceeds the minimum guarantee (the amount described above under the guarantee credit, in other words £130 for a single person or £198.45 for a couple in 2009-10), you lose 40p of savings credit for each extra £1 of income you have built up through your own savings. While that is a lot better than losing Pension Credit on a pound-for-pound basis, it is still like being taxed at 40 per cent.

Your income for Pension Credit

The table shows the main types of income taken into account in working out your entitlement to Pension Credit. The rules are complex – for example, the first part of some types of income is ignored – so this table is only a rough guide. To find out more about Pension Credit, visit the Pension Service website, www.thepensionservice.gov.uk/pensioncredit/home.asp.

Type of income	Included when working out your:	
	Guarantee credit	Savings credit
Pensions		
State Pension	✓	✓
Occupational and personal pensions	✓	✓
Pensions you are not getting because you have deferred starting them	✓	✓
Earnings		
Earnings from a job or self-employment (less tax and half any pension contributions)	✓	✓
Working Tax Credit	✓	
Benefits		
Council Tax Benefit		
Housing Benefit		
Attendance Allowance and Disability Living Allowance		
Carer's Allowance	✓	✓
Payments from social services to pay for care		
Most other state benefits	✓	✓
Savings and investments (your capital)		
Actual interest, dividends, rents from buy-to-let properties and other income from your capital		
Deemed income[a]	✓	✓
Other		
Equity release regular payments (but not sums used for necessary repairs and improvements)	✓	✓
Rent from lodgers who live in your home	✓	✓
Maintenance payments from a former partner	✓	
Regular payments from a charity or relative		
Personal injury awards		

a Each £500 of your capital (and any remainder) in excess of the first £6,000 is deemed to give you an income of £1 a week. Capital normally includes the value of any land and property, but not your own home.

Pension Credit calculator

This calculator estimates the amount of Pension Credit you might get in 2009–10. For a more detailed estimate of the Pension Credit you might get (taking into account the complex income rules), use the online calculator at www.thepensionservice.gov.uk/pensioncredit/calculator/home.asp.
To claim Pension Credit, call the Pension Service on 0800 99 1234.

		Example 1 Single, aged 65 or over	Example 2 Couple, claimant 65 or over	Your figures
Your weekly income on which Pension Credit is assessed (see opposite)	A	£98.00	£218.00	
Guarantee credit (payable from age 60)				
Standard minimum guarantee Enter whichever applies to you: Single £130 Couple £198.45	B	£130.00	£198.45	
Work out B – A	C	£32.00	-£19.55 NO GUARANTEE CREDIT	
If C is zero or less, you do not qualify for any guarantee credit. If C is greater than zero, this is the amount of guarantee credit you get.				
Savings credit (payable from age 65)				
Savings credit starting point Enter whichever applies to you: Single £96 Couple £153.40	D	£96.00	£153.40	
Work out A – D	E	£2.00	£64.60	
If E is zero or less, you do not qualify for any savings credit.				
If E is greater than zero, multiply E by 60%	F	£1.20	£38.76	
Enter whichever applies to you: Single The lower of F or £20.40 Couple The lower of F and £27.03	G	£1.20	£27.03	
If amount C is greater than zero, G is the amount of saving credit you get.				
If C is less than zero, ignore the minus sign and write the amount here	H	n/a	£19.55	
Multiply C by 40%	I	n/a	£7.82	
Work out G – I	J	n/a	£19.21	
If J is zero or less, you do not qualify for any savings credit. If J is greater than zero, this is the amount of savings credit you get.				

YOUR HEALTH

A variety of NHS services, such as sight tests and prescriptions, are free if your income is low. You may qualify automatically if you are getting certain state benefits. If you are not getting these benefits, but nonetheless your income is low, you can apply through the NHS Low Income Scheme. Bear in mind that if you are aged 60 or over you may qualify for free NHS services anyway on the grounds of age (see page 93).

The schemes described in this section are designed to help you with the cost of various NHS treatments, but do not confer any entitlement to receive NHS treatment. For example, if there are no dentists in your area taking on NHS patients, being entitled to free NHS dentistry might not be any help, since the schemes do not cover the cost of private treatment.

NHS services if you are getting certain state benefits

If your income is low, you can qualify for a wider range of financial help regardless of age:

- Free NHS prescriptions.
- Free or reduced-cost NHS dental treatment.
- Free NHS sight tests.
- Voucher towards the cost of glasses or contact lenses.
- Refund of travel costs to hospital to receive NHS treatment.
- Free NHS wigs and fabric supports.

You qualify automatically for any of the above if:

- **You are getting specified means-tested state benefits,** such as the guarantee credit part of Pension Credit. Use the letter you received telling you about your Pension Credit award as proof of eligibility when you pick up a prescription or use other services.
- **You hold a tax credit exemption certificate.** Not all tax credit claimants are eligible for one but, if you are, it is sent to you automatically shortly after you make your tax Ccedits claim. Without children, you qualify only if you are getting Working Tax Credit

To apply for a certificate under the NHS Low Income Scheme, complete form HC1 available from Jobcentre Plus offices, hospitals, some dentists and opticians or by calling 0870 155 5455.

with a disability element and your household income is no more than a set limit (which has been unchanged at £15,050 a year since April 2005).

NHS Low Income Scheme

If you don't get means-tested state benefits or tax credits, but your income is low, you might still qualify for the NHS concessions or at least some reduction in the normal charges through the NHS Low Income Scheme. Your income is assessed against the amount you are deemed to need to live on, taking into account, for example, your housing costs and the extra you need if you are disabled. But you are automatically excluded from this scheme if you have savings worth more than £16,000. If your income and savings are low enough, you will be issued with a certificate (HC2 for full help with costs and HC3 for partial help) that you need to show each time you pick up a prescription or use an NHS service.

BILLS

Getting Pension Credit acts as a passport to a range of benefits, which you can apply for simultaneously with your Pension Credit claim.

- **Council Tax Benefit.** You will qualify for this benefit to an amount equal to your whole bill.

- **Housing Benefit.** You can claim for part or all of your rent.
- **Mortgage interest.** If you are an owner-occupier, you may be able to get extra Pension Credit to help with housing costs, such as mortgage interest.
- **Cold Weather Payment.** This is extra cash (£25 in winter 2008–9) to help with heating if temperatures are below zero for seven consecutive days or more. It is paid automatically with your Pension Credit (or other benefits) – you don't make a claim.

The Social Fund

If you get Pension Credit (or some other means-tested benefits), you are also eligible to apply for a range of grants and loans from the Social Fund (part of the benefits system that considers requests

If you do not get the guarantee part of Pension Credit, but your income is low, you might still be entitled to Council Tax Benefit and/or Housing Benefit, but you will have to apply separately and they might cover only part of your bills.

To find out more about the Social Fund get booklet SB16 'A guide to the social fund' at www.dwp.gov.uk/advisers/sb16. For further information or to make a claim, contact the Pension Service at www.thepensionservice.gov.uk or, if you are under 60, Jobcentre Plus at www.jobcentreplus.gov.uk.

for one-off payments and loans). For example, you could apply for a budgeting loan to help you spread the cost of a large expense; a community care grant to cover, say, the cost of travelling to visit your partner in hospital; or a funeral payment if you have to pay for someone's funeral and cannot afford it. If you are aged 60 or over, contact the Pension Service for information or to apply. If you are under 60, contact Jobcentre Plus.

YOUR HOME

Heating improvements

If you are getting Working Tax Credit with a disability element (see page 87) or you are 60-plus and getting Pension Credit, Council Tax Benefit, Housing Benefit or certain other means-tested benefits, you may be able to get a grant worth up to £2,700 to install loft insulation, cavity wall insulation, central heating and/or make other heating improvements. This scheme is run by Warm Front in England (see below).

Your local home improvement agency (see page 95) can give you advice and support regarding any repairs, improvements and adaptations to your home, including advice on the range of grants, loans and other schemes available in your area.

> **“ You could apply for a budgeting loan to help you spread the cost of a large expense. ”**

If you live in England, to find out about Warm Front grants, call 0800 316 2805 and see Useful addresses on page 215 for equivalent schemes in the rest of the UK. To find your local home improvements agency, see www.foundations.uk.com.

Money-saving ideas

Check out the tips on the following four pages for cutting out financial waste, using your income more effectively and staying within budget without becoming fortress frugal.

1 Shop around for cheaper utilities

Loyalty seldom pays. If you stay with the same fuel suppliers year in, year out, you are likely to be paying over the odds. Use the SwitchwithWhich service (www.switchwithwhich.co.uk or call 0800 533 031) to compare over 5,000 tariffs and see if you can get a better deal.

2 Cheaper phone and broadband

The same applies with your landline, mobile and internet connection

> **Comparison sites are an effective way of finding the most cost-effective deal.**

packages. There is a bewildering array of different deals on offer. Comparison sites, such as www.uswitch.com and www.moneysupermarket.com can help you find the most cost-effective deal for you.

3 Stay in touch by internet

You can save on phone bills if you already have an internet connection and keep in touch by email. If you and the person you are calling both have a service like Skype (www.skype.com), you can make free voice calls to each other – and see each other too if you have a webcam.

4 Save energy

With the cost of fuel so high these days, a key way to save is to cut the amount of energy you use. Visit the Energy Saving Trust website, www.energysavingtrust.org.uk, for loads of ideas, including some that are very cheap and simple – see overleaf.

 For further money-saving tips – but relating to tax – see pages 177–80. See also Which?'s product comparison site at www.whichcompare.co.uk.

Save energy, save money

What you can do	How much you might save a year
Switch to a condensing boiler with full heating controls	£250
Loft insulation (0–270mm)	£205
Cavity wall insulation	£160
Double glazing	£140
Heating controls upgrade	£105
Fit solar water heating system	£50
Floor insulation	£50
Hot water tank jacket	£40
Switch to most energy-efficient fridge freezer	£34
Switch to most energy-efficient tumble drier	£30
Draught proof doors, windows and letter boxes	£30
Switching five 100W bulbs to low-energy bulbs	£29
Turn off all appliances instead of using standby	£28
Filling gaps between floor and skirting board	£25
Insulate main pipes	£10

Sources: Energy Saving Trust (www.energysavingtrust.org.uk/Home-improvements Accessed 30 October 2008); Which?

5 Consider a water meter

If the family have left home, chances are you could save on water bills by switching to a water meter instead of paying rates. Use the OFWAT calculator at www.ofwat.gov.uk/consumerissues/ meters to see how much money you might save.

6 Pay bills by direct debit or online

Some suppliers charge extra if you pay phone or household bills quarterly by cheque, and if you pay by monthly direct debit, instead, you usually you get a discount of around 5 per cent. With these schemes, you pay a fixed sum each month, which builds up to pay your quarterly bills as they fall due. This is a neat arrangement provided your monthly payment is not set too high. Check to make sure you are not building up a surplus in your account. If you are, ask for a refund and get your monthly payment reduced to a more reasonable level. Suppliers usually give a discount to customers who manage their account and pay their bills online.

7 Watch out for insurance instalments

By contrast, you will usually pay extra if you opt to pay car or home insurance by monthly direct debit instead of a single annual premium. The provider views this as lending you money and typically charges a hefty double-digit interest rate.

8 Cancel unwanted insurances

As you get older, you may not need some types of insurance any more. Provided you have made sure your partner will have enough pension if you go first, life cover may be redundant. You are very unlikely to need life insurance if you live alone and no one is financially dependent on you. Private medical insurance may seem reassuring, but bear in mind that it generally will not pay out for the cost of treating long-term chronic health conditions or pre-existing health problems. Think carefully and check the small print before being persuaded to take out loan protection

insurance or extended warranties – is a claim likely, would your circumstances be covered if you did need to claim?

9 Emergency fund

However little you can save each week or month, try to build up some savings – the table , below, shows how even small amounts build up. This will give you a fund to dip into in an emergency instead of borrowing. Use the Financial Services Authority's (FSA) comparative tables, www.fsa.gov.uk/tables to find the best savings account.

10 Control your credit card

Don't pay through the nose for credit. If possible, pay off your credit card in full each month – in that way you get the convenience of a short interest-free loan at no cost. If you can't manage full repayments, pay off as much as you can. Don't just pay the minimum – the longer the debt drags on, the more you pay for it in total. Set up a direct debit to make

How your savings might grow

This table assumes you save in a tax-free Individual Savings Account (ISA) (see page 117) paying 6% a year interest.

Amount you save each week	Value of your savings after			
	6 months	1 year	3 years	5 years
50p	£3.05	£6.19	£19.72	£34.91
£1	£6.10	£12.39	£39.43	£69.82
£5	£30.52	£61.93	£197.17	£349.12
£10	£61.03	£123.87	£394.34	£698.24
£20	£122.06	£247.73	£788.68	£1,396.48

your monthly payments so you never miss the due date (which will cost you up to £12 a time plus extra interest).

11 Shop around when you borrow

Use comparison sites like www.moneyfacts.co.uk and www.moneysupermarket.com to find the cheapest credit card deals and personal loans. Check out Zopa (http://uk.zopa.com/ZopaWeb). This is a website that brings together people who want to borrow money and savers who are willing to lend – so it is, in effect, an online marketplace for lending and saving. Because it cuts out the middleman – in other words the banks – and operates solely through the internet, there is the potential for rates to be more competitive than you could get from a bank.

Check whether there is a **credit union** in your area that you could join (see www.abcul.org or ask your local authority).

Jargon buster

Credit union A mutual self-help organisation where members build up savings and can borrow at reasonable rates. Members are linked by a 'common bond', which means they all, for example, live in the same area, work for the same company, attend the same church, and so on

12 Weed out direct debits

Once a year, ask your bank for a list of your direct debits and cancel any for things you no longer use, for example the gym you no longer visit, the magazines that pile up unread and the premium TV channels you never have time to watch.

13 Pay less for petrol

Before you fill up, check where in your area is selling the cheapest fuel using web comparison sites, such as www.petrolprices.com.

14 Buy online

It is well known that lots of items are cheaper if you buy them online rather than in the shops – and you may be saving on petrol too – but don't forget to add on postage and packing charges. The internet can be useful even if you like old-fashioned shopping, because some retailers let you check and reserve items online before you visit their real-word shop, which can save wasted trips.

15 Put food shopping on a diet

Do your food shop just once a week and take a list. That way, you will be less tempted to make impulse buys that can really add up. A list will help you to plan meals, which you can focus around cheaper seasonal produce. Shop with a friend, so you can take advantage of BOGOFs and other bulk deals without having to eat yoghurt and tuna fish for a month.

Income from your home

In retirement, many people find themselves 'asset-rich-income-poor'. Your income might be restricted but maybe you have wealth tied up in a home you own. There are various ways you can make this asset work for you to provide a cash lump sum or regular boost to your income. Even if you rent your home, taking in a lodger or running a small bed-and-breakfast business could be a source of extra income.

Downsize or stay put?

Planning ahead to use your home as a pension is a risky strategy and not recommended. But, if having retired you need extra income, downsizing could be worth considering.

The 2008 housing market downturn has been a reminder that property, like most other investments, can go down as well as up, so putting all your investment eggs in that one basket is risky. Therefore, perhaps unsurprisingly, research by Baring Asset Management shows the number of people who say they will be relying just on property to fund their pension had dropped from 3.2 million in 2007 to less than 0.9 million by mid-2008.

Falling property prices are just one potential problem if your intention is to sell up to release capital. Typically, your aim might be to sell the family home and switch to a smaller, more convenient property, such as a bungalow or maybe sheltered housing. But these properties are not necessarily cheaper than the family home you are selling. To find a significantly cheaper home, you may need to move to another part of the country or even abroad. In that case, you need to think carefully about the emotional and social aspects of relocating. For example, can you choose an area where you already have friends or family? Do you have interests that will help you to meet people and make new friends? Does the area have the type of health, social and other facilities you want? Will you be dependent on a car? What will happen if later on you have to give up driving?

Bear in mind, too, that the costs of selling, buying and moving eat into any equity you plan to extract from your home. The table opposite gives an idea of these costs and the case study

---

Pit your wits **Answers**

Question 6
How could you turn a house you own into extra income without moving home?
A: You could consider, for example, equity release (see pages 117-24), taking in a lodger or starting a bed-and-breakfast business (see pages 125-9) or selling part of your garden (see page 130).

> " The costs of buying, selling and moving eat into any equity that you plan to extract from your home. "

The cost of selling, buying and moving

Use this table to give you an idea of the costs of downsizing.

	Cost	Example 1: selling home for £250,000 and buying for £150,000	Example 2: selling home for £600,000 and buying for £250,000
As a seller			
Estate agent's fee	1.5% to 2% of price	£4,375[a]	£10,500[a]
Home information pack	£350	£350	£350
As a buyer			
Stamp Duty Land Tax	See table below	£0[b]	£2,500
Surveyor's fee	say, £500	£500	£500
Search fees and Land Registry fees	say, £500	£500	£500
As both			
Legal costs	say, £1,500	£1,500	£1,500
Removal costs	say, £600	£600	£600
TOTAL		£7,825	£16,450

a Assuming 1.75% fee.

b Assuming purchase before 3 September 2009, otherwise £1,500.

Stamp Duty Land Tax (SDLT) in 2008–9

Purchase price	Rate[a]
£0–£125,000[b]	No tax
Over £125,000 up to £250,000	1%
Over £250,000 up to £500,000	3%
Over £500,000	4%

a Rate applies to whole property price not just excess over the threshold.

b Increased to £175,000 if you are buying between 3 September 2008 and 2 September 2009 inclusive. Otherwise, increased to £150,000 if you are buying in specified areas that are part of the Government's regeneration plans. You can check whether your property is in a specified area using the search tool at www.hmrc.gov.uk/so/dar/dar-search.htm.

For up-to-date information on budget changes, go to: www.which.co.uk/advice/tax-basics-explained/budget-changes/index.jsp.

Case Study Les and Molly

Les and Molly are selling a £350,000 family home and buying a bungalow for £200,000. Their costs of downsizing are:

- Estate agent's fees (1% x £350,000):   £5,250
- Home Information Pack: £350
- SDLT (1% x £200,000):   £2,000
- Survey: £500
- Search fees, Land Registry fee: £500
- Legal costs on both sale and purchase: £1,500
- Removal costs: £600

This comes to a total of £10,700. The net amount of cash they realise from downsizing is £350,000 - £200,000 - £10,700 = £139,300.

above shows how they could reduce the cash you release.

The big advantages of downsizing are that, apart from costs, you realise the full value of the home you are selling (in contrast to equity release schemes – see opposite) and, if selling your own home, the money you release is tax-free.

If you have invested in a second home or buy-to-let property that you are now selling, you do not have the problems of relocating and re-buying, but you will usually have to pay Capital Gains Tax on the proceeds of your sale (see pages 169–73) and this can take a hefty chunk out of your profit.

Equity release schemes

Equity release is a way of realising capital locked up in your home without having to move. The main drawback is that you will not get the full value of the part of your home that you sell or mortgage.

If you invested, say £10,000 to be repaid on a distant but uncertain date – say, five, ten or 20 years' time – would you expect to get £10,000 back or a larger sum? Almost certainly your answer is: a larger sum because, if you invest, you expect to get a return as compensation for giving up the immediate use of your money and for any risks involved. That is a fundamental principle embedded in the pricing of equity release schemes. These schemes offer you a lump sum or income now but you – or more likely your estate – have to pay back a larger sum later to compensate the investors (the equity release companies) who supplied the money. Provided you are comfortable with that, equity release schemes could be worth looking into if you need to raise money, but do not want to move home. There are, however, other drawbacks to equity release schemes that you should be aware of and these are discussed further in this section. Moreover, you should also look at possible alternatives (see page 121) and consider carefully the impact on any state benefits and your tax position (see page 122).

Equity release schemes come in two basic forms: lifetime mortgages and home reversion schemes.

 If your income is tight, make sure you are claiming all the state benefits to which you may be entitled (see Chapter 4). Any income and capital you draw from your home by downsizing, equity release or taking in lodgers (see page 125) can affect your entitlement to benefits. Although the proceeds from selling your own home are normally tax-free, any income from investing the proceeds, from some types of equity release scheme or from lodgers will generally affect your tax bill – see Chapter 7 for further details.

❝ Look at possible alternatives and consider carefully the impact on any state benefits and your tax position. ❞

LIFETIME MORTGAGE

With a lifetime mortgage, you borrow against the value of your home but the capital and usually the interest too are repaid only when the home is sold on your death or when you move out permanently (for example, because you move into a care home). Lifetime mortgages can be taken out jointly with your spouse or other partner, in which case the loan does not have to be repaid until the second death.

You can use a lifetime mortgage to raise a single, large cash lump sum. If you want an income, you can either draw out a series of smaller lump sums or use a single lump sum to buy an investment, such as an annuity. The former is usually more tax-efficient, because part or all of the return from an investment will normally be taxable (see Chapters 6 and 7), whereas the money raised through a series of small lump sum loans will be tax-free.

 It is essential to make sure that any lifetime mortgage you take out has a no-negative-equity guarantee. The guarantee ensures that, however rapidly your loan grows and whatever happens to house prices, the maximum you or your estate must repay will not exceed the proceeds from the eventual sale of your home. Check the terms of the guarantee carefully – some include selling costs within the guarantee, but others could leave you or your estate to meet the selling costs.

Types of lifetime mortgage

With the most common form of lifetime loan – a 'roll-up loan' – interest is added each month to the amount you owe. You are charged interest not just on the amount you originally borrowed, but also the interest that has already been added to the outstanding balance. This means the total that you owe can grow rapidly – see the table, opposite. The interest rate is often fixed for the whole life of the loan, or may be variable.

What happens when your home is sold

When your home is eventually sold, the proceeds are used to repay the outstanding loan and what is left over – if anything – goes to you or your estate.

Eligibility conditions

Different providers set different age limits, but you must be at least 55 or 60 with most schemes (but 70 with some) to be eligible for a lifetime mortgage. In addition, the value of your home less any

How the loan balance could grow

The table shows, for each £10,000 you borrow through a lifetime mortgage, how the amount you owe could grow when interest is rolled up – in other words added to the outstanding balance.

After this many years:	The balance would be this much if you were charged interest fixed at a yearly rate of:				
	5%	6%	7%	8%	9%
5	£12,834	£13,489	£14,176	£14,898	£15,657
10	£16,470	£18,194	£20,097	£22,196	£24,514
15	£21,137	£24,541	£28,489	£33,069	£38,380
20	£27,126	£33,102	£40,387	£49,268	£60,092

debts already secured against it (in other words the equity you own) needs to be worth at least a minimum amount, generally in the range £50,000–£100,000. If you have an existing mortgage, you will usually be required to use part of the lifetime mortgage to pay it off.

There will also be restrictions on the amount you can borrow, which generally vary with your age. The older you are, the greater the sum you can borrow, but the absolute maximum for a roll-up loan is unlikely to be more than half the value of your home.

❝ The total you owe can grow rapidly. ❞

Case Study Hannah

Hannah is 70 and owns her own home, worth £240,000. She is considering a lifetime mortgage and has been offered a maximum loan of 40 per cent of the value of her home, which would be 40% x £240,000 = £96,000. Interest, at a fixed rate of 7 per cent, will be rolled up and repaid when the mortgage comes to an end. If Hannah experiences the average life expectancy for a woman aged 70, which is 18 years, the outstanding loan will reach £337,200. This will be repaid from the proceeds of selling the home. How much, if anything, remains for her heirs depends on how house prices change over the 18 years. Hannah has been careful to choose a lifetime mortgage with a no-negative-equity guarantee. This means that if the sale proceeds are lower than the outstanding loan, Hannah's heirs will inherit nothing from the house but equally the lender will have no further claim against Hannah's estate or anyone else.

Equity release providers that are members of the trade body, Safe Home Income Plans (SHIP), all offer no-negative-equity guarantees on their lifetime mortgages and have agreed to abide by a code of good business practice – see www.ship-ltd.org.

REVERSION SCHEME

With a reversion scheme you sell part or all of your home, but retain the right to carry on living there either rent-free or for a token rent. When the home is eventually sold, the reversion company takes a percentage of the sale proceeds (or the whole amount if you sold 100 per cent of your home). This means that the reversion company, not you or your estate, gets the benefit of any appreciation in value of the part of the home you sold. But, equally, the reversion company has to accept any reduction in value of that part if house prices have fallen. A reversion scheme can be taken out jointly with your spouse or other partner, in which case it continues until the second death.

As with lifetime mortgages, reversion schemes can pay you a single lump sum or a series of smaller lump sums. Alternatively, they may be combined with an annuity or other investment to provide you with a regular income. In general, investment income is taxable (see Chapter 7) but lump sums from the sale of your home are not, so opting for a lump sum or series of lump sums will usually be the more tax-efficient option.

The money you get when you take out the scheme will be smaller than the value of the part of the home you sell. For example, a woman aged 70 might get, say, £4,500 for every £10,000 she sells (see the case study, right). The difference (between £10,000 and £4,500 in this example) is the return to the reversion company, reflecting the delay until it can expect to get its money back and the fact that it earns no rent

from the property (or only a tiny amount) in the meantime.

A key factor that the reversion company uses in deciding how much to offer is how long it expects to wait to get its money back, which, in turn, depends on the average life expectancy for someone of your age and sex. Therefore, the older you are when you take out the scheme, the larger the sum you should get for each £10,000 you sell, and men tend to get slightly more than women.

Eligibility conditions

Terms and conditions vary from one provider to another. To qualify for a home reversion scheme, you must usually be aged at least 65 or 70 years. Your home must be in reasonable condition (or you must be intending to use some or all of the money raised to bring your home back to a good condition) and worth a minimum amount, typically £75,000.

Case Study   Joan

Joan is 70 years old. She owns her home outright and currently it is valued at £240,000. She is considering a home reversion scheme. If she sells 90 per cent her home (worth 90% x £240,000 = £216,000), she has been offered a lump sum of £97,200. When her home is eventually sold (likely to be on Joan's death), the reversion company will take 90 per cent of the sale proceeds. The remaining 10 per cent will go to Joan's estate.

Is equity release for you?

Equity release is not the only option if you need to raise cash or income and is not suitable for everyone. This is a complicated area, so get advice. The most obvious alternative to equity release is downsizing, but, even If you want to stay in your current home, equity release is not necessarily your only option.

ALTERNATIVES TO EQUITY RELEASE

A common reason for considering equity release is to raise extra income for everyday living. If this is your motive, first you should check that you are getting all the income due to you. For example, are you:

- Claiming all the state benefits you may be eligible for, such as Pension Credit, Council Tax Benefit and Attendance Allowance (see Chapter 4)?
- Taking steps to trace any lost private pensions you could now be claiming (see below)?
- Exploiting the potential of your home – for example, could you take in a lodger (see page 125)?
- Making sure you are not spending more than you need to (see Chapter 4, pages 109–12)?
- Paying too much tax (see Chapter 7)?

Another important reason for needing extra cash is to pay for essential repairs or improvements to your home. If you are an older person or have a disability, you might qualify for a grant from your local authority or other source (see pages 94–5 and 100).

Interest-only mortgage

You cannot normally use equity release to raise a lump sum below, say, £10,000. If your need is for a smaller amount, another option could be to take out an interest-only mortgage against your home. Like a lifetime mortgage, the amount you borrow does not have to be repaid until you no longer need the home. But, unlike a lifetime mortgage, you pay interest every month, so the outstanding balance does not grow.

In general, you need to make sure you can afford the interest out of your current income – and to think about whether you

To check if you are eligible for any benefits, visit your local Citizens Advice bureau (www.citizensadvice.org.uk). To track down a lost private pension, contact the Pension Tracing Service www.thepensionservice.gov.uk/atoz/atozdetailed/pensiontracing.asp.

121

can cope with an increase in payments if the interest rate is variable.

However, if the loan is to pay for essential repairs and your income is low enough for you to qualify for the guarantee credit part of Pension Credit (see page 103), then your Pension Credit might be increased to cover the interest. You need to check carefully whether this might apply in your case, in particular what types of work on your home would count as essential.

The Pension Service can advise you on the interaction of Pension Credit and loans for essential home repairs. Your local home improvement agency can help you find out about grants and interest-only mortgages if you are an older homeowner or have a disability.

STATE BENEFITS AND TAX

If you are getting means-tested state benefits, such as Pension Credit, Council Tax Benefit or Housing Benefit (see pages 101–7), any income or lump sum you raise through equity release could cause a reduction in your benefit. Your local Citizens Advice Bureau (CAB), the Pension Service and some independent financial advisers (IFAs) can help you work out whether your benefit would be affected and by how much.

Be aware too that any extra income (but not capital sums) could have a disproportionately large effect on your tax bill if your income is above a certain level (£22,900 in 2009–10). This happens if the extra income triggers a reduction in the amount of age allowance you get (see page 163). Any independent adviser helping you with your equity release decision should check this.

OTHER FACTORS TO CONSIDER

These are some other factors you should think about before going down the equity release route.

Charges

Check what fees and charges you will have to pay. Typically, there will be an arrangement fee, valuation fee and legal costs. Find out whether any have to be paid in advance or whether they can be deducted from the amount of equity you release. If you opt to take a series of small lump sums, there may be a separate administration fee each time you draw a payment.

Check what happens if you want to end the scheme early. There may be hefty early repayment charges with a lifetime mortgage. Normally there are no early repayment charges with a reversion scheme – in fact, the provider will be happy to get its money sooner than it had expected.

To find your local office for **The Pension Service**, go to www.thepensionservice.gov.uk. You can find your local home improvement agency from www.foundations.uk.com.

Maintaining your home

If you take out a lifetime mortgage, as with any mortgage, the lender will want to be satisfied that your home is good security for the loan. This might mean you have to use some of the money raised to bring your home up to a reasonable state of repair if maintenance has been neglected for a long time.

With a reversion scheme, ownership of part or all of your home passes from you to the reversion company, so it has an even more direct interest in the ongoing upkeep of the property. Essentially you become a tenant and you should check carefully what obligations the agreement with the reversion company places on you. In particular, check what rights the reversion company has to inspect the property and who is responsible for arranging and paying for necessary repairs.

Changing circumstances

An equity release scheme might be transferable to a new property. If you move home, provided that property is acceptable to the equity release provider. However, moving could be a problem if you want to shift to a smaller, less valuable property or, say, sheltered housing (which often is not eligible property). If, alternatively, you pay off the equity release scheme, there is a danger that you will be left with too little equity to buy a replacement home.

If you are a couple at the outset, you will probably opt for a scheme that continues until neither of you needs the home anymore. If you are single, be aware that anyone who later moves in

with you is unlikely to have any rights to stay in the home once you have ceased to live there.

Your family

Taking out an equity release scheme means that all or part of the value of your home will eventually pass to the equity release company, leaving less of your wealth to be passed on to your heirs. To avoid false expectations, you might want to discuss your plans with your family.

Sometimes equity release schemes are marketed as a way of saving Inheritance Tax (IHT) (see pages 198–203). But, while equity release certainly reduces the value of your estate and the amount of tax that may be due on it, this is because part of the value of your estate has passed to the equity release company instead. Check carefully that there really is a significant net benefit to your heirs.

VALUE FOR MONEY?

There has been much debate about whether equity release schemes represent good value for money and the answer depends to a large extent on how you expect house prices to move over the time you have a scheme. Equity

Key facts illustration

The Financial Services Authority (FSA) rules require the equity release provider or adviser to supply you with a key facts illustration for any scheme you are considering. This sets out the main features, costs and risks of the scheme in a standard format making it easier for you to compare one scheme with another.

release has been evolving over the years, for example:

- Following the house price crash at the end of the 1980s, the focus was on the issue of negative equity as elderly homeowners were left with lifetime mortgages larger than the value of their property. This led to the welcome introduction of no-negative-equity guarantees and a shift away from some higher-risk types of scheme.
- In the later 1990s and early part of this decade, new types of lifetime mortgage were tried out where instead of being charged interest, the lender took a percentage of any rise in the value of your home between taking out the loan and the mortgage coming to an end. As house prices rose, this provoked suspicion that providers of these mortgages and of reversion schemes were making excess profits. The mortgages ceased to be offered and, although reversion schemes continued, they account for only a small proportion of the market.
- In 2008, house prices started to fall once again, making it is easier to see that equity release is not a risk-free business for the providers.

A 2006 study for the Joseph Rowntree Foundation (an independent research organisation) suggested that reasonably priced equity release schemes had become readily available. But this is a controversial view and it is clear that not every scheme on the market offers a good deal. You need to make your decisions in this area with care and you are strongly recommended to get professional advice.

GET ADVICE

If you take out a home reversion scheme, the value put on your property will be crucial in determining the deal you get. Financial Services Authority (FSA) rules require that the valuation is carried out by a professional valuer acting for you and who is independent of the provider.

Whether you take out a lifetime mortgage or reversion scheme, you will need to employ a solicitor. With a reversion scheme, it is essential that your legal adviser carefully checks the terms of your tenancy agreement with the reversion company.

Equity release is a complex area of financial planning. Get help from an independent financial adviser (IFA). Among other aspects, FSA rules require the adviser either to check whether your entitlement to state benefits could be affected or to refer you to another expert for those checks.

 Deciding whether an equity release scheme is appropriate for you is a complex decision and there are many variations on the standard equity release schemes described in this section. Always get advice from an IFA. To find local IFAs who can advise you on this area, see www.impartial.co.uk.

Lodgers and B&B

If you have the space and are happy to share your home, you can make up to £4,250 tax-free each year in rental income from lodgers and bed-and-breakfast guests.

Another way to make money from your home is to let out a spare room or two either on a reasonably permanent basis to a lodger or temporarily to bed-and-breakfast guests. These options are possible whether you own your own home or rent it. However, if you have a mortgage or equity release scheme (see page 117), you should check that the lender or reversion company is happy with the arrangement. Similarly, if you rent, you need to get the agreement of your landlord. In either case, also let your buildings and contents insurers know in case your cover or premium need amending.

The table overleaf summarises the main issues you need to consider before taking in a lodger or starting a bed-and-breakfast business. If you employ staff (for example, someone to help with breakfasts), you will need to comply with additional regulations and your local authority can advise on this. Consider carefully whether you are happy opening your home to strangers.

YOUR LODGERS' OR GUESTS' RIGHTS

When you invite someone to stay in your home, they have some legal rights, particularly concerning the living space they can call their own and the amount of notice you must give if you want them to leave (see table, overleaf). These rights vary depending on the agreement you make with them. Bed-and-breakfast guests and often lodgers will have the right to occupy a room in your home, but that will not prevent you having access, for example, to change bed linen, take out rubbish, and so on. But you could make an agreement with a lodger that gives him or her greater rights – for example, the right to 24 hours' notice if you need to enter the room. This is a complicated area – for more information and guidance on the type of agreement to choose, get the free booklet 'Letting rooms in your home' from the Department for Communities and Local Government (www.communities.gov.uk/publications/housing/lettingrooms).

 To find out about the legal aspects of running a bed-and-breakfast business, contact your nearest tourist information centre (see *The Phone Book*). They will be able to put you in touch with the tourism officer at your local authority.

Letting out rooms: things to remember

	Lodger	Bed-and-breakfast
Planning permission	Not needed for up to two lodgers. If more, check with local authority.	May be needed. Check with local authority.
Other permission	Mortgage lender, equity release provider, landlord.	Mortgage lender, equity release provider, landlord
Gas appliances	Maintain in good order. Annual safety check by CORGI-registered installer required.	Maintain in good order. Annual safety check by CORGI-registered installer required.
Electrical appliances	Ensure safety and carry out any necessary repairs.	Ensure safety and carry out any necessary repairs.
Furniture and furnishings	Must meet fire resistance standards (unless pre-1950).	Must meet fire resistance standards (unless pre-1950).
Standards and maintenance	General duty to ensure accommodation is habitable.	General duty to ensure accommodation is habitable. Duty to carry out risk assessment and decide on appropriate precautions.
Fire safety	Usually no special requirements, but sensible to have smoke alarms, fire extinguisher, fire blanket and planned escape routes.	Duty to carry out fire risk assessment and decide on appropriate precautions. Sensible to have smoke alarms, fire extinguisher, fire blanket and planned escape routes.
Food safety	No special requirements.	Must register with local authority and comply with food hygiene regulations.
Your safety	Always take up references, for example, from previous landlords, employer and/or bank.	No particular precautions. Use your judgement.
Written agreement	Not required, but recommended.	Must keep register of guests.
Term	You and lodger agree this – could be fixed term or open-ended.	Short, temporary stay.
Rent	You and lodger agree the amount, rent period (eg weekly, monthly) and when to review. Usually pay one rent period in advance.	You set your overnight rate.
Deposit	You and your lodger agree this – typically, one month's rent.	None.
Access to rooms	Depending on agreement, could be on 24 hours' notice.	At any time.
Notice to quit	Depends on the type of agreement you have. For example, if your lodger is staying indefinitely, usually a month's notice or one rent period. If staying for an agreed fixed period, you can't usually end the agreement early unless your lodger agrees.	Whatever you previously agreed or whatever is reasonable.
Eviction	Get legal advice.	Get legal advice.

State benefits

If you are getting means-tested state benefits, such as **Pension Credit**, **Council Tax Benefit** or **Housing Benefit** (see pages 101-7), any extra income from lodgers or bed-and-breakfast guests could cause a reduction in your benefit. Your local **Citizens Advice** bureau or the **Pension Service** can help you work out whether your benefit would be affected and by how much.

THE INCOME TAX POSITION

In general, rents from lodgers or bed-and-breakfast guests are taxable income, although you can deduct various expenses, such as extra heating and lighting, cost of providing meals, hiring a cleaner, advertising for tenants or guests, and so on. You pay tax only on the profit that remains.

Rent-a-Room Scheme

Alternatively, you can instead opt to be taxed under the Rent-a-Room Scheme, an option under the Income Tax rules that lets you receive a certain amount of rent tax-free. Under the scheme, you cannot deduct any expenses but the first £4,250 a year of gross receipts are

tax-free. For this purpose, gross receipts means the rent and also any payments you get for related services, such as meals, laundry and cleaning. If these receipts are £4,250 or less, you pay no tax at all. If your receipts are more than £4,250, you have a choice:

- Deduct £4,250 from your gross receipts and declare the remaining balance for tax.
- Work out your tax bill in the normal way by adding up your rents and related payments, deducting actual expenses and declaring the resulting profit for tax.

If two or more people share the income from the lettings, the Rent-a-Room Scheme limit is split with each person (regardless of how many they are) being allowed to get £2,125 tax-free.

To use the Rent-a-Room Scheme, you must be letting furnished residential accommodation in your only or main home. You cannot claim rent-a-room relief for letting a separate self-contained unit, letting space in a second home or renting to a business.

❝ The first £4,250 a year of gross receipts are tax-free. ❞

 For a free guide to the legal aspects of taking in a lodger – see www.communities. gov.uk/publications/housing/lettingrooms. To learn more about running a bed-and-breakfast business, contact your local authority, national tourist board or Business Link or its local equivalent (see Useful addresses on pages 211-15).

COUNCIL TAX AND BUSINESS RATES

Taking in lodgers will not normally affect your Council Tax position. However, bear in mind that, if you have been living alone, you will lose the 25 per cent sole-occupancy discount (see page 94) from the date you start to share with lodgers.

Technically, you will be treated as running a business if you take in bed-and-breakfast guests. However, business rates will not normally apply, provided:

- The guests stay in your only or main home.
- The property remains primarily a home. (As a guide, if half or more is used for bed-and-breakfast, you will probably have to pay business rates.)
- You have no more than six guests at any time.

CAPITAL GAINS TAX (CGT)

When you eventually sell your only or main home, there is usually no tax on any profit you make because you get private residence relief. Some of the relief is lost if you have used part of your home for business purposes. The rules here relate to CGT and apply regardless of whether or not you have claimed rent-a-room relief for Income Tax.

Taking in a single lodger who shares your living space does not count as business use and so there should be no CGT implications. If you take in two or more lodgers, however, you are likely to be treated as having run a lodging house business and, in that case, there could be some CGT to pay (see page 169).

Taking in bed-and-breakfast guests does count as a business, but you lose private residence relief only in respect of those parts of your home used *exclusively* for business. For example, a bedroom might be exclusively set aside for guests during part of the year but it is likely that breakfasts will be prepared in a kitchen that doubles up for your own private use as well. Very minor private use – for example, just storing a few

Jargon buster

Private residence relief Exemption from CGT on any profit you make from selling your only or main home. You may lose some of the relief if, for example, you use your home for business (see page 171)

> **&& There should be no CGT implications if you take in a single lodger who shares your living space. &&**

personal possessions in a guest room – is likely to be disregarded.

To work out the part of any gain on selling your home that relates to business use, you need to agree a basis with your tax office. If the amount of tax involved is small, any reasonable basis is likely to be acceptable, such as the proportion of rooms involved.

Where letting out part of your home results in the loss of some private residence relief, you might nevertheless still have no tax to pay because of letting relief (see box, below).

Letting relief

Normally there is no CGT on any profit you make from selling your only or main home – this exemption is called private residence relief. You may lose some of the relief if, for example, you let part or all of your home as residential accommodation. In that case, CGT could be charged on part of the profit in proportion to the amount of your home you let out and/or the time period for which you let it. However, where CGT may be due because you have let out part

or all of your only or main home, you can usually claim letting relief. Any part of the gain covered by letting relief is tax-free. The maximum amount of relief is the lower of:

- The gain made because of the letting.
- The amount of private residence relief given; or
- £40,000.

See the case study, below, for an example.

Case Study   Shirley

Shirley sold her four-bedroom house in Oxford in August 2008. £162,500 of the £200,000 gain she made on the sale was covered by private residence relief and so tax-free. But she had run a bed-and-breakfast business for ten years and £37,500 of the gain was deemed to be related to the business. However, she qualifies for letting relief equal to the lower of:

- The gain made because of the letting: £37,500.
- The amount of private residence relief given: £162,500, or
- £40,000.

The letting relief is £37,500, meaning she has no CGT to pay.

To find out more about the Rent-a-Room Scheme, see www.hmrc.gov.uk/individuals/tmarent-a-room-scheme.shtml. For more information about CGT, see Chapter 7 and the *Which? Essential Guide: Tax Handbook 2009/10*, published in Spring 2009.

Cash from your garden

If you have a large garden, selling part of it for development might be a way of raising some extra cash, but take care not to trigger a Capital Gains Tax (CGT) bill.

The credit squeeze of 2008 put the brakes on new housing development for a while. But the Government is still encouraging efficient land use, including reuse of **brownfield sites**. Therefore, it seems likely that development opportunities will re-emerge and could be a source of extra cash in retirement.

TAX AND TAX RELIEF

As outlined on page 128, when you sell your only or main home, any gain you make is normally free of CGT because you get the benefit of private residence relief. This relief covers your home and garden, provided the whole plot is no more than half a hectare (about 1.2 acres) or, if larger, is the sort of garden required for reasonable enjoyment of the home, bearing in mind its size and character.

Normally, of course, you would sell the garden along with the home. But private residence relief can still apply where you sell part of the garden while keeping the home. The part you sell must still have the characteristics of a garden and simply getting planning permission does not affect this. But, if you have started to build or even just roped off a building plot, the land will no longer be garden and private residence relief will not apply. Any gain from the garden sale would then be chargeable to CGT.

It is difficult to get relief where you sell part of a garden that is larger than 1.2 hectares. The very fact that you are selling part of the grounds suggests that they are not, in practice, required for the reasonable enjoyment of the home.

Exceptionally, HM Revenue & Customs might accept that the sale should, in fact, qualify for relief if you are selling to, say, a close relative whose presence in a new home in the garden would not detract from your enjoyment of your home or if you are having to sell because of financial hardship.

Jargon buster

Brownfield site Land that is classified as already developed, including the gardens of existing homes

 See pages 169-73 for details of how CGT is worked out. The section covers defining CGT, claiming reliefs, dealing with losses and how to work out your tax bill.

Investments

With some knowledge of investments and a systematic strategy you can enhance your financial security, achieve your goals and protect yourself from scams and mis-selling. There is plenty of scope for a do-it-yourself approach but, in some areas, you may want the help of a financial adviser.

Investments and risk

Following a basic strategy will help you to choose investments that match your goals and particular circumstances. A crucial part of the process is understanding risk.

Whatever stage of life you have reached, the basics of investing (see the basic investment strategy chart, opposite) are the same and form the framework for the ideas in this chapter:

- **The Risk self-assessment test** on pages 134–6 will help you decide on your attitude towards risk and page 137 onwards describes the different types of risk you need to balance when you are choosing how to save or invest.
- **Pages 144–53 consider some of the typical goals at this stage of life** and suggest broad ways you might invest to achieve them.
- **Because many older people own second homes,** pages 154–7 looks at the particular issues involved in using property as an investment.

The first section of this chapter focuses on risk because risk is fundamental to making the right choice of investments and often at the heart of any problems. If things go wrong, the cause is often a mismatch – either accidental or deliberate – between the risk an investor is comfortable taking and the risk inherent in the particular product. Understanding risk will sharpen your investment choices and arm you against both glossy marketing and outright fraud.

 It would not be appropriate for a book of this kind to recommend specific investments and providers - what will be suitable for you depends on your own particular circumstances and preferences. We point out sources to help you shop around for yourself and, on page 160, explain how to find and get the best from an independent financial adviser (IFA).

❝Risk is fundamental to making the right choice of investments and often at the heart of any problems. ❞

A basic investment strategy

Goals

Decide on your goals. In retirement, a common goal is extra income, but you might also be looking at building up a lump sum over a short or longer period for a variety of reasons (see pages 144–53).

Constraints

Assess the constraints on your choice of investments. This will be a mix of practical and personal factors, including for example how much you can afford to invest, your attitude towards risk, your tax position and your health. For a detailed look at risk, see pages 137–9. For guidance on tax, see Chapter 7.

Types of investment and/or strategy

Identify the broad types of investment or strategy that you could use to meet your goals given the constraints. This involves understanding the different types of product and their inherent features, such as risk, charges and tax treatment, and rejecting those products that are not suitable. See pages 140–53 for examples.

Specific products

Shop around for the best specific products. For help with this or any of the stage above, contact an independent financial adviser (see page 160).

66 Understand the different types of product and their inherent features, such as risk, charges and tax treatment. 99

Risk self-assessment test

Use this test to check your attitude towards risk before you read the section starting on page 137. It will help you to consider whether your natural instincts tend to help or hinder your investment decisions.

1 You are a long-term investor and the charts below show the share price of some shares you own.

a) Looking at Share X, what would you do when the share price reached point A: buy some more, hold or sell?

b) Looking at Share Y, what would you do when the share price reached point B: buy some more, hold or sell?

SHARE X
Share price over last ten years

SHARE Y
Share price over last year

2 Which of these three games would you rather play: A, B or C?

Game A: You give me £1. I toss a coin and give you £1.50p if the coin is tails, but just 50p if it is heads.

Game B: You give me £1 and I invite you to draw one ball from a bag that contains three blue balls and seven white ones. I'll give you £5 if you draw a blue ball, but nothing if you draw a white.

Game C: You give me £1 and I invite you to draw one straw from a bunch of ten. There is just one long straw and I'll give you £8 if you choose it, but nothing if you draw a short straw.

❝Consider whether your natural instincts tend to help or hinder your investment decisions.❞

3 You inherit £100,000. Which of the three portfolios below represents the way you would be most likely to invest the money for the long term: A, B or C?

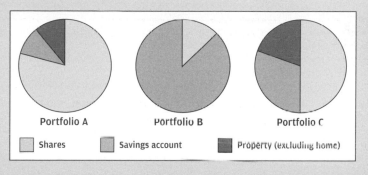

Portfolio A   Portfolio B   Portfolio C

☐ Shares   ☐ Savings account   ☐ Property (excluding home)

4 If inflation were averaging 5 per cent a year, which of these investments would you prefer?

Portfolio A: You invest £1,000 and get back £1,280 in two years' time.
Portfolio B: You invest £1,000 and get back £1,460 in four years' time.
Portfolio C: You invest £1,000 and get back £1,910 in 10 years' time.

How to score your answers

Work out your total score from the upside-down answers below.

Question	How each answer scores	Your score
4	A = 1 B = 2 C = 3	
3	A = 3 B = 1 C = 2	
2	Game A = 1 Game B = 2 Game C = 3	
1b	Buy = 2 Hold = 2 Sell = 1	
1a	Buy = 3 Hold = 2 Sell = 2	

Score 6 to 8 ➝ Cautious investor

Score 9 to 11 ➝ Balanced investor

Score 12 to 14 ➝ Adventurous investor

For information on what your answers tell you, see overleaf.

What your answers tell you

Question 1

Chart X shows the share price of Company X over the last ten years. It has shown good growth over the whole period.

Cautious and balanced investor: No one can know how the share might perform in future, so either holding or selling to take a profit now could be a moderate response to the situation.

Adventurous investor: Buying more shares when the price is already so high could be an adventurous strategy.

Of course, in real life, you would want a lot more information before making any decision.

Chart Y shows the price performance of a share, this time over just one year. The sharp dip in the price could just be a temporary adjustment.

Cautious investor: It is common for people who are uncomfortable with risk, to sell when share prices fall.

Balanced and adventurous investors: In general, long-term investors should ignore short-term fluctuations – or you might even view it as a good buying opportunity.

Question 2

These are all games of chance.

Cautious investor: Game A might appeal to you. Here you have a 50-50 chance of getting back either 50p or £1.50 so you always get at least some money back. But, if you played the game many times, you would only break even, so you cannot expect to make a profit.

Balanced investor: Game B gives you a 70 per cent chance of losing all your money but a 30 per cent chance of making £5. If you played this game repeatedly, you could expect to average £1.50 a game, which is more than the £1 stake, so this game could be a good choice.

Adventurous investor: In Game C, you have a 10 per cent chance of winning £8 but a 90 per cent risk of losing your money. Although the £8 looks tempting, if you played this game repeatedly, you could expect your average win to be 80p per game, which is less than your stake. So chasing the £8 win looks like a high-risk strategy.

Question 3

Cautious investor: You might feel happier putting most of your money into savings accounts, but bear in mind that you are then vulnerable to inflation and may be missing out on higher returns (see opposite).

Balanced investor: Generally a balanced approach is to spread your money across different types of investments (see page 153).

Adventurous investor: You may be tempted to put most or all or your money in shares and other higher-risk investments.

Question 4

Cautious investor: The future is uncertain and understandably you may prefer to secure your gains sooner rather than later, opting for the two-year deal.

Balanced investor: You have probably considered the impact of inflation and worked out that the return that has the highest buying power in terms of today's price levels is the four-year deal. The £1,460 would buy as much as £1,201 today compared with £1,161 and £1,173 from the two- and ten-year deals, respectively (see opposite).

Adventurous investor: You may be drawn to the promise of the highest cash sum even though it means holding on for ten years.

DIFFERENT TYPES OF RISK

Mention 'risk' in connection with investments and most people think of losing some or all of the money they invested (their capital). But being overly cautious about losing capital can leave you heavily exposed to other risks that have the potential to do as much or more damage to your financial wellbeing.

Capital risk

Capital risk means the risk of losing part or all of the money you originally invested or losing part or all of gains that you have previously built up. Capital risk is inherent in investments, such as shares, which are traded on a market and whose price can go down as well as up.

Share prices can be very volatile in the short term. Therefore, if you are investing for say five years or less, generally you should avoid capital risk – for example, by choosing deposit-based investments – such as bank and building society accounts or National Savings and Investments (NS&I) products – where there is little or no risk of failing to get your capital back.

Despite the short-term volatility, over long periods (say, ten years or more) the return on shares has tended to exceed the return on deposits by a wide margin. For example, research by Barclays Capital looking at UK investment returns over the last 108 years shows the average return before tax, but after inflation from shares was 5.3 per cent a year compared with just 1 per cent a year from deposits. Therefore, if you are

investing for the longer term, it usually makes sense to have at least part of your money in share-based investments.

Regardless of term, the amount of capital risk you are willing to take tends to decrease with age, because your ability to replace any lost capital reduces once you cease to work. Your temperament will also dictate the amount of capital risk you are comfortable taking, but you do need to realise that opting for low capital risk may increase your exposure to other risks, particularly inflation.

Inflation risk

Your retirement could easily last 20 or 30 years. Looking back over the last 30 years, annual inflation in the UK has ranged from a low of 1.5 per cent to a high of 18 per cent. The average inflation rate over the last 30 years has been 5 per cent. The chart on page 47 shows how the buying power of money

Pit your wits **Answers**

Questions 7 and 8

7 If you have a fixed income and inflation averages 4 per cent a year, how much buying power would your income have lost after 20 years?
A: c) Half. The buying power of each £1,000 of a fixed income would have fallen to £675 after ten years and just £456 after 20 years.

8 For someone aged 70, what proportion of their wealth should they sensibly invest in share-based investments?
A: Some experts would suggest around 30 per cent, but there is no single correct answer – see page 151.

137

would fall over the years ahead, given different rates of inflation. For example, at 5 per cent a year inflation, the buying power of £100 would have fallen to £61 after ten years, £38 after 20 years and £23 after 30 years. In terms of your investments, the impact of inflation is important because:

- **Even if you reinvest the interest** or other income from your investments, if the after-tax return is lower than inflation, your wealth will be diminishing as time goes by.
- **If you are drawing an income from your investments,** the buying power of your capital will be decreasing with inflation. Moreover, the income it produces is likely to buy less and less each year, so your standard of living will fall (see case study on page 47).

The main way to reduce inflation risk is to invest at least part of your money in investments that have tended over the long term to produce returns that are high enough after any tax to beat inflation. These tend to be share-based investments which, as outlined above, also involve capital risk. Alternatively, a few investments are designed specifically to give inflation-linked returns – see the entries for index-linked investments in table overleaf – but, except in times of high inflation, tend to offer relatively low returns compared with, say, shares.

Another way to increase your return, and so your chances of beating inflation, is to choose investments that are tax-free (see pages 177 and 180).

Shortfall risk

Shortfall risk is the possibility that your investment or savings will not produce enough to meet a goal. To increase your chance of saving enough, you may have to opt for those investments that have tended to produce higher returns, such as shares, but this means accepting extra capital risk. For example, when you are building up a pension, it might be tempting to invest in deposits but, if history is any indication, the return from deposits will be so low that you would need to save huge amounts each month to achieve a reasonable pension target. To make saving more affordable, you are likely to have to put at least some of your money into share-based investments. Bear in mind that taking on capital risk is not suitable if you are investing over the short-term.

Fixed/variable risk

Some investments give you the chance to lock into a fixed return usually for a set term. This can turn out to be a good choice, if over the term, the return on

 The Retail Prices Index (RPI) is a measure of inflation based on how the average household spends its money. If you spend your money differently, your personal inflation rate may be higher or lower. To explore your personal inflation rate, see www.statistics.gov.uk/pic.

Jargon buster

Bond An investment where you are, in effect, lending to the Government, company or other organisation that issued the bond. Your loan earns interest at a fixed rate and, in most cases, will eventually be repaid on a set date, called the redemption date. However, before then, you can sell the bonds on the stock market but, in that case, you cannot be sure what price you will get and could get back either more or less than you originally invested

Asset allocation Adjusting the amount of risk you take (especially when investing for the long term) by spreading your

money across several different types of investments, such as deposits (often called cash), bonds, property and shares (called equities) – see page 151 for more information

Cash individual savings account (ISA) Bank, building society or NS&I deposit that pays tax-free interest. You can invest up to £3,600 a year in a cash ISA – see Chapter 7 for details

National Savings & Investments (NS&I) An agency issuing savings products on behalf of the Government, which ultimately guarantees the return of your money, making NS&I products very safe

competing investments falls, but will have been a poor choice if other returns rise. You may be happy to accept this risk if you value the certainty of a fixed return, but bear in mind that fixed returns can also be especially vulnerable to inflation.

Similarly, you might choose investments that offer a variable return. You then have the opportunity to share in any increase in returns generally (for example, if general interest rates rise), but equally you are exposed to any fall in returns.

❝ If the after-tax return is lower than inflation, your wealth will be diminishing as time goes by. ❞

 For more information about the different types of saving and investment outlined overleaf, see the *Which? Essential Guide: Save and Invest*. To compare savings and investments from different providers, check out comparison websites, such as www.fsa.gov.uk/tables and www.moneyfacts.co.uk.

Main types of investments

This is an overview of the main types of investments available listed broadly in order of increasing risk. Pages 144–53 show how they may be applied to some common investment goals. For details of the tax treatment, see Chapter 7.

Investment		Description	Mainly useful for
Index-linked investments	RPI-linked annuity	Provides an income that increases each year in line with inflation (see page 57).	Income
	NS&I index-linked savings certificates	Bonds with a term of three or five years, at the end of which, you get a tax-free return guaranteed to be a small percentage over and above inflation. See www.nsandi.com.	Growth
	Index-linked gilts	Government bonds where both the income and repayment at redemption are increased in line with inflation. If you hold the gilts until redemption, the real return you get is fixed and guaranteed. You can sell before then on the stock market, in which case you may get back more or less than you invested. See www.dmo.gov.uk.	Income
Bank and building society accounts, most NS&I products	Easy access account	Accounts where you can get your money back at any time. Cash individual savings accounts (ISAs) – see page 177 – are often this type of account.	Income, growth
	Notice account	Accounts where you can get your money back on giving, say, 30, 60 or more days' notice. May be able to get your money back earlier but lose interest.	Income, growth
	Term account and bonds	Accounts where you invest for a set period, often for a fixed rate of interest. Might not be able to get your money back early.	Income, growth
	Guaranteed equity bonds	Accounts that earn interest, but the amount is linked to the performance of a stock-market index or basket of shares. But whatever happens to the index or shares, you are promised your original capital back in full.	Growth

Investment		Description	Mainly useful for
Individual gilts		Government bonds that pay you interest and usually return a fixed sum on a set date (the redemption date). If you hold the gilts until redemption, your return is fixed and guaranteed. You can sell before then on the stock-market, in which case you may get back more or less than you invested. See www.dmo.gov.uk.	Income
Annuities		Traditional versions provide a fixed income either for a set period or for life (see page 57).	Income
Investment funds investing in gilts and/or bonds	Unit trusts and open-ended investment companies (OEICs)	A ready-made portfolio of gilts and/or corporate bonds. You invest by buying units, the price of which varies directly with the value of the investments in the fund. Unlike investing direct in gilts or corporate bonds, your return is not fixed.	Income, asset allocation
	Investment trusts	A company whose business is investing in a portfolio of gilts and/or corporate bonds. You invest by buying shares in the investment trust. The price of the shares is indirectly linked to the value of the investments in the fund and also influenced by the relative demand for the shares. Unlike investing direct in gilts or corporate bonds, your return is not fixed.	Income, asset allocation
	Exchange traded funds (ETFs)	A company whose business is providing a return linke to a portfolio of gilts and/or corporate bonds. You invest by buying shares in the exchange traded fund. The price of the shares is directly linked to the value of the underlying investments. Charges tend to be lower than for unit trusts, OEICs or investment trusts. Unlike investing direct in gilts or corporate bonds, your return is not fixed.	Growth, asset allocation
	Insurance funds	A ready-made portfolio of gilts and/or corporate bonds. You invest by paying premiums for an insurance policy. After deduction of any up-front fees, the remainder of your money is allocated to units in one or more investment funds of your choice. The price of the units varies directly with the value of the investments in the fund. Unlike investing direct in gilts or corporate bonds, your return is not fixed.	Income, growth, asset allocation

Investment		Description	Mainly useful for
Individual corporate bonds	Permanent interest-bearing shares (PIBs)	Bonds issued by building societies or banks that used to be societies (in which case the bonds are called perpetual sub-bonds or PSBs). They pay interest but have no redemption date so the only way to get any money back is to sell on the stock market. The price you get may be more or less than the amount you invested.	Income, asset allocation
	Other bonds	Bonds issued by companies. They work in a similar way to gilts (see page 141) but are more risky because, unlike the UK government, a company might renege and fail to pay the promised interest or repayment on redemption.	
Investment funds investing in shares or property	Real estate investment trusts (REITs)	Type of investment trust that invests directly in property or the shares of property companies. Provided most of the fund's income is paid out to investors (and other conditions are met), the tax treatment is particularly favourable (see page 176).	Income, asset allocation
	Property authorised investment funds (PAIFs)	Type of unit trust or OEIC that invests directly in property or the shares of property companies. Provided most of the fund's income is paid out to investors (and other conditions are met), the tax treatment is particularly favourable (see page 176).	
		A ready-made portfolio of shares or property. There is a wide choice of funds, for example, investing in shares of companies in a particular country or involved in a particular type of business. Funds may be unit trusts, OEICs, investment trusts, exchange traded funds or insurance funds – see under *Investment funds investing in gilts and/or bonds* on page 141 for the broad difference between these.	Income, growth, asset allocation

Investment	Other funds	Description	Mainly useful for
Single property		For example, a buy-to-let property that you rent out. It is more risky than investing in a spread of different properties (see page 154).	Income, growth
Individual shares	Preference shares	Shares in a company where you have the right to receive dividends before any payment is made to the ordinary shareholders, but there is no guarantee that any dividend will be paid. If the company goes bust, you also have the right to get any money back ahead of the ordinary shareholders, but you could still lose all that you invested.	Income
	Ordinary shares	Ordinary shareholders are the ultimate owners of a company. Your return is a share of the company's profits paid out as dividends (but there is no guarantee that any dividends will be paid) and any gain you make from selling the shares on the stock market for more than you paid.	Income, growth, asset allocation
Higher risk investments	Hedge funds	Investment funds that use sophisticated strategies – for example, using derivatives (see below) to enhance the returns that you might get.	Income, growth, asset allocation
	Derivatives	Instead of investing direct in, say, shares (but also other investments), derivatives let you speculate not just on how the price of the underlying shares will move, but that the movement will happen within a set period of time. Derivatives can be used to reduce the risks of, say, an existing portfolio of shares or alternatively as a high-risk investment.	Growth
	Alternative investments	This is a loose term used to mean things like art, antiques, fine wines and classic cars. You are essentially gambling on future tastes and popularity in the hope of making a capital gain. In the meantime, there may be costs of ownership, such as storage and insurance.	Growth, asset allocation

Investment goals

There is no limit to the possible goals you might have for saving and investing. This section looks at four goals that are particularly likely to be relevant in later life: ensuring you have extra income.

SAVING FOR AN EMERGENCY FUND

While an emergency fund gives you security against the financial effects of a disaster, it also provides you with the chance to be impulsive when a good opportunity comes along.

While you will have your own personal needs, hopes and dreams, nearly everyone shares some basic goals that fall into a fairly standard hierarchy, starting with paying off problem debts. Provided you can do this, the next goal is to stay out of debt by having a cushion of money to draw on for, say, unexpected house or car repairs or when something good comes along, such as the chance to go on holiday with friends or a bargain offer on garden furniture.

An emergency fund can also be an alternative to taking out some types of insurance. For example, rather than taking out extended warranties on satellite TV equipment or home computers, you could instead save the premiums you would have paid and use them to pay-as-you-go if repairs are needed. If you are still working and cannot afford **income protection insurance** or want to keep its cost down, you can at least build up an emergency

To shop around for the best easy access or notice accounts, see www.fsa.gov.uk/tables or other comparison websites, such as www.moneyfacts.co.uk.

fund equal to, say, three or six months' take-home pay that could tide you over a temporary period off work.

As you can see, there is no hard-and-fast rule about how much to have in your emergency fund. It depends on your particular circumstances and how you intend to use the fund. Somewhere between one and six months' income is likely to be enough for most people.

Where to invest

You want immediate access to your emergency fund. Usually that means choosing an instant access account from a bank, building society or National Savings and Investments (NS&I). If you have not already used your cash ISA allowance for the year (see page 177), this could be a good choice.

If you are comfortable using a credit card in an emergency, you could put your emergency fund into an account where you have to give a short period of notice before getting your money back. If you are getting benefits because your income is low, you may qualify for a Savings Gateway account from 2010 – the Government will add 50p for every £1 you save.

Amounts up to £50,000 per person per UK institution are fully protected in the event of a bank or building society become insolvent – see page 159.

SAVING UP FOR SOMETHING

Whatever your reason for saving, if you may need your money back within the next five years, stick to investments where you cannot lose your capital.

You may be saving for a cruise, deposit on a second home, home improvements, added financial security or a multiplicity of other reasons. The table, overleaf, summarises a range of investments that could be suitable. Some let you invest on a regular basis. With others, you would need to set aside a lump sum or periodically invest a series of smaller lump sums.

INVESTING FOR GRANDCHILDREN

For children born from September 2002 onwards, the Child Trust Fund (CTF) offers a tax-efficient way to save. There is also a range of other options for older children.

❝ If you might need your money back within five years, stick to investments where you cannot lose your capital. ❞

For full details of NS&I products, see www.nsandi.com. Click on the 'our range' tab and a long list appears from which you can choose to find out further information.

Short-term savings

RISK	Type of investment	Minimum	Description/points to note	From
	If you might need your money back at any time			
LOWER RISK	Easy or instant access accounts	Often any amount from £1. If set up as regular savings accounts, often £10 or £20 a month.	• Can get your money back in full at any time. • Earns interest usually at a variable rate. Best rates tend to be from internet accounts. • Tax-free return if you opt for a cash ISA, otherwise interest is taxable at your top rate (see Chapter 7).	Banks, building societies, NS&I
HIGHER RISK	Notice accounts	Often any amount from £1. If set up as regular savings accounts, from £10 upwards.	• Can get your money on giving a specified amount of notice (for example, 30, 60, 90 or 120 days). Interest penalty if on withdrawals without notice. • Earns interest usually at a variable rate. • Tax-free return if you opt for a cash ISA, otherwise interest is taxable at your top rate (see Chapter 7).	Banks and building societies
	If you will need your money back at a set future time			
LOWER RISK	NS&I fixed-rate certificates	£100	• You invest for a set term (two or five years) at the end of which you get your capital back plus a fixed return. • No interest if you cash in during the first year and reduced return if you otherwise cash in early. • Return is tax-free.	NS&I
	NS&I index-linked certificates	£100	• You invest for a set term (three or five years) at the end of which you get your capital back plus a return that is a fixed percentage plus inflation. • No interest if you cash in during the first year and reduced return if you otherwise cash in early. • Return is tax-free.	NS&I
	NS&I guaranteed growth bonds	£500	• You invest for a set term (one, three or five years) at the end of which you get back interest at a fixed rate. • 90-day interest penalty if you want your money back early. • Interest is taxable at your top rate (see Chapter 7).	NS&I

RISK	Type of investment	Minimum	Description/points to note	From
	Term accounts (also called bonds)	Minimum varies, say £500 upwards. If set up as regular savings accounts, typically £10 a month upwards.	• Can get your money at the end of a specified term (usually one to five years). Usually possible to get your money back early but interest penalty. • Earns interest usually at a fixed rate. • Tax-free return if you opt for a cash ISA, otherwise interest is taxable at your top rate (see Chapter 7).	Banks and building societies
	Guaranteed growth bonds	Varies, say £5,000 upwards	• You invest for a set term (from one to ten years) at the end of which you get back your capital plus a fixed return. • Usually high charges if you want your money back early. • The insurance company has paid tax already and there is no further tax for you to pay unless you are a higher-rate taxpayer (see Chapter 7).	Insurance companies (or the insurance subsidiaries of other organisations, such as banks)
HIGHER RISK	Guaranteed equity bonds	Varies, say £500 upwards	• Terms typically range from one to six years. With some you cannot get your money back early, others charge a fee. • Each bond is typically on offer for only a limited period. • Let you participate in stock-market growth but with the guarantee that you will get all your capital back or your capital plus a minimum return[a]. • The bonds work in a variety of ways, but essentially the price of the guarantee is that, if the underlying stock-market index or basket of shares rises, you get back less than you would have done by investing in that index or those shares direct. • Return usually taxed as interest in the year you receive it and taxable at your top rate (see Chapter 7), but tax-free if in a cash ISA.	Mainly banks and building societies, a few insurance companies[b]

a But check under what circumstances the guarantee might fail.

b But do not confuse with other capital protected products from insurance companies where you can lose some or all of your capital if the underlying stock market index or shares fall by more than a specified amount.

The Child Trust Fund (CTF)

Across the UK, a CTF account is opened for every child born from 1 September 2002 onwards. The account receives an initial endowment from the Government of £250 (or £500 for families on a low income) and a further £250 (£500) when the child reaches the age of seven years. Parents, grandparents, friends and anyone else can add a further £1,200 a year to the account and the money invested grows until the child reaches the age of 18 years. At that stage, the child can use the money in any way he or she wants, including rolling over the savings into an individual savings account (ISA). The tax treatment of ISAs is the same as that for CTFs – see box, below.

The aim of this government scheme is twofold:

- To ensure that every young person has at least a small amount of capital to help them make the most of the opportunities they face as they reach adulthood.

- To stimulate young people's interest in saving as part of a national drive to increase financial capability.

Tax and children's savings

Every person from age zero onwards has his or her own separate identity as a taxpayer. This means a child, however young, has his or her own allowances to set against Income Tax and Capital Gains Tax in the same way as an adult does. There is an anti-avoidance rule to guard against parents exploiting their child's tax allowances as an artificial device to save Income Tax. If a parent makes gifts to the child and these gifts produce an income of more than £100 a year, the whole of the income is taxed as if it belongs to the parent rather than the child. However, the rule does not apply to money the parent invests in a Child Trust Fund or most tax-free investments (but not cash ISAs), or to returns in the form of capital gains rather than income. The rule does not apply to gifts from anyone other than parents – for example, grandparents.

How CTFs are invested and taxed

There are three ways a CTF can be invested:

- Savings account. The interest is completely tax-free. Bear in mind that an 18-year investment is long term so a savings account might not be the most appropriate choice (see page 137).
- Stocks-and-shares account. Typically this means investing in a fund of shares, bonds, and so on. Income from shares is taxed, but the rest of the return is tax-free.
- Stakeholder account. Invested on a stocks-and-shares basis (as above) until age 13 and then gradually shifted to bonds and savings as age 18 approaches to lock in earlier gains and guard against a slump in value if stock markets fall shortly before age 18 years.

Investments for children

RISK	Type of investment	Description/points to note	From
LOWER RISK	Children's bonus bonds	• For young people aged 0–21 years. Each bond offers tax-free fixed return over five years. Minimum investment £25. • Not caught by the parental income anti-avoidance rule (see opposite).	NS&I
	Savings account	• Can help child to learn about managing money. • Assuming child is a non-taxpayer (most are), register to receive interest without tax deducted (see page 174). • Some accounts are designed especially for children with free gifts.	Banks, building societies, NS&I
	Cash ISA	• Open to young people from age 16 onwards. • Despite being otherwise tax-free, income is caught by the parental income anti-avoidance rule (see opposite).	See www.fsa.gov.uk/ tables to compare accounts
	Child Trust Fund	• Tax-efficient saving from birth to age 18 (see information opposite) • Not caught by the parental income anti-avoidance rule (see opposite).	See www.childtrustfund.gov.uk for list of providers
	'Baby bonds' and similar plans	• For regular savings up to a maximum £270 a year (though lump sum arrangements also available). • Money goes into an investment fund where income from shares is taxed but rest of return is tax-free. • Not caught by the parental income anti-avoidance rule (see opposite). • Any fixed charges can eat heavily into the relatively small investment.	Friendly societies
HIGHER RISK	Unit trusts and other investment funds	• Can be opened in the name of a child but operated on their behalf by an adult. Income is caught by the parental income anti-avoidance rule (see above), but not capital gains.	See, for example, www.trustnet.com to compare funds

> **66** If a parent makes gifts to the child and these produce more than £100 a year, the income is taxed as if it belongs to the parent. **99**

Grandparents and CTFs

The maximum investment in a CTF (on top of the Government endowments) is £1,200 in total. Given the anti-avoidance rule for income from parental gifts, in general it makes sense for parents to take priority paying into a child's CTF and for grandparents and others to look at alternatives (see table, page 149). But, if the parents are not using the full CTF allowance, this could be a good home for gifts from other people too.

INVESTING FOR INCOME

Choosing a spread of different investments can help you meet the challenge of providing a reliable income that will not lose its buying power as the years go by. Extra income is often a key goal as you get older and a particularly

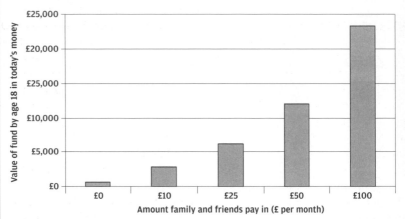

How a CTF could grow[a]

The chart shows how a child's CTF could grow by age 18 given the Government endowments and different levels of monthly saving from other people. All amounts are shown in today's money.

Value of fund by age 18 in today's money

Amount family and friends pay in (£ per month)

[a] Assumes: money is invested in a stakeholder account; for first 13 years, fund grows at 7 per cent a year less charges at 1.5 per cent a year; during last five years, fund grows at 5 per cent a year (with no explicit charges); inflation over the whole 18-year term averages 2.5 per cent a year.

 For information about CTFs, including a list of providers, see www.childtrustfund. gov.uk. For an estimate of how much your child's fund might be worth by age 18 in today's money, go to www.fsa.gov.uk/financial_capability/pgtm/parents/choose-a-calculator.html.

difficult one. Once you retire, it is natural to be wary of capital risk because your ability to replace lost money may be limited. On the other hand, if you will be relying on this income throughout retirement, you need an investment strategy that will protect you from inflation. Retired people, more than any other group, are on a quest for high returns (in this case high income) with no risk. A fundamental rule of all investing is that risk and return go hand in hand. If an investment offers you a higher-than-average income, you should immediately be asking what is the cost in terms of higher risks and/or higher charges.

Asset allocation

A classic approach to the problem of simultaneously pursuing a reasonable and sustainable income while managing your exposure to capital risk is to spread your money across a range of different types of investment. Typically, investments are divided into four classes:

- Cash (deposits).
- Bonds (gilts and corporate bonds).
- Property (usually commercial).
- Equities (shares).

Asset allocation means building yourself a portfolio that has elements from all or several of these classes. The idea is that:

- **Some exposure to equities and possibly property** gives you the potential for growing your capital and income in order at least to keep pace with inflation, but
- **If share prices fall, this will tend to be offset by better performance** by some or all of the other asset classes.

Deciding on the relative balance of asset classes in your portfolio will depend on your precise needs, your attitude towards risk, your age, how much you have to invest and other factors. What is right for one investor will be different from the best solution for another. There is no neat formula to work it out and you may want to get help from an IFA or stockbroker (see below). If your resources are limited, it may not be appropriate for you to take any capital risk at all.

Off-the-peg asset allocation

You may want to choose for yourself investments from each asset class. But, if you would prefer an off-the-peg solution, there are various investment bonds and funds that give you a ready-made portfolio with a built-in spread of assets – see table, pages 152–3.

 To find an IFA in your area, see www.unbiased.co.uk. To find a stockbroker or investment manager, see www.apcims.co.uk. See also the *Which? Essential Guide: Save and Invest*.

Investments

Selected income-producing investments

RISK	Type of investment	Description/points to note	From
		Bonds	
LOWER RISK	NS&I guaranteed income bond	• You invest for a set term (one, three or five years) during which you get a fixed income. • There is 90-day interest penalty if you want your money back early.	NS&I
	NS&I income bond	• No set term. You invest and get an income each month, which will vary as interest rates go up and down. • You can get your money back at any time without penalty.	NS&I
	Guaranteed income bond	• You invest for a set term (between one and ten years), during which you get a fixed income. At the end of the term you get back your capital in full. • Usually high charges if you want your money back early.	Insurance companies
	With-profits bond	• You take out an insurance policy whose value grows as bonuses are added. The amount of bonus depends indirectly but mainly on the performance of an underlying investment fund that is invested in equities, bonds, property and cash. • You can draw an income from the bond, typically a maximum 5 per cent a year. If the amount you draw in income exceeds the bonuses, you will not get your capital back in full.	Insurance companies
	Distribution bond	• You take out an insurance policy and your money is invested with typically 60 per cent going into a bond fund (for income) and 40 per cent into equities (for growth). The fund's income is paid out to you. • The amount of capital you get back depends on the performance of the underlying investment funds.	Insurance companies
HIGHER RISK	High income bond	• You take out an insurance policy and your money is invested in one or more investment funds. You draw a regular income that can vary (often up to a maximum of 5 per cent a year of the amount you invested but can be higher). • The amount of capital you get back depends on the performance of the underlying investment funds.	Insurance companies

RISK	Type of investment	Description/points to note	From
		Investment funds	
LOWER RISK	Bond fund	• Invests in gilts, corporate bonds and/or similar medium-risk income-producing investments.	Unit trusts, OEICs, investment trusts, ETFs (see page 141)
	Managed fund	• Invests in a range of assets from different classes. Cautious managed funds are aimed at low-risk investors; balanced managed funds pursue a higher risk strategy.	Unit trusts, OEICs, investment trusts
	Distribution fund	• Typically invested 60 per cent in bonds (for income) and 40 per cent to equities (for growth).	Unit trusts, OEICs
	Fund of funds	• Invests in a range of other investment funds often from a variety of different asset classes. • The main drawback is that you pay two sets of charges: to the fund-of-funds manager and to the managers of the underlying funds.	Unit trusts, OEICs, investment trusts
	Property investment fund	• Invests directly in commercial property (such as shopping centres and office blocks) and/or in the shares of property companies. The income you can draw off is underpinned by the fund's rental income.	Unit trusts, OEICs, investment trusts
HIGH-ER RISK	Equity income fund	• Invests in shares mainly of large well-established companies that have a reliable record of paying dividends, which underpin the income you draw.	Unit trusts, OEICs, investment trusts

❝Choosing a spread of investments can help you meet the challenge of providing a reliable income that will not lose its buying power.❞

Income from property

Owning a second home either in the UK or abroad is an opportunity to create investment income as well as the possibility of a capital gain when you sell.

In 2008, the house price bubble finally burst not just in the UK but also in some popular holiday-home areas, such as Spain. Making a tidy profit when you sell – or even being able to find a buyer at all in the short term – ceased to look so certain. However, there is another way to make money from a second home: rent it out. You might be looking to let the property on a long-term basis if, say, you plan eventually to retire to your second home but don't need it yet, or you are retiring abroad and want to let out your former UK home. Alternatively, you might be looking at combining holiday lets with the intention of also using the property yourself.

LONG-TERM UK LETS

A home that originally you chose for your own use is not necessarily an ideal proposition for long-term UK lets. The property needs the right characteristics to meet the business purpose of letting, for example:

- **Location.** Is it in a good rental area – for example, close to a university if you are letting to students; close to jobs or transport links if you are letting to young professionals; close to good schools if your tenants will be families? If the home is in a coastal or scenic area, holiday letting might be a realistic (see opposite).
- **Size and character.** Is the property suitable for renting out? Large houses with lots of bedrooms may suit students. Smaller, more upmarket properties with small gardens may suit professionals. Families will want more space and a garden.

❝ Property needs the right characteristics to meet the business purpose of letting. ❞

To find a letting agent, contact the Association of Residential Letting Agents, www.arla.co.uk. To find an accountant, see Useful addresses (page 211). For a detailed guide to renting out your second home, get the *Which? Essential Guide to Renting and Letting.*

You must also be prepared to alter the property to suit tenants rather than you – for example, neutral décor, removing furniture that does not meet fire safety regulations, and you may need to upgrade the bathroom and kitchen.

Do not underestimate the work involved in letting a property. There are essentially six aspects to a rental business:

- **Preparing your property** to rent out.
- **Finding tenants.**
- **Collecting rents.**
- **Maintaining and repairing** the property.
- **Dealing with problems,** such as a tenant upsetting neighbours or refusing to leave.
- **Keeping accounts** and sorting out your tax bill.

If you are looking to maximise your profit, you may be thinking about running your rental business yourself. But, unless you are looking for what may turn out to be a full-time job, it will be worth paying for a letting agent to do at least some of the work and you might want an accountant to handle the administration and tax.

HOLIDAY LETS

Renting out your holiday home is likely to be an easier task because it is probably

❝Do not underestimate the time involved in keeping everything in excellent working order. ❞

already in an ideal location to attract holidaymakers. On the other hand, there is often a distinct holiday season, so you may not be getting rents all year round.

Once again, do not underestimate the work involved. Having prepared the property for letting, there is considerable ongoing maintenance, such as gardening and minor repairs, because holidaymakers expect a property to be well presented with everything in excellent working order. At each switchover – which could be as often as every week – you will need to check the property and its contents for faults; clean; change the linen; prepare any welcome pack, and greet your new guests. Back in the office, you need to advertise your property, manage bookings, take deposits, maintain accounts and keep up with tax. Once again, if you are not keen on this level of commitment, using a letting agent for some of these tasks is likely to be the answer and essential if you are not within easy reach of the property.

Letting a property abroad has all the advantages and drawbacks of a UK

Agents offering letting services for properties abroad who are members of the Association of International Property Professionals (AIPP) abide by a code of practice – see www.aipp.org.uk.

holiday let plus some added dangers, such as being aware of local laws and the problems of maintenance at a distance.

TAX AND RENTAL PROPERTY

You have to declare any profit you make from letting out property and any gain you make when you sell. When you first start up, you have until 5 October following the end of the tax year to do this. Thereafter, your tax office will prompt you to send in a tax return each year.

Income Tax

Your profits are the rental income less allowable expenses, which include, for example, letting agent's fees; travel to the property to carry out work there; cost of hiring say a gardener (but nothing for your own time if you do the work yourself); cost of repairs; Council Tax and business rates; water rates; insurance; office expenses related to the letting, such as stationery and phone bills; and so on.

Buying capital items – such as a computer you use for the rental business, a lawnmower, ladders and tools used at the property, installing central heating – is not an allowable expense, but you get tax relief in a different way. The general rule is that you have an Annual Investment Allowance (AIA) – £50,000 in 2008–9. In working out your profit, you can deduct up to the full amount of the amount you spend up to your AIA.

Furnished UK holiday lettings

If you let a furnished holiday property in the UK, you can qualify for some tax advantages:

- If you make a loss it can be offset against other income you have for the same year. With other types of letting, you can only carry the loss forward to set against future gains.
- You can claim the AIA, even for spending on furniture and equipment for use in the property.
- The property counts as a business asset, which you can pass on free of Inheritance Tax (IHT), provided the business use continues (see Chapter 9).

To qualify, the property must be available for letting on a commercial basis for at least 140 days a year, actually let for 70 days and where any periods of long-term accommodation (defined as continuous periods of more than 31 days) do not exceed 155 days a year. Note that, although the sale of such a property before 6 April 2008 qualified for reduced Capital Gains Tax, this no longer applies – see Chapter 7.

If you spend more than your AIA for the year, you write off the excess in subsequent years at a rate of 20 per cent of the remaining balance (or 10 per cent if the things you bought are treated as integral to the fabric of the property, such as heating, lighting, water systems and so on).

The capital spending rules are different where you are spending on items – such as a fridge, cooker or furniture – to be used by tenants in a furnished letting (unless it counts as a furnished UK holiday let – see box opposite). In that case, you can choose either to write off the full cost of each replacement item as you renew it or you can deduct a wear-and-tear allowance each year (equal to 10 per cent of your rental income).

Capital Gains Tax (CGT)

If you sell a second home or holiday property that has never been your only or main home, any gain you make is fully exposed to CGT (charged at 18 per cent in 2008–9.) Where the property has been your main home for any period, you may be able to reduce the tax bill by claiming letting relief (see page 129).

Tax on foreign lettings

If you are a UK resident, UK tax is due on all your worldwide income, including rents from a property abroad. This applies whether or not you bring the money into the UK. Similarly, you are liable for UK CGT on any profit your make when you sell the property. Typically you will also have to pay local taxes in the country where the property is situated but you can usually offset these against the UK tax due. HMRC has been clamping down on UK residents who fail to declare overseas income. If you are caught, you face fines, interest on unpaid taxes and possible imprisonment.

❝ HMRC has been clamping down on UK residents who fail to declare overseas income. ❞

For more information about the taxation of property income, see HMRC's booklet SA105 (Notes) 'Notes on UK Property' from www.hmrc.gov.uk/sa (follow the link to Tax returns, forms and helpsheets). See also the *Which? Essential Guide: Property Investor's Handbook*.

Complaints and compensation

You have no comeback if an investment turns out badly because of risks that you accepted at the outset. But provided you are dealing with an authorised firm, if you have been misled, badly advised or lost money because of poor administration, you have grounds to complain and can claim compensation.

MAKING A COMPLAINT

1 Go back to the company at fault – this might be the provider or an adviser. Keep a copy of any letter you send and make notes of any phone conversations.
2 If the firm does not offer a satisfactory response, say that you want to complain using the formal complaints mechanism. The financial regulations under which they operate require them to have a formal procedure.
3 If you are not happy with their reply or they have not come back to you within eight weeks, take your complaint to the Financial Ombudsman Service (FOS).

FOS is an independent complaints body that is free for consumers. It will try to mediate or arbitrate between you and the firm and has the power to order the firm to take whatever action is needed to put the situation right, including compensation (up to a maximum of £100,000). If appropriate, FOS will look at both the legal rights involved and other relevant factors, such as normal industry practice, in coming to its decision. Instead of going to FOS, or if you are unhappy with the FOS outcome, you could take your case to court. However, court cases tend to be lengthy and expensive.

If a firm goes out of business owing you compensation, you may instead be able to get redress from the Financial Services Compensation Scheme (FSCS). The table, opposite, shows the maximum amounts of compensation payable.

 You have the protection of the FOS and FSCS only if you use an authorised firm (see opposite).

 For further information about FOS, see www.financial-ombudsman.org.uk. For more details about the compensation scheme, see www.fscs.org.uk.

Compensation from FSCS

The FSCS may pay out if a firm has gone bust owing you money. The limits shown apply per person per organisation. For example, if you have two accounts with the same bank, the sum of the accounts is covered up to £50,000. If you have a joint account, the limit applies to each of you, in other words up to a maximum of £100,000 in the account. Note that different limits generally apply if you deal with a non-UK-based firm.

Type of investment	Level of cover	Maximum payment
Deposits, such as bank and building society accounts	100% of the first £50,000[a]	£50,000
Insurance-based personal pensions, annuities and investment-type life insurance	100% of the first £2,000 and 90 per cent of the remainder	Unlimited
Unit trusts, shares and other investments	100% of the first £30,000 and 90% of the next £20,000	£48,000

a Applies from 7 October 2008. Lower limits applied before that date. The FSA is consulting on further increases to the limit.

AUTHORISED FIRMS

An authorised firm is an investment business that is legally allowed to do business with UK customers. To become authorised the firm must satisfy the Financial Services Authority (FSA) that it is run by fit and proper people, solvent and will comply with the FSA's rules. The rules include a requirement that the firm operates a proper complaints procedure and, if needed, customers have access to a compensation scheme.

Getting help

If you need advice on any stage of your investment strategy, such as working out your goals and constraints, choosing your broad strategy and/or selecting specific products, get help from an independent financial adviser.

You might be perfectly happy working through the four steps of the basic investment strategy outlined on page 133. Alternatively, you may feel you need some help with some or all of the steps and this is where an investment adviser can help.

There are essentially two types of adviser: tied advisers, who sell the products of one or a handful of providers; and independent advisers, who can recommend the most suitable products from any provider on the market. If you seek advice from, say, your local bank or building society, it will nearly always be tied advice. For independent advice, choose an IFA.

COST

These vary depending on what type of adviser you choose to work with.

- **Tied advisers** normally receive commission each time they sell products, such as investment-type

life insurance and unit trusts – as do some advisers who can select products from the whole of the market.
- **Fee-paying advisers.** To use the title 'independent', an adviser must either charge a fee for their advice and rebate any commissions to you or offer you the option of paying by fee as an alternative to commission. Fees vary from around £75–£250 per hour but many advisers offer a free first consultation.

The advantage for you of using a fee-paying adviser is that there is no risk of 'commission bias'. This is the tendency of an adviser to recommend: one product rather than another because it pays higher commission; you switch products unnecessarily; you take out products you don't really need; or you buy more of a product than you really need.

The disadvantage of paying by fee is that you have to pay a possibly large sum at the time you get the advice.

 To find an IFA, see www.unbiased.co.uk. To check that an adviser is authorised, use the FSA Register at www.fsa.gov.uk/register/home.do.

Tax

It is galling to work at maximising your income and wealth, only to see a large chunk disappear into the Government's hands. For many people, a perk of reaching the age of 65 is a higher tax-free allowance for income. But whatever your age, there are opportunities for saving tax both on income and when you sell something, such as a second home or collectable items.

How your income is taxed

Some types of income are tax-free. You can claim a variety of reliefs and allowances that reduce the tax due on the rest of your income. Allowances are often higher once you reach the age of 65, so you could find that you do not have to pay any Income Tax at all.

Income Tax basics

This chart summarises how your tax bill for a year is worked out.

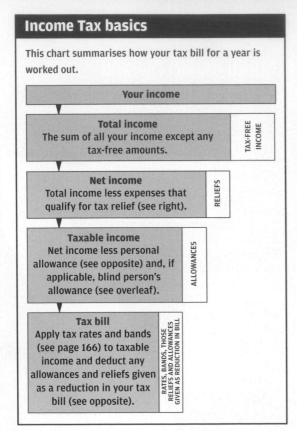

Your income

Total income
The sum of all your income except any tax-free amounts.

TAX-FREE INCOME

Net income
Total income less expenses that qualify for tax relief (see right).

RELIEFS

Taxable income
Net income less personal allowance (see opposite) and, if applicable, blind person's allowance (see overleaf).

ALLOWANCES

Tax bill
Apply tax rates and bands (see page 166) to taxable income and deduct any allowances and reliefs given as a reduction in your tax bill (see opposite).

RATES, BANDS, THOSE RELIEFS AND ALLOWANCES GIVEN AS REDUCTION IN BILL

Each person is taxed as a separate individual and tax is based on your income for a tax year. The chart, left, gives a quick summary of how your tax bill is worked out.

INCOME

Some types of income are tax-free (see box on page 165). All the rest are potentially taxable – this includes earnings from a job, profits from self-employment, state and private pensions, some state benefits, rents from letting property, interest from savings, dividends from shares and share-based investments and income from most other types of investment.

TAX RELIEF FOR EXPENSES

The Government encourages some types of spending by letting you claim tax relief on it. Tax relief is given in two main ways:

- By deducting the expense from your total income, thus reducing the amount of income left to be taxed. This applies to contributions to occupational pension

As well as Income Tax, you may have to pay National Insurance contributions on earnings from a job (see page 84).

schemes and donations to charity through payroll giving.

- **Through tax relief at source**. You deduct tax relief from the payment you are making and hand over the remaining reduced amount. If you are a higher-rate taxpayer, you can claim extra relief. This method applies to contributions to personal pensions and charitable donations by Gift Aid.

ALLOWANCES

Everyone has a personal allowance. This means that some income that would otherwise be taxable is tax-free. You might qualify for other allowances as well, the most common of which are described below.

Personal allowance

The table below shows the personal allowances for the 2008–9 and 2009–10 tax years. The allowances are higher for people aged 65-74 and higher again for people aged 75 and over, but you lose this extra age-related allowance if your income exceeds the threshold shown in the table.

The extra allowance is reduced by £1 for every £2 by which your income exceeds the threshold until it is reduced to the level of the under-65 allowance.

Income Tax personal allowances

If you reach this age during the tax year:	2008-9	2009-10
Under 65	£6,035	£6,475
65-74	£9,030	£9,490
75 or over	£9,180	£9,640
Income threshold at which age-related allowance starts to be lost	£21,800	£22,900
Income level at which all the extra age-related allowance is lost and you just get the under-65 allowance:[a]		
65-74	£27,790	£28,930
75 or over	£28,090	£29,230

a This income level will be higher if you are married or in a civil partnership and you or your spouse or partner were born before 6 April 1935 (see Married couples allowance, overleaf).

Tax

Blind person's allowance

You can get extra personal allowance, called blind person's allowance, if you are registered blind (England and Wales) or would be unable to carry out any work for which eyesight is essential (Scotland and Northern Ireland). In either case, this means that you have been certified as blind or severely sight-impaired by a consultant ophthalmologist. If you become registered in one tax year but were certified in the previous year, you can claim blind person's allowance for the earlier tax year as well. The allowance is £1,800 in 2008-9 and £1,890 in 2009-10.

If your income is too low for you to be able to use part or all of your blind person's allowance, you can ask your tax office to transfer the surplus to your spouse or civil partner to reduce the tax they pay.

Married couple's allowance

This allowance is restricted to married couples and civil partners where one or both of the couple were born before 6 April 1935 (so aged 75 or over in 2009–10). In 2009–10, married couple's allowance is £6,965. In 2008–9, there were two rates: £6,625 for age 75 or over and £6,535 for age 74. Married couple's allowance works differently from the other allowances: you get a reduction in your tax bill equal to 10 per cent of the allowance or the amount needed to reduce your tax bill to zero (whichever is lower).

Married couple's allowance is initially given to the husband (if you were married before 5 December 2005 or whoever has the higher income where your marriage or civil partnership took place on or after that date. If the person who gets the allowance has income above the age-related allowance threshold (£21,800 in 2008–9 and £22,900 in 2009–10), the married couple's allowance is reduced by £1 for every £2 of income over the threshold. However, married couple's allowance is never reduced below a basic amount (£2,540 in 2008-9 and £2,670 in

 For more detailed information about tax, see the *Which? Essential Guide: Tax Handbook 2009/10*, published in Spring 2009.

Tax-free income

These are the main types of income likely to be relevant in later life that are free from Income Tax.

Pensions and state benefits

- £10 Christmas bonus for State Pensioners and one-off £60 bonus from January 2009.
- Winter Fuel Payment (see page 93).
- Pension Credit (see page 101).
- Working Tax Credit (see page 86).
- Housing Benefit (see page 107).
- Bereavement payment (a lump sum for widows and widowers).
- Council Tax Benefit (see page 107).
- Disability Living Allowance and Attendance Allowance (see page 97).
- Any extra occupational pension that you get as a result of retiring because of a work-related injury or disability.
- Tax-free lump sum from a pension scheme (see page 52).

Income from an employer

- Some fringe benefits, such as contributions your employer pays towards your pension (see page 31).
- Mileage allowance (up to 40p a mile for the first 10,000 miles and 25p thereafter).
- Up to £30,000 in redundancy money as long as it was not part of your contract or customary for employees in your position.
- Up to £3 a week to cover the extra costs of working from home.
- Many other expenses payments that reimburse money you have spent on work.
- Long-service award worth up to £50 that is not cash and has been given for 20 or more years' service.
- Lump sum death benefit from life insurance provided through work.

Savings and investments

- Interest from National Savings & Investments (NS&I) certificates (see page 146) and Premium Bonds.
- Interest from cash individual savings accounts (ISAs) (see page 177).
- Income from savings and bond-based investments held within stocks-and-shares ISAs, CTFs and tax-efficient friendly society plans (see pages 180, 148 and 149). Income from share-based investments held in ISAs, CTFs and these friendly society plans has been taxed at 10 per cent, which cannot be reclaimed.
- That part of the income from a purchased life annuity that represents the return of your capital (see page 52-3).
- Income from an annuity paid direct to a care provider (see page 192).

Other income

- Up to £4,250 from letting room(s) in your home through the Rent-a-Room Scheme (see page 127).
- Pay-outs from mortgage payment protection policies and other loan protection policies.
- Payout from an income protection policy you have arranged for yourself (but not such insurance provided by your employer).
- Payment to your survivors from a term insurance policy following your death.

Income Tax bands and rates

Your taxable income is split into a maximum of three different tax bands:

- The starting rate.
- The basic rate.
- The higher rate.

Your personal allowance and the three tax bands are set against your income in a strict order as shown in the table, below. This order is important because, within the same band, different types of income are taxed at different rates.

If your allowance or a band has been used up against the type(s) of income that have first priority, there is then none left to set against the next type of income. For example, if the whole of the starting-rate band is used up by 'Other income' (taxed at 20 per cent in that band), none of the band is left for savings income and so you cannot benefit from the 10 per cent rate that applies when savings income falls within that band. However, if only part of the starting-rate band were used by 'Other income', the remainder of the band would be available to set against any 'Savings income'. The two case studies, right, show how this works.

In 2008–9, the starting rate band is £2,320 and £2,440 in 2009–10; the basic rate band is normally £32,480 in 2008–9 and £34,960 in 2009–10, but may be extended to give higher-rate tax relief on personal pension contributions or Gift Aid donations (see Case study: Rasheed, right); the higher-rate band covers the remainder.

Tax rates in 2008–9 and 2009–10

	Type of income			
	Other income[a]	Savings income	Dividend income	Life insurance gains
Order in which personal allowance and bands are set against income	First	Second	Third	Fourth
Personal allowance	0%	0%	10%[b]	20%[b]
Starting-rate band	20%	10%	10%[b]	20%[b]
Basic-rate band	20%	20%	10%[b]	20%[b]
Higher-rate band	40%	40%	32.5%[c]	20% or 40%[c], [d]

a In other words, income other than savings income, dividend income and life insurance gains.
b Tax already deducted and cannot be reclaimed.
c Total including tax already deducted.
d Tax rate depends on type of policy (see page 176).

In 2009–10, Bettina, aged 66, has income of £5,000 State Pension, £3,000 occupational pension, £1,000 interest from cash ISAs and £2,000 interest from other savings accounts. The interest from the ISAs is tax-free. The tax bill of £51 on her other income is worked out as shown below.

	Other income	Savings income
Income	£8,000	£2,000
Personal allowance (£9,490)	£8,000	£1,490
Starting-rate band (£2,440)	£0	£510 taxed at 10% = £51

Bettina's £2,000 interest from other savings accounts was paid with tax at 20 per cent (£400) already deducted. Therefore, she claims back £400 – £51 = £349 from her tax office using form R40 (see page 174).

In 2009–10, Rasheed's income comprises £7,000 State Pension, £38,000 occupational pension together with £10,000 interest from savings accounts and £5,000 in dividends. He is aged 66 but still paying contributions to a personal pension. In 2009–10, he paid £10,000 into his personal pension. This counts as a net contribution and so the pension provider claims basic-rate tax relief from HMRC and adds it to Rasheed's plan, making an overall gross contribution of £12,500 (see Chapter 1, page 33). Because Rasheed is a higher-rate taxpayer, he also qualifies for higher-rate tax relief on this pension contribution. The way the tax legislation works to give him this relief is to extend his basic-rate tax band by the amount of his gross pension contribution (£12,500). This has the effect of taking £12,500 of his income out of the higher-rate tax band, reducing his tax bill by 40%–20%=20% of £12,500. His total tax bill of £488 + £6,614 + £2,000 + £439 + £198.25 = £9,739.25 is worked out as shown below.

	Other income	Savings income	Dividend income
Income	£45,000	£10,000	£5,000
Personal allowance (£9,490)	£9,490	£0	£0
Starting-rate band (£2,440)	£2,440 taxed at 20% = £488	£0	£0
Basic-rate band (£32,480 + £12,500 = £44,980)	£33,070 taxed at 20% = £6,614	£10,000 taxed at 20% = £2,000	£4,390 taxed at 10% = £439
Higher-rate band	£0	£0	£610 taxed at 32.5% = £198.25

2009–10). Age-related personal allowance is reduced before any married couple's allowance.

Whoever initially gets the married couple's allowance, part or all of the basic amount can be transferred to the other spouse or partner. If your income is too low to use part or all of your married couple's allowance, you can ask your tax office to transfer the unused part to your spouse or partner to reduce his or her tax bill.

HOW YOU PAY INCOME TAX

There are essentially three ways in which you may receive income:

- **Gross** (without any tax deducted) – for example, the State Pension. If you should pay tax on this income, it will be collected either through the Pay As You Earn (PAYE) system or self-assessment (see above right).
- **With tax deducted at source**. Most savings income, dividends and some other types of income are paid with some tax deducted. If you are a basic-rate taxpayer, you have no further tax to pay. Higher-rate taxpayers must pay extra either through self-assessment or the PAYE system. In some cases, other taxpayers can reclaim some or all of the tax – see page 174 for more information.

- **Through PAYE.** Your employer or the pension provider deducts the correct amount of tax from your pay or pension. This system may be used to collect tax you owe, for example on income paid gross (see below left).

You must use the self-assessment system to sort out any income (and capital gains) that remain to be taxed. This means completing a tax return, which must reach your tax office by 31 October following the end of the tax year if you complete a paper return, or the following 31 January if you file your return online. Any tax outstanding is also due on 31 January (though you may be required to pay some tax earlier through two instalments).

❝ A tax return must reach your tax office by 31 October if you complete a paper return. ❞

For more information about reporting and paying tax through the self-assessment system, see the HM Revenue & Customs website at www.hmrc.gov.uk/sa.

How capital gains are taxed

If you sell something for a profit, you may have to pay Capital Gains Tax (CGT), but some gains are tax-free and everyone has a substantial annual CGT allowance.

CGT used to be extremely complicated but, where you sell or give something away on or after 6 April 2008, the rules are now much simpler. The chart below summarises the basic steps. At the time of writing, CGT rates for 2009-10 had not been published. Therefore 2008-9 rates are used in this section.

Capital Gains Tax basics

This chart summarises how the tax bill when you sell or give away an item is worked out.

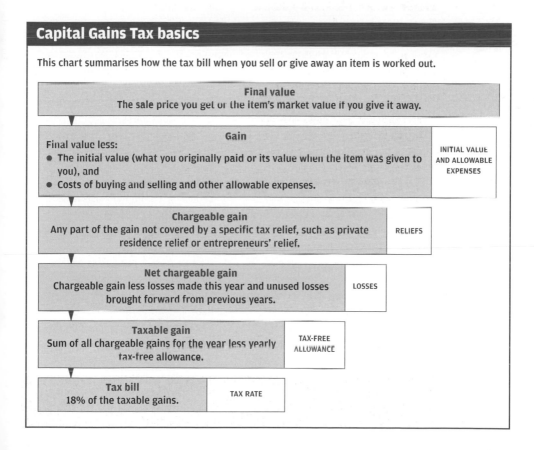

Final value
The sale price you get or the item's market value if you give it away.

Gain
Final value less:
- The initial value (what you originally paid or its value when the item was given to you), and
- Costs of buying and selling and other allowable expenses.

INITIAL VALUE AND ALLOWABLE EXPENSES

Chargeable gain
Any part of the gain not covered by a specific tax relief, such as private residence relief or entrepreneurs' relief.

RELIEFS

Net chargeable gain
Chargeable gain less losses made this year and unused losses brought forward from previous years.

LOSSES

Taxable gain
Sum of all chargeable gains for the year less yearly tax-free allowance.

TAX-FREE ALLOWANCE

Tax bill
18% of the taxable gains.

TAX RATE

WORKING OUT THE GAIN

Any gain on some types of assets and transactions is completely tax-free (see box on page 173). With other assets, usually the first step in working out whether there might be tax to pay is to take the proceeds you get from selling the item (final value) and deduct the amount you paid (initial value). However, if you give the asset away or it was given to you, instead you will need to use the market value on the date of the gift. And, if you started to own the item before 31 March 1982, you substitute the market value on that date for the actual initial value. You can also deduct a variety of expenses, including:

- **Costs of buying and selling**, such as commission, valuation fee, advertising to find a buyer, legal costs and Stamp Duty Land Tax.
- **Cost of defending your** title to the asset.
- **Amounts spent on the item to improve its state** and enhance its value, provided the enhancement is still reflected in the value when you dispose of the item – for example, adding a conservatory to a house, having a picture cleaned or a clock restored. But you cannot claim the cost of your own time spent on the enhancement.

If the final value less initial value and allowable losses comes to less than zero, you have made a loss. This must be set against any gains you make on the disposal of other assets during the same tax year. But losses that cannot be set

off in this way are then carried forward for use in future tax years (see Losses, overleaf).

RELIEFS

There is no CGT on a gain or part of a gain that is covered by a tax relief. The following are two common situations when such reliefs might apply.

Retiring from business

If you are self-employed or run your own company, you need to decide what to do with your business when you retire. There are three main options: give the business away, sell it, or close down.

- **If you give away the business** to an individual or a trust – for example, you might be handing down the business to your children – you and the new owner can jointly claim **hold-over relief** from CGT. This means any gain you have made while owning the business is transferred to the new owner by deducting it from the initial value at which they are treated as having acquired the business. When the new owner eventually disposes of the business, his or her gain is worked out using this adjusted initial value. Whether or not any tax is then due depends on the rules and circumstances prevailing at that time. Hold-over relief is not given automatically and you and the new owner must make your joint claim within five years of the 31 January following the end of the tax year in which the business was transferred.

- If you sell your business as a going concern or you close it down and sell off the assets within the following three years, you may be able to claim **entrepreneurs' relief**. This allows you to ignore 4/9ths of any gain – in effect reducing the tax rate you pay from 18 to 10 per cent. However, the business gains over your whole lifetime (since 6 April 2008) on which you can claim this relief are limited to a maximum of £1 million. Relief is not given automatically. You must claim it within one year of 31 January following the tax year in which the business or asset were disposed of.

Selling your home

In general, there is no CGT when you sell your only or main home because any gain is covered by private residence relief (see page 128). However, in some situations, private residence relief may be restricted – for example, if you are absent from home for a prolonged period; you use part of your home exclusively for business; or you have let your home (see pages 128–9). Some periods away from home do not cause a reduction in private residence relief:

- The first year (sometimes two) of ownership if you are renovating or rebuilding the property.
- The last three years of ownership.

Case Study   **Ming**

Ming sells his shop in 2008-9 making a profit of £270,000. He has made no previous claims for entrepreneurs' relief, so this is well within the £1 million lifetime limit. Claiming the relief, only 5/9 x £270,000 = £150,000 of the gain is taxable. He has no losses to set against the gain, but can deduct his tax-free allowance of £9,600, leaving £140,400 to be taxed. Tax comes to 18% x £140,400 = £25,200, leaving Ming with an after-tax sum of £244,800.

Jargon buster

Entrepreneurs' relief A reduction in a capital gain you make when you sell or close down your business, which reduces the effective rate of CGT on the gain to 10 per cent (instead of the usual 18 per cent)

Hold-over relief An election you can make at the time you give away your business. The election transfers a gain on the business assets to the recipient so that any CGT bill is put off until a future date and paid by the new owner rather than you

 If you are selling or closing down a business, get advice from an accountant or tax adviser (see Useful addresses on pages 211-15). Claim hold-over relief or entrepreneurs' relief through your tax return or contact your usual tax office.

- Periods of any length when you were working abroad and periods totalling up to four years when, because of your work in the UK, you have had to live away. In both cases, you must have lived in the home both before the first absence and after the last.
- Periods when you have to live in job-related accommodation elsewhere, provided you intend to live in your own home eventually.
- Any other periods of absence that together add up to no more than three years as long as you lived in the home both before the first absence and after the last.

Private residence relief covers just your only or main home, not any second or subsequent property. However, if you do have more than one home, you can elect which is to be treated as your main home, provided you do this within two years of acquiring the second (or subsequent) home. Having made the election, you can then change it at any time. The home you elect does not have to be the one where you spend the majority of your time. A married couple or civil partners can have just one main home between them. Unmarried partners, even if they live together, can each elect a different property as their main home. If you do not make an election, which of two or more properties is your main home must be decided on the facts – for example, where you are registered to vote and have your post sent.

Case Study Jay

Jay makes a gain of £150,000 on the sale of his flat in 2008–9. Throughout the time he lived there, he used one of the six rooms exclusively for his book-keeping business. Therefore, 1/6 x £150,000 = £25,000 of the gain is chargeable to CGT. After deducting his tax-free allowance of £9,600, he has to pay CGT of 18% x £15,400 = £2,772.

Case Study Richard and Elaine

Richard and Elaine are married and have owned a weekend cottage in Devon for ten years. In 2008–9 they want to sell it and expect to make a gain of £100,000. Years ago they made an election to treat their Basingstoke home as their main home. They can now alter the election to nominate the Devon home as their main home. Even if the nomination lasts only, say, two weeks, that is enough for the last three years of the ten-year ownership period to qualify for private residence relief. Almost immediately, they can switch the nomination back to their Basingstoke home ensuring that the restriction of relief on that property will be negligible. Because three of the ten years' ownership are now eligible for relief, the chargeable gain on the Devon home relates only to the remaining seven out of ten years and becomes (£100,000 x 7/10) = £70,000. After the tax-free allowance, the CGT bill is (£70,000 – £9,600) x 18% = £10,872.

LOSSES

Any losses you make on selling or giving away assets must be deducted from gains made in the same tax year. Once the gains have been reduced to zero, any remaining losses are carried forward to future years. (Note that reducing your gains right down to zero means any tax-free allowance for the year is wasted.)

If you still have some chargeable gains, next you deduct any unused losses brought forward from previous years.

But you deduct only so much as is needed to reduce the chargeable gains to the level of your tax-free allowance. Any remaining losses continue to be carried forward for use in a subsequent year.

YOUR TAX BILL

Having deducted all the expenses, reliefs and losses you can, you next subtract your annual tax-free allowance (£9,600 in 2008–9) and pay CGT at a single rate of 18 per cent on whatever remains.

CGT-free gains

These are the most common gains and transactions on which you do not pay CGT:

- Whatever you leave on death (though Inheritance Tax (IHT) may be payable, see page 198)
- Gifts to your spouse or civil partner, provided you live together. These are made on what is called a 'no-gain/no-loss basis'. This means that the final value that you are deemed to get is set exactly equal to your initial value plus allowable expenses and any reliefs (see page 170 for an explanation of all these terms), so your gain is zero. The initial value at which your spouse or partner is deemed to have acquired the asset is set to that same amount.
- Gifts to charity and local sports clubs that are eligible to be treated in the same way as charities.
- Your only or main home (but see pages 128 and 171).
- Private cars.
- Assets that are deemed to have a useful life of 50 years or less (called 'wasting assets'). This would include, say, a caravan or boat.
- More durable personal belongings with a final value of less than £6,000. This would include, for example, many paintings, antiques and other collectables.
- Foreign currency for personal spending abroad and British money including post-1837 sovereigns.
- Gambling and lottery wins.
- Gains on certain investments, including any held within an individual savings account or Child Trust Fund, gilts and many corporate bonds.

For more information about CGT, see the *Which? Essential Guide: Tax Handbook 2009/10*, published in Spring 2009.

Tax and investments

The return you personally get from an investment depends crucially on the interaction between your personal tax situation and the way the chosen investment is taxed.

Making good investment decisions requires an understanding of whether the return will be taxed as income or capital gain and how much tax will be deducted either in your own hands or before the return reaches you.

TAX ON SAVINGS

Bank and building society accounts and National Savings & Investments (NS&I) products all pay income in the form of interest and no capital gain. The interest from most of these products is paid with tax at 20 per cent already deducted. If you are a basic-rate taxpayer, this exactly

satisfies your tax bill. If you are a higher-rate taxpayer you have extra tax to pay. A starting-rate taxpayer can reclaim half the tax deducted – do this on form R40. Non-taxpayers can reclaim all the tax or, better still, register to receive the interest gross by completing form R85 available from the account provider.

A few NS&I products are taxable but pay interest without any tax deducted, which is very convenient if you are a non-taxpayer. Some NS&I products and all cash individual savings accounts (ISAs) pay tax-free interest, which is particularly valuable for higher-rate taxpayers.

Return on savings

If you get a net or tax-free return of:	It would be equivalent to a gross return of this much, if you were a:			
	Non-taxpayer	Starting-rate taxpayer	Basic-rate taxpayer	Higher-rate taxpayer
1%	1%	1.11%	1.25%	1.67%
3%	3%	3.33%	3.75%	5.00%
5%	5%	5.55%	6.25%	8.33%
7%	7%	7.77%	8.75%	11.67%

 To claim back Income Tax overpaid on your savings, use form R40 available from your tax office or the HM Revenue & Customs website, www.hmrc.gov.uk (follow the 'Find a form' link).

TAX ON GILTS AND BONDS

Usually, interest from gilts and corporate bonds is paid gross. If you are a taxpayer, you need to declare this income on your tax return or, if you do not get a return, to your tax office by 5 October following the end of the tax year. Tax is due at 10 per cent if you are a starting-rate taxpayer, 20 per cent basic-rate or 40 per cent higher-rate. Any capital gain is normally tax-free. The whole return, including interest, is tax-free if you hold these investments through a tax-efficient wrapper, such as a stocks-and shares ISA.

TAX ON SHARES

Dividends from shares are the distribution of some or all of a company's profits, which have already been taxed. Along with the amount you receive (the net dividend), you get a 10 per cent tax credit for the tax already deducted. The net dividend plus tax credit is the gross dividend.

The tax credit exactly matches the tax due if you are a basic-rate taxpayer. If you are a higher-rate taxpayer, you have to pay a further 22.5 per cent of the gross dividend to pay. Non-taxpayers cannot reclaim any of the tax credit. Capital gains from selling shares at a profit are taxable. However, if you hold the shares through a tax-efficient wrapper, such as a stocks-and-shares ISA, gains are tax-free, though income is still taxed at 10 per cent.

Jargon buster

Tax-efficient wrapper If you hold investments through an ISA, pension scheme, Child Trust Fund or some types of friendly society plan, there is little or no tax on the return you get. The ISA, pension scheme and so on is not itself an investment, but can be thought of as a wrapper around the investments that creates this favourable tax treatment

TAX ON INVESTMENT FUNDS

Distributions from unit trusts and open-ended investment companies (OEICs) that invest mainly in gilts and/or corporate bonds are taxed in the same way as savings income (see opposite) and paid with 20 per cent tax already deducted. Distributions from share-based unit trusts and OEICs are taxed in the same way as share dividends (see left). Gains are taxable, unless the investment fund is held through a tax-efficient wrapper.

Case Study **Paul**

In 2009-10, Paul receives a net dividend of £90 plus a £10 tax credit. He is a higher-rate taxpayer, so has extra tax to pay of 22.5% x (£90 + £10) = £22.50. Including the tax credit, he has paid total tax of £32.50 (32.5 per cent).

For more information about how investments are taxed, see the *Which? Essential Guide: Save and Invest.*

Investment trusts and exchange traded funds are companies quoted on the stock exchange and so their return is taxed in the same way as income and gains from any other type of share (see page 175).

TAX ON INVESTMENT-TYPE LIFE INSURANCE

Insurance companies offer a variety of contracts where you pay a premium and aim to get a payout that, typically, is linked directly or indirectly to the performance of one or more funds run by the insurance company. The company rather than you owns the investments in the funds and has to pay tax on both the income and gains they produce. Therefore the payout is already net of some tax, which is deemed to be equivalent to tax at the basic rate (20 per cent in 2009–10). If you are a basic-rate taxpayer, there is no further tax to pay. If you are a higher-rate taxpayer, there could be extra tax (see below). If you are a non-taxpayer, you cannot reclaim any of the tax paid by the company.

Insurance contracts where you pay regular premiums year after year are usually 'qualifying policies'. With these, there is no further tax bill for higher-rate taxpayers. Contracts where you pay a single premium are always 'non-qualifying policies'. Special tax rules apply to non-qualifying policies. In particular, for a maximum of 20 years, you can have a payout of up to 5 per cent a year of the amount you have paid in premium(s) without any immediate tax bill. Tax becomes due only when the policy comes to an end and depends on your tax position at that time – so if by then you are no longer a higher-rate taxpayer, no extra tax would be due.

PROPERTY FUNDS

In general, property funds are taxed like any other investment trust or stocks-and-shares-based unit trust or OEIC (see above). In particular, the fund accounts for tax on the income and you receive distributions with a tax credit. This is very different from the way in which you would be taxed if you invested direct in a property (see pages 156–7). There are two special types of property fund that aim to put you in more or less the same tax position that you would be in as a direct property investor. They are real-estate investment trusts (REITs) and property authorised investment funds (PAIFs, which are set up as unit trusts or OEICs). With both of these, provided the fund pays out the majority of the rental income it gets from property as distributions to investors, the fund itself pays no tax on the income. You receive the distributions with tax at the basic rate (20 per cent) already deducted and there is extra to pay if you are a higher-rate taxpayer. But if you are a non-taxpayer, you can reclaim the tax.

For more information about property funds, contact the Association of Real Estate Funds (AREF) at www.aput.co.uk, or the Investment Management Association at www.investmentuk.org.

Tax-saving tips

These tax-saving ideas can help ensure that you keep your Income Tax and Capital Gains Tax bills to a minimum, so that you rather than the taxman benefit from your hard-won cash!

1 Use your cash ISA allowance

Everyone needs some readily accessible savings (see page 144). You can put up to £3,600 a year into a cash ISA but, if you don't use this allowance, it cannot be carried forward so is lost for good. Cash ISAs come in a variety of accounts – easy access, notice, variable interest, fixed – and the interest is tax-free not just now but, under current government intentions, for as long as you leave your money invested. Even if you are a non taxpayer, cash ISAs can be a good choice because the rates are often very competitive and you are sheltered from tax should you become a taxpayer in future.

> **❝ There is a variety of cash ISAs – easy access, notice, variable interest and fixed. ❞**

2 If you are losing age allowance, switch to tax-free income

If your income is in the range where you are losing age allowance (see page 163), your top rate of tax is effectively 30 per cent. Switching to tax-free sources of income is therefore very tax-efficient (see case study, right).

ISA investment limits

Overall ISA limit	up to £7,200
– of which, this much can be invested in a cash ISA	up to £3,600
– of which this much can be invested in a stocks-and-shares ISA	up to £7,200 less whatever you invest in a cash ISA

Case Study Ralph

In 2009-10, Ralph, 65, has Income of £23,900. This is £1,000 above the £22,900 threshold at which age allowance starts to be lost. As a result, his personal allowance is £8,990 and he pays £2,982 tax.

If he transferred enough savings to a tax-free source – for example, ISAs or National Savings & Investments certificates (see page 146) – so that £1,000 of his income becomes tax free, Ralph would then get the full personal allowance of £9,490 and his tax bill would fall to £2,682, which is a tax saving of £300.

3 Consider investing for capital gains rather than income

For example, those unit trusts or other investments funds that aim to produce capital growth or even expensive pictures and antiques. You have a sizeable tax-free CGT allowance (£9,600 in 2008–9) that is often wasted. At 18 per cent, the tax rate on gains is often lower than you would pay on income.

❝ You have a sizeable tax-free CGT allowance that is often wasted. At 18 per cent, tax on gains is often lower than on income. ❞

4 If you work, consider tax-free perks instead of pay

On wages, you pay Income Tax and, if you are under State Pension age, National Insurance too (see page 84). But there is no National Insurance on perks and, on some, no Income Tax either. These include: mileage allowance up to 40p per mile (whatever the actual cost to you), contributions your employer pays into a pension scheme for you, the loan of a bicycle, free or subsidised meals at work, staff sports facilities, routine medical screening and check-ups, equipment (such as a wheelchair or hearing aid) primarily to help you do your job if disabled, and help with the cost of education or training necessary or beneficial to your work.

5 Claim Rent-a-Room relief if you let rooms in your home

You can have up to £4,250 income a year tax-free from taking in lodgers or running a bed-and-breakfast (see page 127).

6 Consider Gift Aid if you are a taxpayer and give to charity

Using the Gift Aid scheme (the charity concerned will explain how to do this), means the charity can claim back basic-rate tax relief on the amount you donate and, if you are a higher-rate taxpayer, you can claim extra tax relief through your tax return. But don't use Gift Aid if you are a non-taxpayer because HM Revenue & Customs can make you pay for the tax relief that the charity will still get.

7 Claim all your allowable expenses when working out a capital gain

Keep records of everything you spend on buying and selling an asset and enhancing its value because they reduce the amount of CGT you may have to pay (see page 170).

8 Weigh up business expenses against CGT if you work from home

If you use part of your home exclusively for business, there could be some CGT to pay when you sell the home (see page 171). You can avoid this by combining the space you use for business with private use too, but then you will only be able to claim a proportion of the expenses associated with the space when working out your taxable business profits. So weigh up the CGT you might save against the Income Tax relief that you would lose.

9 If you have two (or more) homes, make sure you elect one as your main home

When you acquire a new home (which could be one you own or one you rent), you have two years in which to elect which will be your main home for the purpose of relief from CGT (see page 172). Once made, you can switch the election at any time which gives you the flexibility to maximise your CGT savings (see, for example, Case study. Richard and Elaine on page 172). If you don't make the election, your main home is decided on the facts and cannot be switched.

10 If you are an unmarried couple with two homes, choose a different main home each

That way you can have two homes between you that are both free of CGT when you sell.

11 If you are selling a business, claim entrepreneurs' relief

You can make up to £1 million of gains from selling businesses during your lifetime, on which CGT is reduced to 10 per cent (see page 171).

❝ There is no tax on a gain from selling small collectables. ❞

12 If you are passing on a business to the next generation, claim hold-over relief

Any CGT you would normally have to pay can be deferred until they eventually sell the business (see page 170).

13 Collectables can be a tax-free investment

There is no tax on a gain from selling a personal belonging for less than £6,000. This can comfortably cover the sale of many small collectables, such as silver items and rare books. There are rules to prevent you artificially splitting sets – such as a set of chairs or chessmen – to squeeze under the limit. To find out more, see HMRC helpsheet HS293 'Chattels and Capital Gains Tax' from www.hmrc. gov.uk/sa/forms/content.htm.

14 Share your income and wealth with your spouse or civil partner

If your spouse or civil partner pays Income Tax at a lower rate than you, shifting income-producing assets to him or her can collectively save you tax. There is no CGT (or Inheritance Tax – see page 198) on gifts between spouses and civil partners.

15 Claim back tax overpaid on savings

Interest from most types of savings is paid with tax at 20 per cent already deducted. If you are a non-taxpayer or a starting-rate taxpayer (see page 166), make sure you claim all or part of the tax back – see page 174.

16 Register for gross interest on any savings if you are a non-taxpayer

To do this, ask the provider for form R85.

17 Take care using stocks-and-shares ISAs

With an ISA invested largely in shares, income is taxed at 10 per cent and gains are tax-free (see pages 165 and 173). But, if you are a basic-rate taxpayer with unused CGT allowance, you get exactly the same tax treatment even if you hold shares or share-based investment funds outside the ISA wrapper. So think twice about paying any fees for the ISA wrapper – there will be no offsetting tax advantage unless you are a higher-rate taxpayer and/or normally use up your CGT allowance.

18 Invest through a pension scheme

You get basic-rate tax relief on your investment – so for every £1,000 you invest, £1,250 goes into the scheme –

and extra relief if you are a higher-rate taxpayer. You can take a quarter of the proceeds as a tax-free lump sum, but you need to be happy to draw the rest as taxable pension.

19 Consider investment funds rather than life insurance

Bear in mind that life insurance payouts are net of tax paid by the company, which you cannot reclaim. This includes tax on capital gains made by the underlying funds that might well have been tax-free in your hands. With other types of investment fund, such as unit trusts, tax on income and gains is determined by your personal tax situation, not that of the fund provider.

20 Look after your tax affairs to avoid fines

Be aware of the set dates by which you must declare income and gains and pay tax on them (see below). There are penalties if you miss these dates – for example, £100 for filing a tax return late – and interest on tax paid late.

Key tax dates

5 April 2009	End of 2008–9 tax year
5 October 2009	Deadline for declaring any income or gains received in 2008–9 tax year if HMRC don't already know about them
31 October 2009	Last day for filing 2008–9 paper tax return
31 January 2010	Last day for filing 2008–9 online tax return
31 January 2010	Deadline for paying any tax still due for 2008–9

Decisions about care

Whether you are caring for elderly relatives or thinking about your own care needs, the questions are similar: what form of care; in what setting; how much will it cost; and what help is available from the State? In the case of your own possible future care, you may also be wondering what scope there is to plan ahead.

Care options

A consequence of people generally living longer is that in your later years you may find you are looking after even older, frail parents. As retirement progresses, you may need some degree of care yourself.

Over a third of people aged 65–74 and just under half of people aged 75 and over say they have a long-standing health condition that limits their activities in some way. The ability to carry on living at home, despite disability, often relies on the availability of care. The majority of care is provided informally – for example, government data show that over three-quarters of people with mobility problems are helped by their spouse or another family member.

In 1993, the Government introduced policies designed to help more people live independently in their own homes through the expansion of formal support services. Now over three-quarters of people aged 90 and over still live in their own home and the number moving into residential and nursing homes (collectively referred to as 'care homes' in this chapter) has actually been declining over the past decade.

Pit your wits Answers

Question 10
What proportion of people aged 65 and over are providing informal care to family, friends or neighbours?
A: (b) One in nine. According to government data, more than a million of the 9.6 million or so people aged 65 and over are providing informal care. This includes over 8,000 carers who are themselves aged 90 or older.

❝ Over three-quarters of people aged 90 and over still live in their own home. ❞

 For more information on your choices, see the *Which? Essential Guide* to *Care Options in Retirement*. You can also get in touch with FirstStop at www.firststopcareadvice. org.uk, which is an advisory service about housing and care options for older people, their families and carers.

KEY DECISIONS

These policies have widened the choice of viable care options, but with a growing elderly population there is pressure on how to pay for them both at the individual level and for society as a whole. Whether you are thinking about support for elderly relatives or for yourself, there are two key decisions to make:

- **What form of care to choose,** in particular care at home, possibly in specialist retirement housing (sometimes called sheltered housing), or in a care home.
- **How to pay for care,** in particular what state financial help is available.

This chapter looks at the options and the financial implications.

CARE AT HOME

Most people would like to stay in their own home and retain as much independence as possible for as long as they can. Regardless of your financial situation, if you have care needs, you have a right to ask the social services department of your local authority for a needs assessment. A social worker or care manager from the social services will visit you in your own home to see what needs you have and to recommend a care plan based on your particular disability and home circumstances. A care plan might include, for example:

- **Daily visits from someone** to help you with personal care, such as getting up and going to bed.

- **Help with shopping and housework.** This could be someone to do these jobs for you or someone to take you out shopping in, say, a wheelchair.
- **Equipment,** such as hoists, grab rails, ramps and raised toilet seats, to help you live at home more easily.
- **An emergency call service** to provide help if you have a fall or, say, get stuck in the bath.
- **A place at a day centre** where you can socialise, receive a hot meal and have access to services such as chiropody.
- **Mobile meals service.** Many local authorities have now replaced traditional meals-on-wheels – a daily hot-meal delivery service. Instead you may be offered regular deliveries of frozen meals that you can store in a freezer and heat up in a microwave. If you find it difficult to heat up the meals, usually your care plan can include someone dropping in to help.

Some small items of equipment may be provided free (see Chapter 4, page 99), but usually you will have to pay for the services recommended in your care plan. Local authorities have discretion to decide their own charges but central government has set out a policy on fair charging that local authorities must abide by. For example, under the rules, flat-rate charges are usually not acceptable, so normally the amount you have to pay will be means tested. The local authority will carry out a financial assessment to see whether you qualify for free services and, if not, how much you should pay – see box, overleaf.

Financial assessment

The fairer charging rules set out the minimum standards that local authorities should use to assess whether you should pay part or all of the cost of care services in your own home. Local authorities can adopt more generous rules if they want to. The rules are detailed but include:

- **Charges should not reduce the income you have left below a set level.** If you are aged 60 or over, this is the Pension Credit guarantee credit level plus a buffer, which varies according to where you live in the UK – for example, 25 per cent cent in England and 35 per cent in Wales. For example, in 2008–9, the Pension Credit limit for a single person is £124.05 a week, so after paying care service charges someone in England should still have income of 125% x £124.05 = £155.06 a week. In 2009–10, that limit rises to £162.50.

- **Income for the purpose of the assessment** can include any disability-related benefits, such as Attendance Allowance, but your local authority should then also take into account any disability-related expenditure you have over and above paying for the authority's care services. For example, you might be spending on extra washing, an emergency call service, transport, and so on. Income should not include any Pension Credit savings credit (see page 103) or any earnings if you work.

- **Your savings can be taken into account in deciding your ability to pay,** but capital below a certain level – in 2008–9, £13,500 (England and Northern Ireland), £19,000 (Wales) or £13,000 (Scotland) – should be disregarded. If your capital is above a set level – £22,250 (England and Northern Ireland), £22,000 (Wales), or £21,500 (Scotland) – you will be charged the full amount for your care services. Between the lower and upper capital limits, you are assumed to receive £1 a week of income from each £250 (or part-£250) of capital and this is included as part of your income in determining the minimum you should have left after paying care charges. Your home is not included as part of your capital.

- **The assessment should be based only on your income,** and generally not that of your partner, if you have one, or anyone else. However, local authorities should take into account individual circumstances – for example, where one member has most of the income and is responsible for all or most of the household bills.

If you feel you are paying too much towards your care services, you have the right to ask your local authority to review your financial assessment.

How your care is paid for

In general, local authorities must now offer you the option of receiving cash, which you use to arrange your own care services. This is known as Direct Payment. However, if you prefer, you can instead ask your local authority to arrange the services you need. The Government has also been piloting a system called Individual Budgets. This is similar to Direct Payment, so you receive a cash sum, but it covers a wider range of services, including, for example, help towards paying for a warden in sheltered housing (see page 186) or a Disabled Facilities Grant to adapt your home (see page 100). The aim of both Direct Payment and Individual Budgets is to put you in control of choosing your service providers and shopping around for a good deal.

Other benefits

Separately, you are likely to qualify for Attendance Allowance or, if under 65, Disability Living Allowance (see page 97) to help you cope with the extra costs of coping with a disability – these tax-free benefits are not means tested.

Carer's assessment

If you are a carer, you also have the right to a free needs assessment. The care plan devised by the local authority after the initial assessment may recommend, for example, someone to sit with your relative to give you a few hours off, or respite care (where the disabled person moves temporarily into a care home) to give you a longer break. You will be expected to pay for these services unless your income and savings are low. Check whether you can claim Carer's Allowance (see page 97).

Scotland and Northern Ireland

In Scotland, eligible personal care is free without any means testing when provided in your own home and you are 65 or over.

In Northern Ireland, such care is free if you are 75 or over. Any medical care you need is provided as normal through the NHS, so generally it is free.

If you do not qualify for free prescriptions (see pages 93 and 98), you can buy a pre-payment certificate, which is worth doing if you need more than three prescriptions per three-month period or 14 items a year. The certificate caps your prescription charges at just over £100 a year.

See *The Phone Book* or www.direct.gov.uk for how to contact your local authority. For details of prescription pre-payment certificates, see www.ppa.org.uk/ppa/ppc_intro.htm. Carers may have the right to ask their employer for flexible working – see page 73, for details.

RETIREMENT HOUSING

Retirement housing – also called sheltered housing or warden-assisted or warden-controlled housing – is designed for people aged 60 (sometimes 55) and over. Typically, it is a collection of, say, 20 to 40 flats or bungalows with some communal facilities, such as a lounge and garden, maybe a guest room that can be hired, a laundry, and emergency call system and usually a warden. The duties of the warden vary from one scheme to another but generally include keeping in touch with residents, organising help in an emergency, reporting repair needs and as a central source of information on accessing care and other services.

Some sheltered housing is available to buy – often on a long **lease**, but sometimes **freehold**. You may be able to buy cheaply through a shared-ownership scheme (where you buy part of the home and rent the rest) or through a lifetime lease (where you have the home

for as long as you live but generally get back little if you sell early). Sheltered housing to rent is mainly provided by councils and housing associations and to qualify you will have to show that you need the housing (for example, because of disability or frailty) and are not able to buy. If you rent and your income and savings are low, you may qualify for Housing Benefit (see page 107).

Charges

Whether you buy or rent, you have to pay an ongoing service charge that covers the cost of the communal areas, emergency call system and warden services. Housing Benefit, if you qualify, may cover part of this. If you do not qualify for Housing Benefit but your income is low, you can apply to your local authority for help in paying the service charge.

Ordinary sheltered housing does not itself include care services – you would still have to arrange these as described under Care at home (pages 183–5). Some local authorities and housing associations run extra-care sheltered housing, which does include personal care (such as help with getting up, bathing and so on) and often meals in a communal dining room. Once again, if your income is low, your local authority may help you pay for these extra services.

Jargon buster

Freehold The right to hold a property indefinitely

Leasehold The right to hold a property for a set time period as specified in the lease

For more information about sheltered housing and to check what sheltered homes are available to buy or rent in your area, see the Elderly Accommodation Counsel website at www.housingcare.org.

Moving to a care home

According to Laing & Buisson, an independent provider of healthcare data, in 2007, some 420,000 people were living in care homes or long-stay hospitals. Around two-thirds were funded by the State. The remaining third were paying from their own resources – fees that can easily amount to £500 to £600 a week or more.

STATE HELP WITH CARE HOME FEES

If you move into a home mainly to receive personal care, you may have to pay some or all of the fees yourself, depending on your means. If your main reason is healthcare, the NHS should pay.

NHS care

If the primary reason for your being in a long-stay hospital or nursing home is to receive healthcare, the NHS should pick up the full cost of the fees – this is called NHS continuing care. This was established by the Coughlan case in 1999 and confirmed in a report by the Health Service Ombudsman in 2002. The report found that some health authorities had been misinterpreting the rules and incorrectly handing healthcare patients over to local authority social services departments where help with fees is means tested. The distinction between personal care and healthcare is not clear-cut and, if you think you are being charged incorrectly, you should ask for a review of your case. You are also entitled to free after-care following discharge after a spell in hospital under the Mental Health Act 1983.

In some circumstances you may receive care at home either to avoid admission to hospital or to enable you to leave hospital early. In this case, you are entitled to free care – called intermediate care – which may include a mix of health and social care. The social care element should be free for a maximum of six weeks.

> **❝If the primary reason for being in a nursing home is healthcare, the NHS should pick up the cost. ❞**

 To ask for a review of your own or your relative's care needs if you think the NHS should be funding them, contact your local Primary Care Trust (contact details from NHS Direct on 0845 4647). If you are unhappy with the outcome of the review, you can take your case to the Health Service Ombudsman at www.ombudsman.org.uk.

Who pays your care home fees?

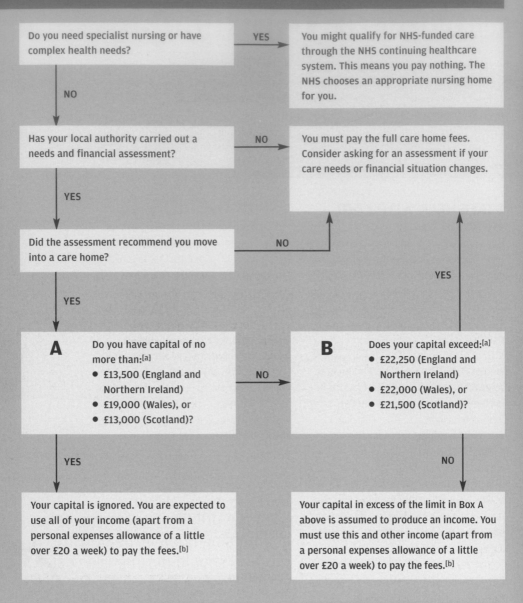

Do you need specialist nursing or have complex health needs?

— YES → You might qualify for NHS-funded care through the NHS continuing healthcare system. This means you pay nothing. The NHS chooses an appropriate nursing home for you.

NO ↓

Has your local authority carried out a needs and financial assessment?

— NO → You must pay the full care home fees. Consider asking for an assessment if your care needs or financial situation changes.

YES ↓

Did the assessment recommend you move into a care home?

— NO →

YES ↓

A Do you have capital of no more than:[a]
- £13,500 (England and Northern Ireland)
- £19,000 (Wales), or
- £13,000 (Scotland)?

— NO →

B Does your capital exceed:[a]
- £22,250 (England and Northern Ireland)
- £22,000 (Wales), or
- £21,500 (Scotland)?

(YES ↑ leads back to "You must pay the full care home fees..." box)

YES ↓ (from A)

Your capital is ignored. You are expected to use all of your income (apart from a personal expenses allowance of a little over £20 a week) to pay the fees.[b]

NO ↓ (from B)

Your capital in excess of the limit in Box A above is assumed to produce an income. You must use this and other income (apart from a personal expenses allowance of a little over £20 a week) to pay the fees.[b]

---

a Capital limits shown are for 2008–9. The limits are likely to increase from 6 April 2009.

b Your local authority meets any shortfall, but only up to whatever maximum the authority has set. If you choose a more expensive home, someone else – family members, say – will have to make up the difference. Alternatively, you may be able to borrow the extra from your local authority to be repaid from the eventual sale of your home or from your estate when you die (this is called a deferred payment agreement).

188

Non-NHS care

If your primary reason for moving to a care home is for help with personal care (getting up, going to bed, bathing, toileting, moving around, preparing meals, and so on), in general you are expected to pay for the fees yourself unless your income and savings are low. In that case, your local authority will carry out a financial assessment (see right) to determine whether you should pay anything at all and, if so, how much. The rules are complex – the chart opposite gives a broad overview.

Even if your main need is personal care, you may require some nursing care too and this is free up to set limits depending on where in the UK you live and, in England, on the extent of nursing care you need. For 2008–9, the limits are:

- **England:** a standard rate of £103.80 a week and a higher rate of £142.80, depending of the extent of nursing care you need
- **Wales:** £117.66 a week.
- **Scotland:** £67 a week.
- **Northern Ireland:** £100 a week.

The Government pays these sums direct to your care provider and the result should be that the care home fees are lower than they would otherwise be.

If you are paying for your care home fees yourself, you are likely to qualify for Attendance Allowance (see page 97). If the NHS or your local authority is paying some or all of the fees, you will not be able to get Attendance Allowance as well.

ASSESSING YOUR FINANCES

Whether or not you can get state funding depends in part on how much capital you have. Capital includes your savings and investments and possibly your home too. But, if your partner (married or not), an elderly or disabled relative or a child under 16 still lives there, the value of your home is disregarded. Your local council also has discretion to ignore your home if, say, your carer will carry on living there.

If you are a couple, the local authority is not allowed to base the financial assessment on your joint resources. It must consider only the capital and income that belongs to you. Therefore, the capital limits in boxes A and B in the chart opposite apply only to your capital, including just your share of any joint capital. In general, if you own joint accounts with your partner or anyone else, you will be treated as owning half the money in the account. If, in fact, you and the other account holder have unequal shares, close the account and replace it with two separate accounts. You will then be treated as owning only the amount in your own account. For example, suppose you and your son have a joint account with a balance of £20,000 of which you contributed £8,000 and your son

Personal care funding in Scotland

If you are in Scotland, the Government also pays £149 a week towards your personal care and pays this direct to the care provider.

£12,000. As long as the money is in the joint account, you will be treated as owning £10,000 (in other words, half the balance). If you close the joint account and distribute £12,000 of the balance to your son and £8,000 to you, you will be treated as owning the correct amount of £8,000.

If you are holding assets on behalf of someone else, you will need to provide proof of this, otherwise the assets will be treated as yours. You can be treated as still owning capital if you are deemed to have deliberately deprived yourself of it – this could be the case if, say, you have given away assets to other family members in advance of applying for a care assessment.

In general, the financial assessment is based solely on the income of the person needing care (or their share of any joint income). However, your partner, if you have one, may be entitled to some of your income. For example, half of any occupational or personal pension you get may be assigned to your partner if it had been supporting you both. Even so, your partner might still have too little to live on and should investigate whether he or she can claim means-tested benefits, such as Pension Credit (see page 101) and Council Tax Benefit (see page 107).

You are required to use most of your income to pay your care home fees and normally you are left with a personal allowance of just over £20 a week that is meant to cover sundries, such as toiletries and confectionary. You can ask your local authority to increase this allowance so that you can give extra financial help to your partner if you are worried that he or she does not have enough to live on, but the local authority does not have to agree to this.

Spouses and civil partners are in law liable to support each other and can be asked to contribute towards the fees, but the local authority should not do this if it would cause financial hardship. The local authority cannot ask an unmarried partner or other family members to contribute.

Case Study — Martin

Martin, who lives in England with his wife in a house they own, has an income of £180 a week (made up of £100 State Pension and £80 a week occupational pension) and £20,000 in savings. Martin has dementia, which is now so bad that he has to move into a care home, charging £500 a week (which is within the maximum limit his local authority will pay). The first £13,500 of Martin's capital is disregarded but he is treated as receiving £1 a week of income from each £250 of capital over that limit, which comes to £26 a week, bringing his total income for the assessment purposes to £206 a week.

Out of this, Martin can keep £21.15 a week personal expense allowance. The rest of his income (£184.85 a week) goes towards the care home fees with the local authority paying the other £315.15 a week. Because Martin is treated as having an income that is higher than his actual income, meeting the payments means that he will have to dip into his savings.

❝ Your partner may be entitled to some of your income. ❞

Planning ahead for care

Long-term care products are expensive. If you end up needing care for only a short period of time, these products could cost more than the care fees would have done. But if you need care for a long time, taking out a long-term care product could work out cheaper than the fees.

You will not necessarily save money taking out a long-term care product, but you will have converted the uncertain cost of paying fees for an unknown length of time into a fixed cost for the long-term care product. This gives you greater certainty over how much money you might have left over to pass on to your heirs.

WHY PLANNING AHEAD IS DIFFICULT

If you do need to move into a care home in later life, the fees could amount to, say, £25,000 a year or more at today's prices. Planning ahead for costs like these is no easy matter for several reasons:

- There is no way of knowing for sure whether you will need care as you get older or for how long. It is reckoned that around a quarter of people aged 65 and over are likely to need significant levels of care. The average stay in a residential home is around five years, but this falls to two to three years for a nursing home.
- Any planning needs to dovetail with the help available from the State. Since most of this is means tested and the rules are complex, it may be hard to work out whether you will get value

from private provision or will simply displace state help that you would otherwise have got.

- Over the last ten years, the Government and other bodies have been reviewing the present state system to look for a less complex, more popular and more financially sustainable alternative. There are no easy answers and it is hard to anticipate what form changes might take, when they might be made and how they might affect the private provision you need.

LONG-TERM CARE PRODUCTS

In addition to these difficulties, there are very few providers of long-term care products, which tend to be expensive.

Long-term care insurance

A classic solution for dealing with uncertain future events is to take out insurance – in other words, before the need arises, you pay premiums in case the worst should happen. If you do need care, the insurance pays out; if you don't, it pays nothing. In the UK there is just one provider of long-term care insurance. It targets healthy individuals aged 50–75 years. With high premiums (for example, around £100 a month for a policy that would pay out a flat-rate £1,000 a month and more for a payout that increases with inflation), it is easy to see why this type of insurance is not popular.

Immediate needs annuities

A handful of providers offer **impaired life annuities** that you buy at the point when you start to need care. You pay a lump sum – perhaps from the sale of your home or by taking out an equity release scheme – and in return get an income that pays either all or a substantial part of your care costs. The income is tax-free, provided it is paid direct to the care provider. The amount you pay for the annuity depends on the monthly payout you need and the annuity provider's assessment of how long it expects you to need care (your life expectancy). Each provider uses its own data and methods to estimate this and the cost of such an annuity can vary by 50 per cent or more from one provider to another, so it is essential to shop around. The advantage

for you is that you have turned the uncertain future costs of care into a known and fixed payment for the annuity.

Long-term care products and your wealth

Under current rules, the State pays your care home fees if your income and capital are low enough. If your capital is above an upper limit (see chart on page 188), you have to meet the full cost of fees yourself until your capital has run down below that limit. At that point, the State starts to help if your income is insufficient to cover the full fees. But local authorities also put a cap on the maximum they are willing to pay. Taking out a long-term care product, then, can be viewed as doing two things:

- **Giving you the ability to pay for a more expensive care home** – in other words, increasing your choice.
- **Helping you to preserve at least some of your capital** to pass on to your heirs or enjoy in other ways.

Because long-term care products are expensive, paying for one will itself use up a big chunk of your capital. But the payout from either insurance or an annuity will continue for as long as you need care so, should you remain in a care home for many years, you make it less likely that your capital will be run down to a very low level.

Jargon buster

Impaired life annuity A lifetime annuity paying a significantly higher than normal income because your poor health means you are likely to have a much shorter life than average

---

Get help with long-term care products from an independent financial adviser – see www.unbiased.co.uk. For more information about care, see the *Which? Essential Guide* to *Care Options in Retirement*.

The next generation

Later life may be a time of increased financial security and an opportunity to help your children and grandchildren cope with the transition to adulthood, first jobs and owning property. It can be a comfort too to realise that your help can continue even when you have passed on. Make sure you are aware of the tax implications and arrange your help in the most tax-efficient way.

Family matters

Make sure you plan your gifts and bequests so the right people benefit and you minimise the amount lost in tax. But don't jeopardise your own financial security.

Like many people, you may feel it is important to leave an inheritance when you die, for example, to ensure that your widow, widower or other partner will be financially secure or to provide for the next generation. You are likely to have two main concerns:

- **Ensuring the right people inherit.** This means writing a will and making sure it is up to date (see opposite). You might also want to consider using **trusts**. According to the National Consumer Council, nearly two-thirds of the UK population, including one-third of people aged 65 and over, have no will.
- **Keeping any Inheritance Tax (IHT) bill to a minimum.** There are a variety of ways to do this (see page 198). In 2008–9, one in 20 estates are expected to pay Inheritance Tax.

One of the key ways to reduce IHT at death is to give away some of your wealth during your lifetime. This may have the added advantage of giving help

to, say, adult children at the time they most need it. Take care to plan your lifetime gifts (see page 201) so that they really do save tax, but most importantly do not give away money or assets that you may need for your own financial security.

> **❝ Plan lifetime gifts to save tax, but do not give away money or assets you may need. ❞**

Pit your wits Answers

Question 11
How much can you leave your family free of Inheritance Tax?
A: In 2008–9, the first £312,000 of what you leave is tax-free. This increases to £350,000 by 2010–11. Spouses and civil partners can jointly leave twice this.

 For a detailed guide to planning tax-efficient gifts during your lifetime and on death, see the *Which? Essential Guide* to *Giving and Inheriting*.

WHY YOU NEED A WILL

If you do not write a will, the law dictates who will inherit whatever you leave on death. The law gives priority to spouses, civil partners and your own children. This may accord with your wishes anyway but not if, for example, you want an unmarried partner or step-children to benefit.

Any share of an asset you own with someone else as 'joint tenants' automatically passes to the surviving owner(s) on your death. Any assets you own outright or your share of assets owned as 'tenants in common' are passed on according to your will or, if no will, the laws of intestacy.

Intestacy rules

The table and box, overleaf, summarise who gets what under the intestacy rules. In general, the rules favour married and civil partners and your biological children. This means unmarried partners and step-children have no automatic right to inherit. It also means that a separated (but not divorced) spouse could inherit rather than the family you are close to now. In addition, property may have to be sold so that your assets can be shared as the law requires and, if you leave children under age 18, costly trusts may have to be set up. You can avoid all these problems by writing a will. If you go to a solicitor, the cost of a simple will starts at around £75.

Jargon buster

Inheritance Tax A tax charged on gifts you make both during your lifetime and on death. However, some gifts are tax-free

Joint tenants A way of sharing ownership of an asset. All the owners have equal shares and rights. On death, your share automatically passes to the remaining owners

Life interest You get the income from or use of an asset during your lifetime. After that, the asset usually passes to someone else

Tenants in common A way of sharing ownership of an asset. Owners have distinct shares that need not be equal. On death, your share is passed on according to your will or the intestacy rules

Trust A legal arrangement that lets you give away assets, but with conditions attached – for example, a trust that lets your surviving spouse use the family home during his or her lifetime after which it is given to your children

> ❝ If you do not write a will, the law dictates who inherits whatever you leave on death. ❞

For more information about intestacy rules and making a will, see the *Which? Essential Guides* to *Giving and Inheriting* and *Wills and Probate*. To find a solicitor, contact the relevant Law Society for your part of the UK – see Useful addresses on page 215.

Intestacy rules

If you were to die intestate, this is what would happen to your estate. For the intestacy rules in Scotland, see box, opposite.

If you were:		Value of estate	This is what the law requires in:	
Marital status[a]	Children?		England and Wales[b]	Northern Ireland[c]
Married	Yes	Up to £250,000	All to spouse. Nothing to children.	All to spouse. Nothing to children.
		More than £250,000	£250,000 to spouse plus life interest in half the remaining estate (which eventually passes to children). Children inherit the rest.	£250,000 to spouse plus half the remaining estate if you have one child or one-third if there are more children. Children inherit the rest.
Married	No	Up to £450,000	All to spouse.	All to spouse.
		More than £450,000	£450,000 to spouse plus half remaining estate. Rest to parents or, if none, siblings[d]. If no siblings, all to spouse.	£450,000 to spouse plus half remaining estate. Rest to parents or, if none, siblings[d]. If no siblings, all to spouse.
Single	Yes	Any	Children inherit in equal shares.	Children inherit in equal shares.
Single	No	Any	Parents inherit or, if none, your siblings[d]. If no siblings, your grandparents. If no grandparents, your aunts and uncles[d]. If none of these, your estate passes to the Crown.	Parents inherit or, if none, your siblings[d]. If no siblings, estate passes to any more remote ancestors. If none, your estate passes to the Crown.

[a] 'Married' includes being in a civil partnership.

[b] The limits here apply from 1 February 2009 onwards.

[c] The limits here apply from 1 January 2008 onwards.

[d] If this relative has died before you, their children or more distant offspring, if any, inherit in their place.

Intestacy rules for Scotland

The law in Scotland work as follows. The amounts stated apply from 1 June 2005 onwards:

- **If you were married with no children.** Your husband or wife has what are called under Scottish law 'prior rights'. These are rights to the family home (provided it is in Scotland) up to a value of £300,000, furniture and household effects up to £24,000 and a cash sum up to £75,000. He or she also has 'legal rights' to half the remaining 'moveable estate' (ie excluding land and buildings). See below for the remaining estate.

- **If you were married with children.** Your husband or wife has prior rights to the family home up to £300,000, furniture and effects up to £24,000 and a cash sum up to £42,000 plus legal rights to share one-third of the remaining moveable estate. The children also have legal rights to share one-third of the moveable estate between them. See below for the remaining estate.

- **If you had a civil partner and no children.** Your civil partner has legal rights to half your moveable estate.

- **If you had a civil partner and children.** Your civil partner has legal rights to one-third of your moveable estate. The children also have a legal right to share a third of the moveable estate between them.

- **If you had children but no husband, wife or civil partner.** The children have legal rights to half the moveable estate.

- **The remaining estate.** Whatever remains after meeting the prior rights, the legal rights (and, in the case of partial intestacy, bequests under a will) is known as 'the dead's part'. It is distributed in the following order of priority: children; parents and siblings; husband or wife; uncles and aunts (or, if they have died, their children); grandparents; more distant relatives; the Crown.

 To find a solicitor, contact the relevant Law Society for your part of the UK – see Useful addresses on page 215.

Inheritance Tax on your estate

What you leave on death is treated as your final gift and may be subject to Inheritance Tax (IHT). However, some gifts and the first slice of your estate are tax-free.

Each gift, including what you leave on death, is not taxed in isolation. Instead, you are taxed on a rolling total of gifts over the last seven years up to the gift in question. So the tax on your estate depends not just on the size of your estate but also gifts you made during the last seven years of your life. However, some gifts are tax-free. See page 201 for tax-free lifetime gifts. For the main gifts that are tax-free at death, see the box, below. Reasonable funeral costs (say, £2,000 or so) can be deducted from the value of the estate before tax is worked out.

IHT on the total of your estate and gifts in the previous seven years is charged at two rates: 0 per cent on the first slice, which is therefore called your nil-rate band; and 40 per cent (in 2008–9) on anything above the nil-rate band. The nil-rate band is £312,000 in 2008–9, £325,000 in 2009–10 and £350,000 in 2010–11.

IHT AND COUPLES

Anything you leave to your spouse or civil partner is usually a tax-free gift, so a family's wealth passes untaxed to the surviving partner on the first death. This used to mean that the nil-rate band of the first to die was wasted and, with just one nil-rate band to set against the family's wealth, there could be a hefty tax bill on the second death. It was possible to get around this problem if couples wrote their wills to leave an amount equal to the nil-rate band to a trust on the first death (with the surviving spouse or civil partner a potential beneficiary of the trust). This used up the nil-rate band of the first to die and prevented all the family's wealth concentrating in the hands of the

---

Main gifts free of IHT on death

- Gifts to your spouse or civil partner (but limited to £55,000 in total if his or her permanent home is not in the UK).
- Lump sum paid to your survivors from your pension scheme or life insurance, provided it is paid at the discretion of the trustees.
- Gifts to charities, political parties and housing associations.
- Gifts of national heritage property.

---

survivor. However, the problem and the need for special planning have been removed for second deaths occurring on or after 9 October 2007, because any nil-rate band unused by the first spouse to die (whatever the date of their death) can now be passed on to the surviving spouse (see Case study: Wies and Gordana for how this works).

Unmarried partners

Bequests to your unmarried partner are not tax-free and you cannot inherit each other's nil-rate band. Anything that unmarried couples leave each other automatically uses up the giver's nil-rate band. The main problem for unmarried couples is that the survivor may be forced to sell the family home in order to pay any tax due on the first death. Other non-married people who live together – such as brothers and sisters,

parents and adult children, frail or disabled people and their carers – face the same problem.

 Equity release schemes (see page 117) are sometimes marketed as a way of saving IHT. Borrowing against your home, by taking out a lifetime mortgage, gives you money to spend or give away now and creates a debt that is deducted from the value of your estate at death. Similarly, selling part or all of your home reduces your assets, releasing cash that you can spend or give away now. While both types of scheme do undoubtedly reduce the value of your estate and so the tax likely to be due on it, bear in mind that you do not realise the full value of your home (see pages 119 and 120). This shortfall could more than offset the tax you save, with no net benefit to your heirs.

The next generation

Case Study Wies and Gordana

Wies died in 2003 (having made no gifts in the seven years before death). He left £100,000 to his daughter, Ewa, and the rest of his estate, valued at £500,000, to his wife Gordana. The bequest to Ewa was covered by his nil-rate band (£255,000 in 2003–4). The bequest to Gordana was a tax-free gift. In February 2009, Gordana dies, leaving an estate of £930,000 (and having made no gifts in the previous seven years). Against this, her executors can set Gordana's own nil-rate band and also Wies' unused band. He had used £100,000 / £255,000 = 39.2% of his band, so Gordana's nil-rate band is increased by 60.8 per cent to £501,696. Tax on her estate comes to (£930,000 – £501,696) x 40% = £171,321.

 For information about transferring the nil-rate band, see HM Revenue & Customs website at www.hmrc.gov.uk/cto/iht/tnrb.htm.

Five ways to save tax on your estate

1   **Use your will to make tax-free gifts,** for example, to your spouse or charity.

2   **Make sure death benefits from your pension scheme and life insurance are tax-free.** Provided these schemes are set up in trust, the trustees rather than you decide who will receive any payout. This means the payout goes direct to the recipient, bypassing your estate and any tax. Typically you will be asked to fill in a form nominating who you would like to benefit and the trustees, although not bound by this, will normally follow your wishes.

3   **Make full use of your nil-rate band.** If you are a couple, to inherit your deceased spouse's or civil partner's nil-rate band, you will need to have the paperwork relating to his or her estate so that you can establish the amount of nil-rate band to be brought forward.

4   **Share assets tax-efficiently.** If you are a couple or, say, parent and adult child living together and the bulk of the family's assets are owned by just one of you, consider spreading them more evenly so that you can both make full use of your nil-rate bands. But, if you are not married or in a civil partnership, be aware of Capital Gains Tax on gifts between you (see page 169) and IHT if you do not survive seven years (see page 202).

5   **Make the most of tax-free lifetime gifts** (see opposite). Making gifts during your lifetime leaves less of your estate to be taxed on death. But only give away assets you can afford to live without.

> ❝ To inherit your deceased spouse's nil-rate band, you will need the paperwork relating to his or her estate. ❞

 IHT is a complex area. It pays to get professional advice from a solicitor, accountant or tax advisers (see Useful addresses on pages 211-15). If your plans involve a substantial sum (say £1 million or more), you might want to use a member of the Society of Trust and Estate Practitioners (www.step.org).

Lifetime gifts

You have enormous scope to make gifts tax-free during your lifetime. But the gifts must be genuine - you can't save tax if you continue to use something you give away.

In theory, any gift you make during your lifetime – pocket money, birthday presents, helping student offspring – could be within the scope of Inheritance Tax (IHT). In practice, some gifts are specifically tax-free – see box, below – which covers most of the normal everyday transfers you might make to

IHT-free lifetime gifts

The following lifetime gifts are free of IHT. However, if you give assets rather than money, there may be Capital Gains Tax to pay - see page 169.

- Gifts to your spouse or civil partner (but limited to £55,000 in total if their permanent home is not in the UK).
- Gifts to charities, political parties and housing associations.
- Gifts of national heritage property.
- Sharing lottery and other gambling proceeds with other members of a syndicate where you have agreed in advance to share any wins.
- Normal expenditure out of income, meaning a regular pattern of gifts funded from your income and leaving you enough to support your usual standard of living. There are no standard limits or rules - what counts as 'normal' will vary from one person to another depending on their particular circumstances. Potentially this is a very valuable exemption that could enable you to make large regular gifts.
- Gifts for the maintenance of your family, meaning your spouse, civil partner, children or other dependent relative if it would be reasonable for you to support them. There are no standard limits. The amount of maintenance that is considered reasonable will vary from family to family depending on their particular circumstances.
- Small gifts up to £250 per person per year. This covers most presents for birthdays, Christmas and so on.
- Wedding gifts - up to £5,000 if you are a parent, £2,500 if you are a grandparent and £1,000 anyone else.
- Up to £3,000 a year of any other gifts. If you don't use the full amount, you can carry the unused part forward for one year only after which it is lost.

family and friends. Other gifts to people are called potentially exempt gifts (PETs) and become tax-free provided you survive for seven years from the date of making them. If you die within the seven years, a PET is reclassified as a chargeable gift and tax may be due after all.

Some lifetime gifts – in particular to most types of trust – are chargeable at the time you make them. Where IHT is due, a gift is not taxed in isolation – tax is based on the rolling total of your gifts over the previous seven years.

TAX ON CHARGEABLE GIFTS

If you make a chargeable lifetime gift – the most common example would be paying money into a trust, for example to benefit your grandchildren, a less common example would be making a gift to a company – the gift is added to any other chargeable gifts you have made within the last seven years. The first part of the total – equal to the nil-rate band for the year (£312,000 in 2008–9) –

is taxed at 0 per cent. Any part of the latest gift not covered by the nil-rate band is taxed at 20 per cent.

If you die within seven years of making the gift, tax is reworked using the nil-rate band and death rate (40 per cent in 2008–9) that apply in the year of death. The tax then due may be reduced

Lifetime gifts and your estate

Tax on PETs and extra tax on other lifetime gifts triggered by death within seven years is completely separate and additional to any tax on the estate. Taper relief can reduce tax on the reassessed lifetime gifts but not tax on the estate.

For more information about lifetime gifts and the tax implications, especially with regard to IHT, taper relief and Pre-Owned Assets Tax, see the *Which? Essential Guide* to *Giving and Inheriting*. For up-to-date information on budget changes, go to: www.which.co.uk/advice/tax-basics-explained/budget-changes/index.jsp.

by **taper relief**. There is no refund if the tax then due comes to less than the tax paid at the time of the gift. But, if it comes to more, HM Revenue & Customs (HMRC) will first seek the extra tax due from the recipient of the gift and, if he or she can't or won't pay, from the estate of the deceased giver.

TAX ON PETS

There is no IHT at the time you make a PET – typically a gift to a person – and none at all if you survive for seven years. If you die within the seven years, the gift is treated as if it had always been taxable after all. Tax is calculated using the running total of gifts over the seven years up to the time you made the PET and the nil-rate band and IHT rate that apply at the time of death. The tax due may be reduced by taper relief. HMRC will first seek to collect the tax due from the recipient of the gift and, if they can't or won't pay, from the estate of the deceased giver.

GIFTS WITH RESERVATION

Giving something away in your lifetime is an obvious way to reduce the value of the estate you leave at death. But your gifts must be genuine. For IHT purposes, you will be treated as still owning something if you give it away but carry on using or benefiting from it – for example, you give away your home, but carry on living there; you give away a holiday cottage, but still carry on using it as normal; you give away a painting, but it still hangs in your home. These are called 'gifts with reservation'. From time

to time, various schemes are devised to get around the gift-with-reservation rules, but these days if you manage to save IHT through such schemes, you will probably instead be caught by **Pre-Owned Assets Tax** (POAT).

Case Study | George

George makes the following gifts during his lifetime:
- 2004-5: £250,000 to his daughter, Grace.
- 2007-8: £150,000 to his only grandchild, Amy.

There was no tax to pay on either of the gifts at the time he made them because they counted as PETs. But, sadly, George died in March 2009. This means the gifts are reassessed as if they had been chargeable gifts all along, though they are taxed at the rate current at the time of George's death: nil on the first £312,000 (the nil-rate band) and 40 per cent on anything more. The tax position of each gift is as follows:

- £250,000 to Grace. George had made no other gifts in the seven years before this one, so the running total is just £250,000. This is completely covered by the nil-rate band of £312,000, so there is no tax to pay on this gift.
- £150,000 to Amy. The only other gift George had made within the previous seven years was the gift to Grace, so the running total is £250,000 + £150,000 = £400,000. Of this, £312,000 is covered by the nil-rate band, but £88,000 of the gift to Amy is left to be taxed at 40 per cent. The tax bill is 40% x £88,000 = £35,200. There is no taper-relief reduction to this bill because George died so soon after making the gift.

In the first instance, Amy is expected to pay the tax but, if she can't, George's estate will have to.

Glossary

Accrual rate: In a salary-related pension scheme, the fraction of yearly pay that you get as pension. Commonly, schemes have accrual rates of 1/60th, 1/80th or 1/100th.

Actuarial reduction: A cut in your salary-related pension if you retire early to reflect the extra cost of paying your pension for longer. Often 6 per cent for each year of early retirement.

Additional pension scheme: Scheme available with salary-related schemes in the public sector where you buy a sum of future pension, paying either by lump sum or regular contributions.

Alternatively secured pension: The name given to a pension from income withdrawal if you are aged 75 or over.

Annuity: An investment where you swap a lump sum (such as your pension scheme) for an income payable for life, but can be for a set period. You cannot get your original investment back as a lump sum.

Annuity rate: Usually expressed as the amount of income (pension) you get each year for each £10,000 of lump sum invested.

Asset allocation: Spreading your money across several different types of investments – such as deposits (often called cash), bonds, property and shares (called equities) – in order to adjust the amount of risk you take.

Attendance Allowance: Tax-free state benefit that is not means-tested, for people aged 65 and over with care needs because of disability.

Authorised firm: An investment business that is legally allowed to do business with UK customers as recorded on the Financial Services Authority (FSA) register.

Bond: An investment where you are, in effect, lending to the Government, company or other organisation that issued the bond. Your loan earns interest at a fixed rate and, in most cases, will eventually be repaid on a set date. Before then, you can usually sell the bonds on the stock market.

Capital Gains Tax (CGT): A tax on the increase in value of an item during the period you have owned it.

Capital-protected annuity: An annuity that is guaranteed to pay out at least as much as you invested. For example, if you paid £10,000 but the annuity had paid out only £8,500 by the time you died, your survivors would get the balance of £1,500.

Capital risk: The risk of losing part or all of the money you originally invested (your capital) and/or part or all of any gains that you had previously built up.

Career average scheme: Salary-related scheme where the pension you are promised is a proportion of your pay for each year you have been in the scheme. Usually, each year's amount is increased in line with inflation up to the time you retire or leave.

Cash Individual Savings Account (cash ISA): Bank, building society or NS&I deposit that pays tax-free interest. You can invest up to £3,600 a year in a cash ISA.

Child Trust Fund (CTF): Scheme for children born on or after 1 September 2002 that gives them a method of building up tax-efficient savings up to the age of 18 years.

Combined benefit statement: A statement from an occupational scheme or personal pension showing forecasts of both the pension you might get from that scheme and the pension you might get from the State Pension scheme given your National Insurance record.

Commutation factor: In salary-related pension schemes, the amount of tax-free lump sum you get for each £1 of pension you give up.

Contracted out: While you are contracted out, instead of building up additional State Pension rights, you build up pension through an employer's occupational scheme or a personal pension. You either pay less in National Insurance or part of your contributions are rebated and paid to the scheme.

Council Tax Benefit: Means-tested state benefit that meets part or all of your Council Tax bill.

Credit union: A mutual self-help organisation where members build up savings and can borrow at reasonable rates. Members are linked by a 'common bond', which means they all, for example, live in the same area, work for the same company, attend the same church, and so on.

Disability Living Allowance: Tax-free state benefit that is not means tested, available to people under age 65 who have care needs or mobility problems because of disability.

Dividends: Payments by a company to its shareholders. They represent a share of the company's profits.

Drawdown: Another name for income withdrawal.

Earmarking (or 'attachment orders'): A divorce court can order that part of one spouse's pension once it starts and/or any tax-free lump sum must be paid to the other.

Enhanced annuity: A lifetime annuity paying a higher than normal income because you are likely to have a shorter than average life due to your lifestyle or a health condition (for example, smoking, diabetes).

Entrepreneurs' relief: A reduction in a capital gain you make when you sell or close down your business that reduces the effective rate of CGT on the gain to 10 per cent (instead of the usual 18 per cent).

Equity release: Arrangement (lifetime mortgage or home reversion scheme) that lets you cash in some or all of the equity in your home without having to move.

Escalating annuity: Annuity where the income paid out increases by a set percentage each year (for example, 3 per cent or 5 per cent a year).

Estate: Everything you own at death, including your personal possessions, home, investments and so on, less everything you owe, such as a mortgage, credit card debts and unpaid tax.

Final salary scheme: Salary-related scheme where the pension you are promised is a proportion of your pay at or near retirement multiplied by your time in the schemes.

Fixed/variable risk: In the context of investments, the risk that you will miss out on increasing general interest rates if you have invested for a fixed return. Alternatively, the risk that your return will fall with general interest rates if you have invested at a variable rate.

Flexible working: Arrangement (such as part-time working, flexi-time or job-sharing) that lets you strike a better balance between working and family duties. Carers and some parents have the right to request flexible working.

Gift with reservation: Something you give away but still continue to use. For Inheritance Tax purposes, you are treated as still owning the item.

Gilt: A type of bond that is a loan to the British Government, which can be bought and sold on the stock market.

Group personal pension scheme (GPPS): A scheme offered through your workplace, but basically the same as any other personal pension. However, your employer may have negotiated favourable terms with the provider, such as lower charges, and might contribute something to the scheme on your behalf. The scheme stays with you even if you change employer.

Hold-over relief: An election you can make at the time you give away your business. The election transfers a gain on the business assets to the recipient so that any CGT bill is put off until a future date and paid by the new owner rather than you.

Home reversion scheme: Type of equity release arrangement where you sell part of your home to raise cash or income and continue to live there rent-free or for a very low rent.

Housing Benefit: Means-tested state benefit that meets part or all of your rent.

Impaired life annuity: A lifetime annuity paying a significantly higher than normal income because your poor health means you are likely to have a much shorter life than average.

Income protection insurance: Insurance that pays out a replacement income if you cannot work because of illness.

Income withdrawal: Pension scheme arrangement where, instead of buying an annuity, you leave your pension fund invested and draw an income from the fund. The income varies with the value of your investments.

Index-linked: Increasing each year in line with inflation.

Inflation risk: The risk that the buying power of your investments will fall over time because the return is insufficient to compensate for inflation.

Inheritance Tax (IHT): A tax charged on gifts you make both during your lifetime and on death. Some gifts are tax free.

Intestacy: Dying without having made a will. The law dictates how your estate will be passed on.

Investment-linked annuity: An annuity where the income varies from year to year in line with an underlying fund of investments, offering the opportunity of an increasing income but risk of a fall in income.

Joint tenants: A way of sharing ownership of an asset. All the owners have equal shares and rights. On death, your share automatically passes to the remaining owners.

Level annuity: An annuity where the amount of income paid out stays the same year after year.

Life interest: In the context of a trust, the right to receive the income from or use of an asset during your lifetime. After that, the asset usually passes to someone else.

Lifetime annuity: Investment where you swap a lump sum for an income that continues for the rest of your life, however long you live.

Lifetime mortgage: Type of equity release arrangement where you take out a mortgage against your home to raise cash or income. The loan and usually the interest too are repaid only on your death or if you move permanently into care.

Limited liability: Situation where the maximum you can lose is capped at the amount you have invested.

Means-tested benefit: A state benefit that you can get only if your income and savings are relatively low, for example, the Pension Credit and Housing Benefit.

Money purchase scheme (also called a defined contribution scheme): Type of pension scheme where you build up your own pension fund to be used at retirement to buy a pension. How much pension you get depends on the amount paid in, how the invested contributions grow, how much is deducted in charges and annuity rates at the point of retirement.

National Insurance (NI) contributions: A tax paid by most people who work. Some types of contribution – Classes 1 (full-rate), 2 and 3 – entitle you to build up State Pension.

National Insurance (NI) record: Your history of paying or being credited with National Insurance during your working life.

National Savings & Investments (NS&I): An agency issuing savings products on behalf of the Government, which ultimately guarantees the return of your money, making NS&I products very safe.

No-negative-equity guarantee: A guarantee that the amount to be repaid when a lifetime mortgage ends (including rolled-up interest) will not exceed the proceeds from selling the home.

Offsetting: Part of a divorce settlement, whereby the person with less in pensions may be granted a bigger share of other assets to compensate for the lost pension rights. For example, the wife might be given a large lump sum or the family home and the husband retains his pension rights in full.

Pension annuity: The type of annuity you buy with a pension fund. All the income you get is taxable.

Pension Credit: Means-tested, tax-free state benefit that tops up the income of people aged 60 and over if their income is very low.

Pension sharing: Part of a divorce settlement whereby the court can order that part of the one spouse's pension rights be transferred to the other. The other person then becomes a member of the pension scheme in his or her own right and, except in the case of most public sector schemes, can transfer the rights to another scheme if they want.

Potentially Exempt Transfer (PET): A gift you make during your lifetime – usually to a person – on which there is no Inheritance Tax charge at the time of the gift or if you survive for seven years. On death within seven years, the gift is reassessed and tax may be due.

Pre-Owned Assets Tax (POAT): Income Tax charged on the value of the benefit you are deemed to get from something you use after you have given it away or contributed towards its purchase, unless the item is caught by the gift-with-reservation rules.

Private residence relief: Exemption from CGT on any profit you make from selling your only or main home. You may lose some relief if, for example, you use your home for business.

Purchased life annuity: Type of annuity you buy with your own lump sum. Part of each payment counts as return of your original investment and only the excess is taxed as income.

Qualifying year: A tax year in which you have paid or been credited with enough NI contributions for it to count towards your State Pension.

Relevant earnings: UK earnings on which you have paid tax, including salary, taxable fringe benefits, profits and rental income from commercial furnished holiday lettings but not other property income. Each year, you can get tax relief on contributions to pension schemes up to a maximum of 100 per cent of your relevant earnings or £3,600, whichever is higher.

Rent-a-Room Scheme: Scheme that lets you receive up to £4,250 a year tax-free from renting out room(s) in your home.

Retail Prices Index (RPI): A common measure of price inflation. It measures changes in a basket of goods and services chosen to reflect the way the average household spends its money.

RPI-linked annuity: Annuity where the income paid out increases each year in line with price inflation as measured by the RPI. If prices fell (deflation), the income would fall.

Salary-related pension scheme: Occupational scheme where you are promised a pension at retirement based on your level of pay, for example, a final salary scheme or career average scheme.

Salary sacrifice: Scheme where you give up some basic pay in return for fringe benefits from your job, such as extra pension rights. The tax treatment of pay and perks means that both you and your employer may be better off as a result.

Self-invested personal pension (SIPP): A type of personal pension giving you control over how you invest your pension fund and a wide choice of investments including, for example, investment funds from any provider, direct investment in shares, gilts and corporate bonds and, in some cases, commercial property.

Shortfall risk: The possibility that your investment or savings will not produce enough to meet a specific goal, such

as enough income for a comfortable retirement.

Stakeholder pension scheme: Type of personal pension that meets certain conditions, including, for example, a cap on charges (no more than 1.5 per cent a year for the first ten years and 1 per cent a year thereafter), flexible contributions and no surrender charges if you transfer to a different provider.

State Pension: The basic State Pension is the part that virtually everyone can build up by paying or being credited with enough NI contributions. For people reaching State Pension age from 6 April 2010, the full pension is paid if you have 30 years of contributions and/or credits. The additional State Pension is the part that you can build up if you are an employee or unable to work because of caring for children or other dependants.

State Pension age: Currently 65 for men and 60 for women. For women reaching State Pension age between 2010 and 2020, the age is being gradually increased to 65. Thereafter, pension age for younger people is being increased in stages to 68 years.

Taper relief: A reduction in the Inheritance Tax that may become due on some gifts (chargeable lifetime gifts and Potentially Exempt Transfers), where the giver dies within seven years of making the gift. There is no reduction if death occurs within the first three years, but after that the reduction is 20 per cent for each year.

Tax year: The year starting on 6 April and running through to the following 5 April.

Tax-efficient wrapper: If you hold investments through an Individual Savings Account (ISA), pension scheme, Child Trust Fund or some types of friendly society plan, there is little or no tax on the return you get. The ISA, pension scheme and so on is not itself an investment, but can be thought of a wrapper around the investments that creates this favourable tax treatment.

Tenants in common: A way of sharing ownership of an asset. Owners have distinct shares that need not be equal. On death, your share is passed on according to your will or the intestacy rules.

Third-way product: A product for providing pension income that combines some of the features of annuities and some of the features of income withdrawal to provide a pension that may be flexible and higher than that offered by a traditional annuity, but with lower risk than income withdrawal.

Today's money: Over time, inflation reduces the buying power of a given sum of money. Converting the sum to today's money means showing how much it could buy at today's levels.

Transfer value: The cash sum passed from an old pension scheme to a new one when you transfer your pension rights. If the old scheme is a money purchase scheme, the transfer value is simply the amount you have built up in your pension fund. If the old scheme is a salary-related scheme, the transfer value is the lump sum that would need to be invested today to provide the promised pension given assumptions about, for example, investment growth.

Trust: A legal arrangement that lets you give away assets but with conditions attached – for example, a trust that lets your surviving spouse use the family home during his or her lifetime after which it is given to your children.

Underlying entitlement: In the context of state benefits, an entitlement to a state benefit that you do not actually receive because you are getting some other type of state benefit instead.

Unsecured pension: The name that is given to a pension from income withdrawal if you are under the age of 75 years.

Working life: The tax years from the one in which you reached age 16 up to the last complete tax year before you reach State Pension age. For example, if your State Pension age is 65, your working life is the 49 tax years from age 16 up to 64 inclusive.

Working Tax Credit (WTC): Means-tested, tax-free state benefit designed to top up low earnings and ensure that being in work pays.

Useful addresses

Accountant – to find one

Association of Chartered Certified Accountants
29 Lincoln's Inn Fields
London WC2A 3EE
Tel: 020 7396 7000
www.acca.co.uk

Institute of Chartered Accountants in England and Wales
Chartered Accountants' Hall
PO Box 433
London EC2P 2BJ
Tel: 020 7920 8100
www.icaew.co.uk

Institute of Chartered Accountants in Ireland
Burlington House
Burlington Road
Dublin 4
Republic of Ireland
Tel: (00 353) 1 637 7200
www.icai.ie

Institute of Chartered Accountants of Scotland
CA House
21 Haymarket Yards
Edinburgh EH12 5BH
Tel: 0131 347 0100
www.icas.org.uk

Advisory, Conciliation and Arbitration Service (ACAS)
Helpline: 08457 47 47 47
www.acas.org.uk

Age Concern
Information line: 0800 00 99 66.
For local branch, see *The Phone Book* or www.ageconcern.org.uk

Association of International Property Professionals (AIPP)
94 New Bond Street
London W1S 1SJ
Tel: 020 7409 7061
www.aipp.org.uk

Association of Residential Letting Agents (ARLA)
6 Tournament Court
Edgehill Drive
Warwick CV34 6LG
Tel: 01926 496800
www.arla.co.uk

Business Gateway
Tel: 0845 609 6611
www.bgateway.com

Business Link
Tel: 0845 600 9 006
www.businesslink.gov.uk
See separate entries for: Business Gateway (Scotland), Flexible Support for Business (Wales) and NI Business Info (N. Ireland)

Child Trust Fund
Tel: 0845 302 1470
www.childtrustfund.gov.uk
FSA calculator: www.fsa.gov.uk/financial_capability/pgtm/parents/choose-a-calculator.html

Citizens Advice Bureau
See *The Phone Book* under 'Citizens Advice Bureau'
www.citizensadvice.org.uk
www.adviceguide.org.uk

Comparison websites
www.fsa.gov.uk/tables
www.moneyfacts.co.uk
www.moneysupermarket.com
www.switchwithwhich.co.uk
www.uswitch.com

Consumer Credit Counselling Service
Wade House
Merrion Centre
Leeds LS2 8NG
Tel: 0800 138 1111 (freephone)
www.cccs.co.uk

Credit union – to find one
www.abcul.org

Department for Business Enterprise and Regulatory Reform
Age discrimination questionnaire:
www.berr.gov.uk/files/file32724.pdf

Flexible working:
www.berr.gov.uk/files/file37031.doc

Disability benefits
Benefit Enquiry Line: 0800 88 22 00
www.direct.gov.uk/en/DisabledPeople/index.htm.

Disability and Carers Service
Free car tax: 0845 712 3456

Elderly Accommodation Counsel
3rd Floor
89 Albert Embankment
London SE1 7TP
Advice line: 020 7820 1343
www.housingcare.org

Employment Tribunal
www.employmenttribunals.gov.uk

Energy Saving Trust
Tel: 0800 512 012
www.energysavingtrust.org.uk

Estate agent/land auctioneer
National Association of Estate Agents (NAEA)
www.naea.co.uk/agents/default.asp

Financial Ombudsman Service (FOS)
South Quay Plaza
183 Marsh Wall
London E14 9SR
Tel: 0845 080 1800
www.financial-ombudsman.org.uk

Financial Services Authority (FSA)
25 The North Colonnade
London E14 5HS
FSA Consumer Helpline: 0845 6061234
Compare products: www.fsa.gov.uk/tables
FSA Register:
www.fsa.gov.uk/register/home.do
Consumer website:
www.moneymadeclear.fsa.gov.uk

Financial Services Compensation Scheme (FSCS)
Lloyds Chambers
Portsoken Street
London E1 8BN
Tel: 020 7892 7300
www.fscs.org.uk

Flexible Support for Business
Tel: 03000 6 03000
www.business-support-wales.gov.uk

Help the Aged
FREEPOST LON18542
Oxford OX29 4BR
Advice line: 0500 76 74 76
www.helptheaged.org.uk.

HM Revenue & Customs (HMRC)

Centre for Non-Residency:
www.hmrc.gov.uk/cnr/index.htm

Certificate of Age Exemption: HMRC, National Insurance Contributions Office, Contributor Caseworker, Longbenton, Newcastle upon Tyne NE98 1ZZ

Forms: http://search2.hmrc.gov.uk/kbroker/hmrc/forms/start.jsp

Inheritance Tax – transferring nil-rate band: www.hmrc.gov.uk/cto/iht/tnrb.htm

National Minimum Wage Helpline: 0845 600 0678

Pay As You Earn (PAYE): www.hmrc.gov.uk/paye/index.htm

Rent-a-Room Scheme: www.hmrc.gov.uk/individuals/tmarent-a room-scheme.shtml

Self-employed helpline: 0845 915 4515 www.hmrc.gov.uk/self-employed/register-selfemp.htm

Tax credits helpline: 0845 300 3900 www.hmrc.gov.uk/taxcredits/index.htm

Tax returns and helpsheets: www.hmrc.gov.uk/sa

Your tax office: check recent correspondence or use the search tool at http://search2.hmrc.gov.uk/kbroker/hmrc/locator/locator.jsp

HM Treasury
www.hm-treasury.gov.uk

Home improvements agency (HIA)
England: 01457 891909, www.foundations.uk.com/hiasearch.aspx

Wales – Care & Repair Cymru: 029 20576 286, www.careandrepair.org.uk

Scotland   Care & Repair Forum Scotland: 0141 221 9879, www.careandrepairscotland.co.uk

N. Ireland – Fold Housing Association: 02890 428314, www.foldgroup.co.uk

Identity and Passport Service
Passport adviceline: 0870 521 0410
www.ips.gov.uk/epa1r1a

Independent financial adviser – to find one
IFA Promotion: www.unbiased.co.uk (investments) or www.impartial.co.uk (mortgages)

The Institute of Financial Planning
Whitefriars Centre
Lewins Mead
Bristol BS1 2NT
Tel: 0117 9345 2470
www.financialplanning.org.uk

Personal Finance Society (PFS)
42–48 High Road
South Woodford
London E18 2JP
Tel: 020 8530 0852
www.thepfs.org
For a list of tied and independent financial advisers who all have more than just the basic qualifications

– specialists in annuities
The Annuity Bureau
Tel: 0845 602 6263
www.annuity bureau.co.uk/

Annuity Direct
32 Scrutton Street
London EC2A 4RQ
Tel: 0500 50 65 75 (freephone)
www.annuitydirect.co.uk

Hargreaves Lansdown Annuity Supermarket
Tel: 0845 345 9880
www.h-l.co.uk/pensions_and_retirement/annuities.hl

Inflation – your personal rate
www.statistics.gov.uk/pic

Jobcentre Plus
www.jobcentreplus.gov.uk

Local authority – to find
See *The Phone Book* under the name of
your council
www.direct.gov.uk

Lodgers – legal guidance
www.communities.gov.uk/publications/
housing/lettingrooms

London congestion charge
www.tfl.gov.uk

National Debtline
Tel: 0808 808 4000 (freephone)
www.nationaldebtline.co.uk

**National Health Service Low Income
Scheme**
Tel: 0870 155 5455
Form HC1 available from Jobcentre Plus
offices, hospitals, some dentists and
opticians

**National Savings & Investments
(NS&I)**
Tel: 0845 964 5000
Minicom: 0800 056 0585
www.nsandi.com

NI (N. Ireland) Business Info
Tel: 0800 027 0639
www.nibusinessinfo.co.uk

Pension calculators
MoneyTrail
Age Concern England
Astral House
1268 London Road
London SW16 4ER
www.ageconcern.org.uk/moneytrail
www.pensioncalculator.org.uk

The Pension Service
International Pension Centre:
www.thepensionservice.gov.uk/ipc/
home.asp

Pension Credit: 0800 99 1234
www.thepensionservice.gov.uk/pensioncredit
/calculator/home.asp

Pension Tracing Service:
www.thepensionservice.gov.uk/atoz/
atozdetailed/pensiontracing.asp

Retirement Pension Teleclaim Service:
0845 300 1084
www.thepensionservice.gov.uk/
state-pension/age-calculator.asp

State pension deferral:
www.thepensionservice.gov.uk/pdf/spd/
spd1may08.pdf

State Pension forecast:
www.thepensionservice.gov.uk

*Voluntary contributions (1996–7 to
2001–2):* www.thepensionservice.gov.uk/
resourcecentre/factsheets/home.asp

Winter Fuel Payment: 08459 15 15 15
www.thepensionservice.gov.uk/winterfuel

Prescriptions – pre-payment certificate
England: 0845 850 0030
www.ppa.org.uk/ppa/ppc_intro.htm
Wales: prescriptions are free
Scotland: from most pharmacies
N. Ireland: from most pharmacies

**Prince's Initiative for Mature Enterprise
(PRIME)**
Astral House
1268 London Rd
London SW16 4ER
Tel: 0208 765 7833
www.primeinitiative.org.uk

Recruitment agencies for older applicants
www.agepositive.gov.uk/resource/links.asp

Safe Home Income Plans (SHIP)
83 Victoria Street
London SW1H 0HW
Tel: 0870 241 6060
www.ship-ltd.org

Society of Trust and Estate Practitioners (STEP)
Answerphone for list of members:
020 7340 0506
www.step.org

Solicitor – to find one
The Law Society (England and Wales)
113 Chancery Lane
London WC2A 1PL
Tel: 020 7242 1222
www.lawsociety.co.uk

The Law Society of Scotland
26 Drumsheugh Gardens
Edinburgh EH3 7YR
Tel: 0131 226 7411
www.lawscot.org.uk

The Law Society of Northern Ireland
40 Linehall Street
Belfast BT2 8BA
Tel: 028 90 2316 14
www.lawsoc-ni.org

Stamp duty
Regeneration areas:
www.hmrc.gov.uk/so/dar/dar-search.htm

Stockbroker or investment manager – to find one
Association of Private Client Investment Managers and Stockbrokers (APCIMS)
22 City Road
Finsbury Square
London EC1 2AJ
Tel: 020 7247 7080
www.apcims.co.uk

London Stock Exchange
10 Paternoster Square
London EC4M 7LS
Tel: 020 7797 1000
www.londonstockexchange.com

Switch with Which?
Tel: 0800 533 031
www.switchwithwhich.co.uk

Tax adviser – to find one
Chartered Institute of Taxation
12 Upper Belgrave Street
London SW1X 8BB
Tel: 020 7235 9381
www.tax.org.uk

Society of Trust and Estate Practitioners
(see separate entry)

TV Licensing
Tel: 0844 800 6790
www.tvlicensing.co.uk

Valuations Office Agency
www.voa.gov.uk.

Warm Front grants
England – Warm Front: 0800 316 2805
www.warmfront.co.uk

Wales – Home Energy Efficiency Scheme (HEES): 0800 316 2815
www.heeswales.co.uk

Scotland – Warm Deal: 0800 316 6009
www.chwdp-scottishexecutive.co.uk/warmdeal/warmdeal.php

N. Ireland – Warm Homes Scheme:
0800 181 667
www.eaga.com/government_contracts/warmerhomes.htm

Water meter calculator
www.ofwat.gov.uk/consumerissues/meters

Index

abroad, retiring 40
accrual rate, definition 24
actuarial reduction 28, 29
added years schemes 29, 30
additional pension schemes 29, 30
Additional Voluntary Contributions (AVCs)
    29, 31
age
    decisions at State Pension 42–4
    discrimination legislation 70, 75
    pension 15–16, 28, 71
    proof of 94
    qualifying for help with travel 93
    retirement 28, 70, 71
annuities 49, 55–60, 141
    capital-protected 59–60
    enhanced 56
    escalating 56, 57–8
    guarantees and capital protection 59–60
    immediate needs 192
    impaired life 56, 192
    investment-linked 59
    joint-life-last-survivor 60
    level 56, 57–8
    lifetime 56, 64
    pension 53
    purchased life 53
    rates 57
    RPI-linked 56, 57–8
    short-term 60
annuity rate 49
asset allocation 139, 151
Association for Conciliation and Arbitration
    Services (ACAS) 74
Association of British Insurers 49

attachment orders 36, 37
Attendance Allowance (AA) 97, 98, 185

banks 81–2, 140, 145
bed and breakfast 125–9
benefits 72, 96–8, 122, 127
benefit statements 24, 25, 26
bills, help with 93–4, 100, 107–8
bonds 139, 141, 142, 175
borrowing money 82, 112
brownfield sites 130
building societies 140, 145
business angels 83
businesses, own
    Capital Gains Tax 170–1
    challenges 77
    easing out of 76
    National Insurance 85
    starting 77, 80–3
    structure 78–9
    work-life balance 77
Business Link 77, 83
business rates 128

Capital Gains Tax (CGT) 76, 128–9, 130,
    157, 178
    CGT-free gains 173
    losses 173
    reliefs 170–2
    tax bill 173
    working out the gain 170
care
    financial assessment 99, 184
    at home 183–5
    key decisions 183

in Northern Ireland 185
options 182–6
payment for 185
planning ahead for 191–2
retirement housing 186
in Scotland 185
career average scheme 23–4
care homes 187–90
carers 17–18, 97, 98, 185
Carer's Allowance 97, 98
children, investing for 145–50
Child Trust Fund (CTF) 145–8
civil partners, protecting 51, 60
Cold Weather Payment 107
collectables 179
commutation factor 53
Companies House 79
company, trading as a 78–9
company pension schemes see occupational
    pensions
consolidating pensions 38–9, 48, 50
    money purchase schemes 49
    pension protection 50
    pros and cons 39
    salary-related schemes 48
contracted out, definition 21
corporate bond 56
Council Tax 94, 100, 107, 128
credit cards 111–12
credit unions 112

deficiency letter 20
defined benefit schemes see occupational
    pensions, salary-related
defined contribution scheme see
    occupational pensions, money
    purchase
dependants 73
direct debit 110, 112
disability, financial help for 96–100, 185
Disability Living Allowance (DLA) 97, 98,
    185
Disabled Facilities Grant (DFG) 100

discrimination 70, 75
dividends 78
divorce and pensions 35–7
downsizing 114–16
drawdown 49, 63–5

earmarking 36, 37
earnings, low see low earnings
emergency funds 111, 144–5
employment gaps 18–21
employment tribunal 71, 75
energy saving 109–10
entrepreneurs' relief 171, 179
equity, definition 118
equity release 117–24
    advice 124
    alternatives to 121–2
    case studies 117, 120
    considerations 122–3
    and Inheritance Tax 199
    lifetime mortgage 118–19
    reversion scheme 120
    state benefits and tax 122
family
    business start-up costs 81
    emergencies 73–4
    and equity release schemes 123
    gifts and bequests to 194–7
final salary scheme 23, 29, 30
financial help 90–112
    extras because of age 92–5
    if you have a disability 96–100
    if your income is low 101–8
    main types available 91
    money-saving ideas 109–12
Financial Ombudsman Service (FOS) 158
Financial Services Authority (FSA) 48, 49,
    123, 159
Financial Services Compensation Scheme
    (FSCS) 158–9
flexible working 73–4
freehold 186

garden, cash from your 130
gift aid 178
gifts, lifetime 201–3
gift with reservation 202, 203
gilts 56, 59, 141, 175
grandchildren, investing for 145–50
grants, business 83
group income protection insurance 28
group personal pension scheme 34

health costs help 93, 98–9, 106–7
heating improvements 108
hold-over relief 171, 179
holiday lets 155–6
holidays from work 73
home, help with costs 94–5, 100, 108
home, income from your 114–30
    Capital Gains Tax 171–2
    cash from your garden 130
    downsizing versus staying put
        114–16
    lodgers and B&B 125–9
    see also equity release
home improvement agencies (HIAs) 95,
    100
Home Responsibilities Protection (HRP) 18
hours, working 73
housing benefit 107

income, low *see* low earnings
income protection insurance 144
Income Tax 156–7, 162–8
    allowances 163–8
    bands and rates 166–7
    how you pay 168
    relief 162–3
income withdrawal 49, 63–5
independent financial advisers (IFAs) 38,
    48, 151
index-linking 13, 42, 140
Individual Savings Account (ISA) 111, 139,
    145, 177, 180
inflation 14, 24, 46–7

Inheritance Tax (IHT) 194, 198–200,
    201–3
insulation grants 95, 108
insurance, care 191–2
insurance instalments 111
internet 109, 112
intestacy rules 195–7
investment funds 175–6, 180
investments 132–60
    complaints and compensation 158–9
    goals 144–53
    for grandchildren 145–50
    help and advice 160
    for income 150–3
    main types of 140–3
    property 154–7
    risk 132–43
    strategy 133
    tax and 174–6
investors, business 83

jobs 71–5
joint tenants 195

leasehold 186
letting houses/rooms 125–9, 154–7
letting relief 128
life expectancy 7
life insurance, investment-type 176,
    180
life interest 195
limited liability 78
living alone 10
loans 82, 112
lodgers 125–9
low earnings 101–8
    bills 107–8
    extra income 101–5
    top up 86–8
    your health 106–7
    your home 108
    see also Pension Credit
low earnings threshold (LET) 21

means-tested benefit 14
minimum wage 72
money purchase schemes *see* occupational
    pensions, money purchase
money-saving ideas 109–12
mortgages 107, 121–2

National Health Service (NHS) 93, 106,
    107, 187
National Insurance contributions 17, 84–5
    and basic State Pension 17–21
    credits 19
    divorce 35
    employees 85
    running own business 85
    self-employed 85
    types of 84
National Savings & Investments (NS&I)
    139, 140, 145
needs assessment 99, 184
no-negative-equity guarantee 118

occupational pensions 22–32
    advantages 22
    age to start 27–9
    case studies 24, 27, 29, 31, 32
    deferring retirement 72
    and divorce 36–7
    money purchase 22, 26
        age to start 28
        consolidating 49
        key decisions 45
        transferring from salary-related
        38
    protecting survivors 51
    and retiring abroad 40
    salary-related 22, 23–5, 38
        age to start 28
        benefit statement 24, 25
        case study 24
        consolidating 48
        inflation and 24
        key decisions 45

pension protection 50
    tax-free lump sums 53
    transferring to money purchase 38
  savings limits 23
  topping up 29
Office for National Statistics (ONS) study
    7–10
offsetting 36, 37
overdrafts 81–2
overseas, retiring 40

partners, protecting 51, 60
partnerships, business 78
passports 92–3
pay and benefits 72
Pay As You Earn (PAYE) 168
Pension Credit
    applying for 102
    the basics 101–2
    calculator 105
    case study 103
    guarantee credit 103, 104
    savings credit 103, 104
    unable to get 20
    your income for 104
Pension Protection Fund (PPF) 50
pensions
    building up 12–40
    choices at retirement 42–68
    consolidating *see* consolidating pensions
    and divorce 35–7
    power of 12–13
    protection 50
    saving for 12–13, 22
    see also specific type
Pension Service 15, 35–6, 42, 102
pension sharing 36, 37
personal pensions 33–4
    age to start 34
    and divorce 36–7
    and retiring abroad 40
    savings limits 23
    self-invested 34

Index

personal pensions *(continued)*
    special types 34
    tax relief on contributions 33
pets, tax on 203
phasing retirement 61–2
Pre-Owned Assets Tax (POAT) 202
prescriptions 93, 98–9, 106
Prince's Initiatives for Mature Enterprise
    (PRIME) 83
private pensions 36–7, 40, 44–5
    see also specific type
private residence relief 128
promotion at work 74
property as an investment 142, 143,
    154–7
property funds 176

qualifying year, definition 17

redundancy 74–5
relevant earnings, definition 22
Rent-a-Room Scheme 127, 178
residency and retiring abroad 40
Retail Prices Index (RPI) 56, 57, 138
retirement
    abroad 40
    age 28, 70
    deferring 10, 61–2, 70–88
    housing 186
    income 12–13, 46–7 *(see also*
        pensions)
    length of 7
    pension choices at 42–68
    phasing 61–2
    quiz 8–9
rights, definition 38

Safe Home Income Plans (SHIP) 119
salaries 72
salary-related occupational schemes *see*
    occupational pensions, salary-
    related
salary sacrifice 22, 29, 31–2

saving energy 109–10
savings 111, 145
    children's 148
    pension 12–13, 22
    short-term 146–7
    tax on 174, 179–80
Savings Gateway account 145
self-employment 78, 80, 85
    see also businesses, own
Self-Invested Personal Pension (SIPP) 34
shares 142, 143, 175
sheltered housing 186
sick pay 72
sight tests 93, 99, 106
single people 10
Social Fund 107–8
spending diaries 90
stakeholder scheme 34
Stamp Duty Land Tax (SDLT) 115
State Earnings Related Pension Scheme
    (SERPS) 14, 21
State Pension 14–21
    additional 14, 21
    age to start 15–16
    amount of 14–15
    basic 14, 17–21
    and carers 17–18
    deferring 16, 42–4
    and divorce 35–6
    employment gaps 18–21
    forecast 15, 35–6
    index-linking 42
    key decisions 42–4
    means-tested benefit 14
    and retiring abroad 40
    six-year rule 20–1
    and women 17–18
State Second Pension (S2P) 14, 21
survivors, protecting 51, 60

taper relief 202
tax 162–80
    businesses and 78–9

capital gains *see* Capital Gains Tax (CGT)
cash from your garden 130
and children's savings 148
effect of equity release on 122
effect of lodgers and B&B on 127
income *see* Income Tax
Inheritance Tax (IHT) 194, 198–200, 201–3
and investments 174–6
key dates 180
occupational pensions 22, 32
and pension deferral 44
personal pension contributions 33
on pets 203
and property rental 156–7
and retiring abroad 40
saving tips 177–80
tax-efficient wrapper 175
tax-free income 165, 177
tax-free lump sums 52–4, 65
television licence 94
tenants in common 195
'third way' products 66–8
today's money, definition 24
training, job 74

transfer value 49
travel, help with 92–3, 96
trust 195

underlying entitlement 97, 98
unmarried partners 51
utilities 109–10

wages 72
warden-assisted housing 186
Warm Front grants 94, 95, 108
water meters 110
widows/widowers, protecting 51, 60
wills 195–7
Winter Fuel Payment 93–4
women and State Pension 15–18
work 71–5
working life, definition 17
Working Tax Credit (WTC) 86–8, 101
    amount 86
    assessing 86–7
    calculator 88
    elements 87
    qualification 86
work-life balance 77

Which? is the leading independent consumer champion in the UK.
A not-for-profit organisation, we exist to make individuals as powerful as the
organisations they deal with in everyday life. The next few pages give you a
taster of our many products and services. For more information, log onto
www.which.co.uk or call 0800 252 100.

Which? magazine

Which? magazine has a simple goal in life – to offer truly independent advice to
consumers that they can genuinely trust – from which credit card to use through to
which washing machine to buy. Every month the magazine is packed with 84
advertisement-free pages of expert advice on the latest products. It takes on the biggest
of businesses on behalf of all consumers and is not afraid to tell consumers to avoid their
products. Truly the consumer champion. To subscribe, go to www.which.co.uk.

Which? Online

www.which.co.uk gives you access to all Which? content online and much, much more.
It's updated regularly, so you can read hundreds of product reports and Best Buy
recommendations, keep up to date with Which? campaigns, compare products, use our
financial planning tools and search for the best cars on the market. You can also access
reviews from *The Good Food Guide*, register for email updates and browse our online
shop – so what are you waiting for? To subscribe, go to www.which.co.uk.

Which? Money

Whether you want to boost your pension, make your savings work harder or simply need
to find the best credit card, *Which? Money* has the information you need. *Which? Money*
offers you honest, unbiased reviews of the best (and worst) new personal finance deals,
from bank accounts to loans, credit cards to savings accounts. Throughout the magazine
you will find tips and ideas to make your budget go further plus dozens of Best Buys. To
subscribe, go to www.which.co.uk.

Which? Books

Other books in this series

Care Options in Retirement
Margaret Wallace and Philip Spiers
ISBN: 978 1 84490 053 4
Price: £10.99

Care Options in Retirement is the definitive guide to navigating the many financial and legal considerations of care and accommodation for older people. The book provides vital information on the many types of housing and care available, from care at home and retirement housing to respite care and care homes. Whether you need to know about benefits, support services, renting or buying retirement housing or want advice on how to interpret a care home's inspection report, you will find useful tips and information.

Save and Invest
Jonquil Lowe
ISBN: 978 1 84490 044 2
Price: £10.99

Save and Invest is a detailed guide to all saving and investment avenues suitable for those approaching the markets for the first time and those seeking to improve their portfolio. Jonquil Lowe, an experienced investment analyst, introduces the basics of understanding risk and suggests popular starter investments. Many types of savings accounts are closely analysed, along with more complex investment options, such as venture capital trusts, high-income bonds, hedge funds and spread betting.

NEW EDITION: Tax Handbook 2009/10
Tony Levene
ISBN: 978 1 84490 060 2
Price: £10.99 (Published Spring 2009)

Written by the *Guardian* personal finance journalist and award-winning consumer champion Tony Levene, this guide gives expert advice on all aspects of the UK tax system. It includes information on finding the right accountant and how to get the best from them, NI contributions, VAT and tax credits for families. This new edition also contains updates from the 2009 Budget, disability credits, tax advice on cars, the latest news on the Taxpayers' Charter and step-by-step advice on completing the self-assessment form.

Which? Books

Which? Books provide impartial, expert advice on everyday matters from finance to law, property to major life events. We also publish the country's most trusted restaurant guide, *The Good Food Guide*. To find out more about Which? Books, log on to www.which.co.uk or call 01903 828557.

❝ Which? tackles the issues that really matter to consumers and gives you the advice and active support you need to buy the right products. **❞**